The Bitter Legacy

The Bitter Legacy

African Slavery
Past and Present

Alice Bellagamba, Sandra E. Greene,
and Martin A. Klein, editors

With the Collaboration of Carolyn Brown

Markus Wiener Publishers
Princeton

For information, write to: Markus Wiener Publishers
231 Nassau Street, Princeton, NJ 08542
www.markuswiener.com

Library of Congress Cataloging-in-Publication Data

The bitter legacy : African slavery past and present / Alice Bellagamba, Sandra E. Greene, and Martin A. Klein, editors ; with the collaboration of Carolyn Brown.
    p. cm.
  Includes bibliographical references.
  ISBN 978-1-55876-549-8 (hardcover : alk. paper)
  ISBN 978-1-55876-550-4 (pbk. : alk. paper)
  1. Slavery—Africa, West—History—20th century. 2. Slavery—Africa, West—History. 3. Slaves—Africa, West—Social conditions. 4. Freedmen—Africa, West—Social conditions. 5. Collective memory—Africa, West. 6. Social classes—Africa, West. 7. Discrimination—Africa, West. 8. Stigma (Social psychology)—Africa, West. I. Bellagamba, Alice. II. Greene, Sandra E., 1952- III. Klein, Martin A.
  HT1331.B58 2013
  326.096603—dc23
                            2013002978

Markus Wiener Publishers books are printed in the United States of America on acid-free paper and meet the guidelines for permanence and durability of the Committee on Production Guidelines for Book Longevity of the Council on Library Resources.

Contents

1. Introduction. When the Past Shadows the Present:
The Legacy in Africa of Slavery and the Slave Trade 1
    ALICE BELLAGAMBA, SANDRA E. GREENE,
    AND MARTIN A. KLEIN

2. The Struggle for Political Emancipation of Slave
Descendants in Contemporary Borgu, Northern Benin 29
    ERIC KOMLAVI HAHONOU

3. On Remembering Slavery in Northern Igbo
Proverbial Discourse 57
    DAMIAN U. OPATA

4. To Cut the Rope from One's Neck?
Manumission Documents of Slave Descendants
from Central Malian Fulɓe Society 67
    LOTTE PELCKMANS

5. Memories of Slavery in a Former Slave-Trading
Community: The Aro of the Bight of Biafra 87
    G. UGO NWOKEJI

6. Tabula and Pa Jacob, Two Twentieth-Century
Slave Narratives from Cameroon 119
    ZACHARIE SAHA

7. Songs of Sorrow, Songs of Triumph: Memories of
the Slave Trade among the Bulsa of Ghana 133
    EMMANUEL SABORO

8. Evoking the Past through Material Culture:
The Mami Tchamba Shrine 149
    ALESSANDRA BRIVIO

9. Slave Ancestry and Religious Discrimination
in The Gambia 163
    ALICE BELLAGAMBA AND MARTIN A. KLEIN

10. Memories of Slavery and the Slave Trade
from Futa Toro, Northern Senegal 193
    MAKHROUFI OUSMANE TRAORÉ

Glossary 213

About the Contributors 219

1. Introduction.
When the Past Shadows the Present: The Legacy in Africa of Slavery and the Slave Trade

ALICE BELLAGAMBA, SANDRA E. GREENE,
AND MARTIN A. KLEIN

After almost a thousand years of exporting human beings, enduring connections have developed between Africa, Europe, the Americas, the Middle East, and the Indian Ocean. These connections have long raised strong public and scholarly interests, and today, as the Senegalese historian Ibrahima Thioub has remarked, they play an important part in the image that contemporary Africans build of themselves and of their contribution to world history.[1] Public attention was reinforced by the launch of the UNESCO Slave Route Project in 1994.[2] At the base of this initiative was the idea that, although marked by violence and subjection, the export of slaves from Africa was a major force of historical change that had to be commemorated both to honor the victims and to shed light on the significant social and cultural changes it produced across time and space. In the wake of the Slave Route Project, countries like Senegal, Ghana, Benin, and even the small Republic of The Gambia, have striven to valorize those parts of their historical past that link them with the Atlantic slave trade. European castles along the West African coast, which served as bases for Atlantic slavers, have been restored and opened to the public; tourists' itineraries have been organized; museum exhibitions have been established; and festivals have been organized to promote the return to Africa

1

of men and women, whose erstwhile ancestors were forcibly enslaved.[3]

This burgeoning heritage politics has focused only marginally on the issue of slavery and slave trading within Africa. Yet, the legacy of internal slave dealing and slave holding lingers in contemporary African societies. It has hampered socioeconomic development during and after colonial rule, and it has resurfaced in the civil wars and violence of the second part of the twentieth century.[4]

Unbeknownst to most, more slaves were probably kept within Africa than were ever exported. Beyond the limited academic circles of those who professionally delve into the history of African internal slavery and slave trade, however, any attempt to discuss these topics overtly is still considered politically incorrect by certain people. Some believe that a focus on the slave trade and slavery within Africa only serves to downplay the heavy tribute in labor and human lives that Africa paid for the development of Europe, the Americas, and many other parts of the world. Others object to this view. The historian Ibrahima Thioub has been critical of Senegalese intellectuals, in particular, for having long looked at slave dealing and slave holding as something not really belonging to the past of their nation. But this criticism can also be applied to many other intellectuals, those in the West as well as in other parts of Africa, as recently stressed by the Nigerian writer Wole Soyinka.[5]

While trans-Atlantic slave shipments ended in the nineteenth century, slave raiding, slave trading, and the use of slave labor within Africa continued well into the early colonial period. In spite of legal abolition, in many parts of contemporary Africa, there are people who are still called slaves in the local languages. In some cases, particularly in desert areas, this slavery is not metaphoric or historical, but quite real. People are owned, and can be sold; they are forced to work for others for no or very little compensation; some have no control over their sexuality. This occurs even though where it exists, slavery is illegal. In some areas, it is only vestigial forms of slavery that remain. Former slaves, for example, may feel they still must meet certain obligations to their former masters. Yet, they can leave if they wish, and keep the products of their labor. In many more areas, people will refer to others as slaves, though these so-called slaves are totally free, and sometimes are even wealthier than their former masters because they were often among the first to be educated in colonial Africa. Despite this freedom and wealth, these former slaves are still often expected to treat former masters with deference. The stigma of slave origins persists. In some districts, a visitor can ask, "Where do the slaves live?" and with no objections raised at all, be directed to whole villages or to quarters of larger villages that are inhabited exclusively by people of slave descent, the children and grandchildren of the formerly enslaved. Of course, there are large areas of Africa where memories of slavery have disappeared and others where they lie buried and are only articulated during litigation over inheritance or disputes about succession to chiefly offices. But in those areas where the legacy of slavery persists, it retains a grassroots social significance and intersects in complex ways with the social inequalities of colonial and postcolonial history.

This book offers a fresh look into these delicate issues by presenting a firsthand collection of sources, which gives voice, as far as possible, either to former slaves or to men and women of slave ancestry. As argued in the following pages, the task of collecting this kind of evidence has not been easy.

Slavery before and after the Colonial Conquest

For the past forty years, historians of Africa have pursued the systematic study of African slave systems and their interaction with the external slave trade. It is now clear that slavery existed in Africa before the Atlantic and trans-Saharan export trade as it existed in most of the world. With the increased demand for African slaves, however, which developed as a consequence of external commercial linkages, the production and trading of slaves became major economic enterprises. The Atlantic slave trade contributed to the creation of military states, where power was based on the ability to provide slaves for sale. It was also resisted, which meant that slave traders could respond to the demand for slaves only by pushing trade networks deeper and deeper into Africa, eventually covering most of Africa. These routes expanded south first from the desert's edge, then in all directions from the Atlantic, and finally, in the nineteenth century, from the East and Northeast African coasts. The external trade shaped not only the nature of the state, but it also stimulated the use of slaves within Africa. Those who grew wealthy in the trade wanted not only European trade goods, but the services slaves could provide. Women were preferred both as workers and as members of the harems of the wealthy and powerful. Male slaves became both workers and soldiers, but were often more difficult to control, and thus, constituted a greater proportion of those exported.

Finally, in 1807, Great Britain and the United States abolished the slave trade.[6] Other European nations soon followed suit, though it took more than a half-century for the export of slaves to be completely stopped. Britain, moreover, abolished the institution of slavery throughout its empire in 1833. France did the same in 1848.[7] The abolitionists hoped that both in the plantation colonies of the Americas and in Africa, productive activity would increasingly be based on free labor, but in Africa, that was not to be. The nineteenth-century Industrial Revolution increased the European demand for African products, like peanut and palm oil, but free labor was generally not available. The century increasingly saw the diversion of the trade in slaves away from export markets to internal ones.[8] Within Africa, slaves produced palm oil, harvested cloves, and cultivated peanuts, all for European and Asian markets. Others harvested kola nuts in the forests of West Africa where this commodity was marketed and sold for local consumption. Still others were used as household labor and as carriers to transport the various goods produced to market. Within a generation of one of the world's largest slave traders—Great Britain—ending its trade, prices for slaves within Africa were as high as they had been at the height of the Atlantic slave trade.[9]

Slave raiding and slave trading within Africa remained not only an important form of economic activity after the 1807 British abolition of the slave trade, it accelerated. From the middle of the century, new weapons, particularly breech-loading and repeating rifles, facilitated the slaver's task. The last third of the nineteenth century was the bloodiest period in African history.[10] British and French anti-slavery legislation had ended slavery in the very small areas then under their rule, but both European powers were careful to discourage flight from neighboring African states. When they started extending their colonial domains in the later part of the nineteenth century, they were careful not to abolish slavery.[11] They forged alliances and supported African military leaders, who not only had large slave holdings, but who were unrepentant slave holders, convinced that slave labor was too important for their local economic activities to even consider abolishing it. Even after conquest, European colonizers continued to depend on slave holding African chiefs to administer their new domains. This most often occurred as an interim measure in the period after the colonial conquest, but before the new colonial authorities had established effective control. Over time, colonial officials began following what was called the Indian model. First applied by Britain in India where slavery was also an important social institution, this model was gradualist in that it simply withdrew support for slave owners, but did not formally abolish slavery.[12] Colonial regimes intervened to halt slave raiding and slave trading since these activities created insecurity, and inhibited economic activity. Public opinion in Europe also spurred colonial officials into action. Reports of slave raiding and trading in Africa were widely condemned by a European public, which by the 1880s, had come to regard slavery as immoral, and free labor as the most preferred means of meeting the needs of a productive economy. They also stopped supporting the rights of slave owners. This meant that a master could no longer ask the colonial administrator to return runaway slaves. Still, the first colonial anti-slavery measures were generally weak, and sometimes were not even enforced.[13] Efforts were made in some British areas, for example, to prevent flight by explaining to slaves that laws against the slave trade did not mean their immediate liberation.[14] The Indian model encouraged colonial regimes to believe that by simply preventing slave holders from acquiring new slaves, slavery itself would disappear in the long run, and slaves' emancipation would occur without disruption. As a result, slavery, as a legal and social institution, ended slowly.

A topic on which scholars have only rarely been able to accumulate enough information to produce a book length study is resistance to the slave trade and slavery within Africa.[15] Before the colonial conquest, Africans resisted enslavement in a variety of ways. Communities hid in remote and inaccessible areas; they built stockades to prevent the attacks of slave raiders; they established networks and social connections at the regional and trans-regional level so as to facilitate the ransom of captives. Memories of such resistance efforts have often been kept alive up to the present. Emmanuel Saboro, in chapter 7, "Songs of Sorrow, Songs of Triumph: Memories of the Slave Trade among the Bulsa of Ghana," tells of a group of people in northern Ghana—the Bulsa—whose contemporary identity is based on their successful resistance to Babatu, a major nineteenth-century slave raider. Songs of sorrow remember the suffering of the Bulsa, while those of triumph celebrate their defeat of Babatu.

Slave masters and colonial officials often shared the view of the slaves as passive human beings, who lacked initiative and needed paternalistic guidance and control. Yet, enslaved men and women had their own expectations about the colonial conquest and readily grasped the change of power and the opportunities it offered. Most found slavery intolerably oppressive. With the exception of those who held privileged roles as soldiers or administrators for wealthy or powerful masters, most African slaves were harshly exploited. Those who remembered an earlier home yearned to return. Where the opportunity existed, they took advantage of it. Immediately after the colonial conquest, slaves took flight everywhere, but it was probably in French West Africa where the greatest of such movements took place. When the French stopped returning runaways to their masters, they hoped the slaves would remain where they were, but the news of successful escapes spread quickly. Between 1906 and 1912, there was a massive exodus.[16] Perhaps over a million slaves left slave masters either to return to earlier homes or to find work in the colonial economy. These were mostly slaves who had recently been enslaved and were both physically able to make the journey and remembered their origins. Flights were most numerous in the harshest areas. In German East Africa, where there were an estimated 500,000 slaves in 1890, the Germans issued about 60,000 Freedom Letters between 1890 and 1914. By the end of this period, the actual number of slaves had dropped to about 160,000. Some had died, but most had simply walked away from slavery once it was abolished.[17]

By the 1930s, most colonial regimes had passed legislation to end slavery in their African possessions. In many parts of the continent, however, a small illicit slave trade, largely in children, persisted, both to serve markets within Africa and as a small trade conducted during the pilgrimage to Mecca.[18] Labor recruitment schemes, which strongly resembled the slave trade of the old days, also began to emerge. An indentures system, employed to provide labor to the cocoa plantations of Atlantic islands so resembled slavery that news of its existence generated a humanitarian reform movement so vocal that the League of Nations was forced to intervene. Labor recruiters then had to change their practices.[19] Zacharie Saha, in chapter 6, "Tabula and Pa Jacob, Two Twentieth-Century Slave Narratives from Cameroon," tells of two men who were sold into slavery, one to Fernando Po, and the other within Cameroon. They were freed only after the collapse of colonial rule. Even after slavery ended, many former slaves remained with their masters, either because colonial regimes discouraged flight or because of the insecurity that faced them if they tried to return home. Often, their homeland was far. Many had been born in slavery or enslaved young. They grew up in their masters' society and culture, formed families, and were reluctant to part with the forms of patronage ensured by their belonging to their masters' communities and descent groups. For those who stayed, emancipation translated into a long struggle to overcome the social boundaries that set them apart from the dominant social categories.

Much, of course, changed. Slave masters were limited by fear of further flight. Where state structures were weak and authority dispersed, slavery had rapidly disappeared under the impact of the colonial conquest. In coastal Kenya, for instance, slaves could easily claim land in the hinterland and become farmers,[20] or seek wage labor in rapidly growing cities like Mombasa. In other areas, forms of slavery persisted. In desert regions of Mauritania, Niger, Mali, and the Sudan, colonial regimes were dependent on slave-owning elites and unwilling to commit the military forces that would have been necessary to end slavery. Masters were also able to control the formerly enslaved in areas where slaves had few options and colonial rulers, because of pragmatic necessity, supported powerful slave-owning chiefs, whose alliance they needed to control the territory. Hamman Yaji, a Fula chief, regularly raided for slaves from 1902, until he was deposed by the British in 1927.[21] Not far away, in Adamawa in French Cameroon, a chief passionately defended slavery in the 1950s, and persuaded the French that it was "too soon" to do anything about slavery.[22]

In most areas, the labor obligations of slaves were gradually reduced, but masters were determined to preserve their social and moral superiority. As noted by the historian John Iliffe, colonial conquest actually "increased [slave owners'] sensitivity on issues of honor and vertical rank."[23] This emerges clearly from the sources. In their contribution to this book, Alice Bellagamba and Martin A. Klein use a newspaper article and an interview to explore the post-abolition situation in Badibu, one of the regions of The Gambia considered quite conservative on the issue of slave ancestry. Badibu slave owners, and their descendants, engaged in a long struggle to preserve the social boundaries that elevated them above their former slaves and other people of slave ancestry.

In chapter 4, "To Cut the Rope from One's Neck? Manumission Documents of Slave Descendants from Central Malian Fulbe Society," Lotte Pelckmans describes a similar situation in the Fulbe Muslim communities of Hayre, located in a very arid and isolated part of Mali. Here, until the late twentieth century, men and women of slave ancestry could not make the pilgrimage to Mecca because they found it difficult to obtain from their masters the document they needed to perform the *hajj*. They could not become imams and generally had to sit in the back of the mosque. This pushed former slaves to seek Muslim education, but it also convinced many to accept their own social and cultural inferiority as divinely determined. In other parts of Africa, like the desert regions of Mauritania, Niger, Mali, the Sudan, and also Borgou in northern Benin real forms of slavery survived the legal end of slavery, and countries like Niger and the Sudan have remained under international scrutiny for cases of slave trading and forcible reduction to slavery.[24]

Paths to Social Emancipation

After abolition in colonial times, many former slaves did not migrate to other areas, but remained within their traditional communities. Their subservient status manifested itself in a variety of ways, from restricted access to land to respect of local honor codes that excluded them from community religious and political leadership posts. They controlled their own labor and their family life, however. Freed slaves negotiated their own marriages and women were no longer forced to have sexual relations with their masters. They also benefited from their willingness to work hard and to learn new skills. A myth believed by slaveholders and many colonial officials alike claimed that slaves were lazy and would work only if forced, but their actual willingness and capacity to work for themselves enabled many to accumulate property.

For those who wanted to move up and out, the two best paths were the army and education. The armies that conquered Africa for European colonial powers were largely composed of the enslaved, sometimes freed in exchange for a long-term enlistment. This continued well into the colonial period. For example, the army of African conscripts that fought for France in World War I was about 75 percent former slaves.[25] The cadres of many colonial and postcolonial armies had a large percentage of the once enslaved or their descendants, which meant that numerous military regimes still contain many such men.[26] Education was probably an even more important path of upward social mobility. In the late nineteenth and early twentieth centuries, a large percentage of those who gathered around European Christian mission stations during periods of military conflict were escaped slaves. They thus often became the first Africans educated in European languages. They became the clerks in government and business operations. Their sons and grandsons were a large part of the postcolonial elite. In the process, they often shed memories of slave status and the resulting stigma of slave origins. Christian missions also provided land and new identities, as did Muslim religious communities. "Serin Bamba is our liberator," say many former slave disciples of the Senegalese religious leader, Ahmadu Bamba.[27]

For other slaves and their descendants, one of the most important weapons in their hands was their ability to physically relocate themselves to a different community. After the colonial conquest, no one could force them to stay with their former masters. Desertions occurred, and continue even today as men and women of slave ancestry find strategies to cope with the enduring stigma of their origins and their social marginality. Sometimes, the formerly enslaved only moved short distances when free land was available near their original villages. Other times, groups moved further. Former slaves sought money working as migrant laborers in peanut fields and cocoa plantations. They worked as porters and filled humble positions at the bottom of the colonial labor hierarchy as cleaners, messengers, drivers, and attendants of colonial officials. When there was an opportunity, they acquired artisan skills, which allowed them to enter the growing tertiary sector of colonial urban centers.

Geographic mobility increased after World War II, with the rapid growth of African cities. In search of opportunities, people of slave ancestry joined the rural-urban exodus of the 1960s and 1970s, moving first inside and then outside Africa. This process of social change is explained in the interview on Badibu slavery that Bellagamba and Klein present in their chapter. Many of Badibu slave descendants are today better off than the descendants of slave owners: hard work and migration have radically changed their economic and social standing both at home and in the diaspora. Still, the linkage between migration and social mobility of freed slaves and people of slave ancestry needs to be further explored.[28] Life-course is one of the variables to be considered. Some urban and international immigrants, as they aged, became sick and isolated. Many had to return to communities where their ancestors had lived as slaves to take advantage of local support networks at the price of accepting their own subordinate status.[29] Structural factors, and the specificity of each historical period, are important as well. In the first part of the twentieth century strangers moving into the villages of the Upper River Gambia were usually assumed to be slaves and were incorporated into the slave class.[30] Makhroufi Ousmane Traoré, in chapter 10, "Memories of Slavery and the Slave Trade from Futa Toro, Northern Senegal," presents us with accounts of slavery from both master and slave descendants in contemporary Futa Toro, an area of Senegal where the resilience of old-status distinctions has been long observed in spite of the fact that men and women from Futa Toro early ventured out of their home villages. They sought opportunities in the cities of Senegambia, in other African countries, and in Europe as well. Relocation to other areas has not always obliterated previous slave identities, in part because they often migrated with support networks controlled by traditional elites and re-created traditional hierarchies in their new homes. Migration to Ghana was, for Mossi villagers of the late 1950s, instrumental to the consolidation of homeland hierarchies between nobles, commoners, and former slaves.[31] While carrying out research on the associational life of early 1960s Bamako, Claude Meillassoux, found men and women of slave ancestry who not only retained their identities as slave descendants but who during family celebrations performed the very dances associated with only slaves in earlier days. Old status distinctions were also significant among Futa Toro and Soninke immigrants in Dakar, and in France, which were in the 1960s, important destinations for Futa Toro and Soninke migrations.[32] Recent works on Senegalese Futa Toro have shown that migration has in many cases reinforced existing social inequalities, but migrants of slave background are more likely to invest in the education of their offspring than in their place of origin, unlike members of the elite.[33]

11

Struggles for Democracy and Political Participation

Struggles for independence, which most African states achieved in the 1960s, and the processes of democratization that followed the end of the cold war in the late 1980s, provided people of slave ancestry with opportunities to take part in civic debates on citizenship, political participation, and the role of the state. At independence, most nationalists were anxious to transcend and if possible, ignore divisions of ethnicity and social class. Many new constitutions included prohibitions of slavery. Some of the more radical regimes, like the Tanganyika African National Union, Mali's Union Soudanaise, and Guinea's Parti Democratique de la Guinée, took more forward stances and actively attacked slavery. The anticolonial struggle had mobilized social forces on the margins of the colonial state, like workers, women, youths, and socially excluded groups like slaves. Descendants of slaves, however, still had to struggle against discrimination by former dominant groups. Attitudes proved hard to change, especially in rural areas.[34] In the very conservative Futa Jallon highlands of Guinea, there were slave revolts even in the precolonial period. When during colonial days slavery ceased to be legal, freed slaves and their descendants strove to overcome their subordination to former masters; yet, at the time of Guinean independence in 1958, slavery was such a relevant social issue that the new government restated its abolition. The epithet of "Fulbe of the 28th of September" (the day of national independence) was a way to depreciate that part of the Futa Jallon citizenry which was of slave ancestry. Roger Botte's research, carried out in the late 1980s, testifies to the resentment of Futa Jallon slave descendants toward enduring discrimination as well as to their commitment to keep alive the memory of their enslaved ancestors by not changing surnames in order to hide their origins.[35]

In the last years of the twentieth century, democratization forced African polities to deal with the vestiges of internal slavery.[36] In Ghana, where there have been several peaceful and democratic political transitions and where the heritage tourism industry and the efforts of local scholars have highlighted the existence of indigenous slavery, the stigma of slave origins remains. This is especially true when it comes to traditional chieftaincy matters. In 1995, the Supreme Court of the Republic of Ghana stripped Nana Akuamoah Boaten Ababio, "a highly educated [businessperson] and respected gentleman" of a quite prominent and important chieftaincy position. They did so because he was of slave origins. The court based its ruling on the fact that "customary laws and usages" which barred slave descendants from such positions were recognized as part of the legal code of Ghana in the country's 1992 constitution. In issuing the judgment, the chief justice noted that discrimination by family heads against those members of the same family who were of slave descent "was not repugnant to justice, equity and good conscience." The decision generated an uproar. Some contended that by upholding this traditional practice, the court allowed customary law to "deny [slaves and their descendants] the rights conferred [on them] by the ordinances that set [them] free." These ordinances were the 1874 Abolition of Slavery Ordinance, the 1874 Emancipation of Persons Held in Slavery, and the 1930 Reaffirmation of the Abolition of Slavery Ordinance. Others argued that "while the emancipation ordinances of 1874 pronounced freedom for slaves in the Gold Coast [i.e., Ghana], they did not ... protect their rights to property," in this case access to a traditional political post. Nana Akuamoah Boaten Ababio was removed from office. His slave status barred him from holding such a position. He was informed, in no uncertain terms, that he had no right of access to the property of the family of which he and the descendants of his ancestor had been a part for generations.[37]

In other parts of Africa, the democratic reforms of the 1990s have made a difference. Changes are most evident in countries where traditional hierarchies have been the most rigid. In northern Benin, those of slave descent, who were known as the Gando, continued to suffer considerably under the hegemony of former masters and rulers for a good part of the twentieth century. Gando who obtained higher education most often hid their origins or moved to areas where they could do so. Only after the end of Mathieu Kérékou's socialist regime and the drafting of a new constitution

13

in 1990, did some Gando intellectuals and professionals return home to convince their fellows to become more assertive. From the 2003 municipal elections, an increasing number of Gando were elected to office.[38]

Eric Hahonou, in chapter 2, "The Struggle for Political Emancipation of Slave Descendants in Contemporary Borgu, Northern Benin," tells that story through the words of a deputy of Gando origin, who has put the fight against discrimination at the top of his agenda. Elsewhere, in those areas where the exploitation of slaves continued the longest, militant slave organizations have emerged. One of these organizations is Timidria, which was created in Niger in parallel with the National Conference of 1991; since then, Timidria has worked to raise the awareness of Niger slave descendants and of civil society at large about the persistence of slavery within the country.[39]

In Mauritania, the movement El-Hor was established in 1978, by educated members of the Haratine, a servile group who have often been defined as descendants of slaves. They demanded the abolition of slavery, land reforms, and the modernization of Islamic jurisprudence, which was used to endorse the subjection of slaves to their masters. SOS Esclaves was created in the mid-1990s in order to enlarge the struggle beyond the Haratine and also include the slaves who are of black origin.[40] In Mali, during the Tuareg rebellion of the 1990s, descendants of slaves joined Ganda Koy, a largely Songhay militia that sought to resist the Tuareg nomads who have preyed on riverine and desert-side peoples.[41] Their exemplary actions have spread. In Senegal, for example, descendants of slaves from the Futa Toro areas have formed an organization known as Endam Bilali. Even where the descendants of slaves are not in a majority or have not come together in formal organizations, the quest for their votes often blunts the harsh edges of stigmatization.

As people of slave descent have increasingly chosen to assert their origins rather than trying to hide them, relations can sometime be abrasive. This is illustrated by the incident Damian Opata cites at the beginning of his chapter. At the same time, increasing numbers among the educated are also interested in eliminating distinctions in social status, and they are doing so by confronting that heritage directly. In Senegal, the Centre Africain de Recherches sur les Traites et les Esclavages (CARTE), directed by Thioub, brings together scholars and students from different parts of Francophone Africa and the Caribbean to promote research on slavery and to support activities aimed at ending the stigma associated with slave ancestry.[42] In Cameroon, a traditional chief, the Fon of Bamendjina in central Cameroon, has built a museum, half of which is devoted to the history of slavery.[43] In Ghana and Nigeria, scholars like Emmanuel Saboro, Damian Opata, Ugo Nwokeji, Kofi Anyidoho, and Akosua Perbi have unearthed memories of slavery in these two countries and publicized them via television programs, museum exhibitions, and public symposia. Their efforts have encouraged both families and communities to discuss the past (and its continuing influence on the present) in ways that have heretofore been avoided.[44]

Where Are the Slaves' Voices?

Most of the contributors to this book assess the vitality of memories associated with African internal slavery and the slave trade in contemporary African societies. Dealing with this kind of recollection, however, is difficult. Not only was the end of slavery slow, as was already noted, but it often took place under the cover of silence. There were many reasons for this. Descendants of slaves and nobles have continued to live together, and the need to get along with each other led both to suppress the most painful aspects of their common history. In many areas, from Senegal to Ghana, etiquette required not confronting distinctions of status openly, while in other contexts descendants of slaves, even after legal abolition, continued to refer to the descendants of their ancestors' masters as "fathers." In doing so, they reassert the traditional hierarchy. Where the slave descendant was properly deferential, the descendant of the master could be paternalistic, but where the freed slave did not behave properly, for example, by pursuing and marrying a noble woman or by being disrespectful, the reaction could be harsh. In the case of the Soninke, Yaya Sy reports the story of a slave descendant, who in the latter part of the twentieth century migrated to Europe and eventually married a noble woman. Not only was he excluded from all of the benefits of the community association, but so were his supporters in France and in the village from which they came.[45] Botte, by contrast, describes the reluctance of Futa Jallon slave descendants to let their daughters marry into the former slave-owning class. This kind of marriage lacks reciprocity just as the contrary—a male slave descendant marrying a noble woman—was still not accepted in the late of twentieth century; fathers of slave ancestry explained to Botte that they preferred marriage alliances with families of the same social status.

Whether foreigners or nationals based in the city or university, scholars addressing these issues often find that there are certain questions they are not supposed to ask. Their persistence, in certain cases, has elicited a wall of silence. Of course, the perceptive scholar who lives in a community can learn a great deal about the web of social relations based on slavery, and with time, is often able to obtain a lot of information. Still, there are parts of the past which are simply unrecoverable either because people, even today, do not wish to discuss them or simply because the memories have withered away.

Ousmane Traoré's informants tell us that what they know comes only from what they have seen themselves and what they have been told by their fathers. In some instances, however, especially when allowed by the broader social context, freed slaves deliberately used silence as a strategy of self-emancipation. By not telling their young where they originally came from, they tried to protect them from the feelings of social inferiority inevitably associated with slave ancestry. In avoiding such painful memories and refusing to share them, these people and their descendants lose the genealogies that were an integral part of their very identities. This kind of choice has been an advantage where slave descendants continue to be stigmatized, but it has also prevented the emergence of collective memories of freed slaves and their descendants, which could be used to reconstruct their side of the story.

In addition to individuals and family heads, entire groups have been secretive about their slave-dealing and slave-holding past. Before colonization, the Aro of Southeast Nigeria operated one of the most efficient slave-trading organizations in Africa, but when a member of their own community, Ugo Nwokeji, tried to ferret out truths about their past, they were reticent and chastised him for pushing too hard. It is a tale G. Ugo Nwokeji, in chapter 5, "Memories of Slavery in a Former Slave-Trading Community: The Aro of the Bight of Biafra," tells well in this book. Similarly, Robert M. Baum spent several decades researching a Jola community in southern Senegal. He learned the language and tried to integrate himself in the community. It took eight visits before he uncovered stories of shrines linked to the slave trade and used by Jola elders to deal with the problems associated with the holding of slaves.[46]

Interestingly, even though much about slavery has either been forgotten or remains hidden, fragments of the past can become embedded in a number of different cultural forms. Rosalind Shaw has discussed Sierra Leone memories of slavery retained in witchcraft beliefs,[47] while Nicolas Argenti has shown how slavery and the slave trade have shaped folktales, which children of the Cameroon Grassfields tell one another to this day.[48] In this book, Damian Opata, in chapter 3, "Remembering Slavery in Northern Igbo Proverbial Discourses," gives us a collection of Igbo proverbs that depict relationships that no longer exist as formal structures but still influence how people view each other. Alessandra Brivio, in chapter 8, "Evoking the Past through Material Culture: The Mami Tchamba Shrine," explores a set of memories that are contained within the rituals of Mami Chamba, a vodun religious order in southern Togo.

More direct transmissions have occurred as well. When memories are publicly articulated in the form of historical narratives or oral traditions, other problems confront scholars of slavery. Ousmane Traoré, for instance, gives us an example of how descendants of slaves and masters look differently at their common past. Both are honestly reporting what they think happened. Remembering, however, is a highly selective process. Husbands and wives, brothers and sisters, or good friends will often recollect differently events they witnessed together. No one can remember everything. Our memories are unconsciously filtered by both individual and collective interests, by our values and by the way we feel about how our ancestors acted. Memories are social and cultural constructs, and events that never occurred can be passionately believed as well as those that actually took place.

Documentary records can be equally problematic. When colonial regimes ended slave raiding and trading, the issue of slavery for many colonial officials was no longer a concern. With slave raiders no longer spreading misery and with slave caravans no longer sorrowfully trudging across the African landscape, colonial governments were rarely under pressure from abolitionist groups in Europe to continue to address the issue. The problem of slavery was supposedly solved. Colonial sources after the early colonial period hardly mention the topic of slavery at all. What followed in reality was a persistent struggle between slaves, masters, and their descendants often over the issue of honor; bravery, generosity, and standards of how to behave continued to be considered as a prerogative of former slave-owning groups. In areas committed to a rigorous Muslim morality, dancing has been sometimes prohibited or allowed only for low-status people as it was a prerogative of slaves and their descendants before abolition. In countries like Mauritania, Senegal, and Mali, people of noble ancestry are not to speak loudly and nor are they supposed to openly discuss sexual matters. Publicly asking for money or gifts is seen as appropriate only for slaves. A true noble did not beg though nobles are sometimes forced by circumstances to behave in ways not appropriate to their status in order to survive.[49] In the aftermath of abolition, many freed slaves and slave descendants conformed to noble behavioral codes in striving to obtain the accoutrements of honor. They achieved a Muslim education. They enrolled in European missionary schools. They refused to beg. They built mosques and churches and sought to behave as a "noble" or chief would.

While many noble elites have clung to status distinctions, others have sought reconciliation with the enslaved and their descendants. Few scholars have focused on this topic except when it involved reconciliation efforts by contemporary African chiefs and politicians to establish better relations with the descendants of those who were sold into the Atlantic slave trade.[50] Among the few scholars who have focused on reconciliation within Africa is Zacharie Saha. In his contribution to this book, he writes of the Cameroonian Tabula, who lived most of his life in slavery dreaming of a return home. After being freed, he met a business person from his home region who arranged for his return. He was received and ennobled by a descendant of the man who sent him into servitude. Similarly, Brivio documents how the cult of Mami Chamba is concerned with setting to rest the unhappy spirits of captives from northern Benin and Togo who died away from their families and homes in the South. In this religious order, the descendants of enslavers essentially worship those their forefathers enslaved, all in the interest of a spiritual reconciliation.[51]

Acknowledgments

The chapters presented in this book are all the product of a larger project to collect African sources on slavery and the slave trade, which the three editors launched in 2006, together with Carolyn Brown of Rutgers University. In 2007, they organized an international workshop at the Bellagio Centre of the Rockefeller Foundation and a conference in Toronto in 2009. Both events focused on African voices on slavery and the slave trade, as much as on the legacy of slavery in contemporary Africa. Martin A. Klein then organized a conference in Buea in Cameroon in December 2010, in collaboration with Stephen Denis Fomin and Idrissou Alioum.

We would like to thank those who supported this project. For the 2007 workshop in Bellagio, we are indebted to the Rockefeller Foundation and the staff at the Bellagio Conference Center, particularly Laura Podio, who provided a welcoming environment conducive to debate and reflection. They also generously provided funds to bring four colleagues from Africa. For the Toronto conference, we are particularly grateful to the Jackman Humanities Institute, which provided financial support, and to Rick Halpern, then Principal of New College, who provided advice, financial assistance, and a comfortable working environment. New College staff, particularly Krishnan Mehta, were also invaluable. We also thank Paul Lovejoy and the Harriet Tubman Institute for Research on the Global Migrations of African Peoples, the Connaught Foundation, and the Centre for Transnational and Diaspora Studies at the University of Toronto. We particularly appreciated the work of our web-master, Yacine Daddi Addoun. The Italian Ethnological Mission in Bénin and West Africa (MEBAO) supported the fieldwork research and the travel expenses of Italian participants, while in various ways, the three universities of Cornell, Rutgers, and Milan-Bicocca aided the participation of Greene, Brown, and Bellagamba in the conferences and editorial meetings that led to the creation of this book. Finally, we thank everyone who participated in the two conferences, including our team of student volunteers, along with the legion of African colleagues, oral historians, archivists, scholars, and ritual specialists who enabled our authors' access to the sources included in this book.

Notes

1. Ibrahima Thioub, "Regard critique sur les lectures Africaines de l'esclavage et de la traite atlantique," in *Les historiens Africains et la mondialisation,* eds. Issiaka Mandé and Blandine Stefanson (Paris: Karthala, 2005), 271-92.
2. See UNESCO official website: http://www.unesco.org/new/en/culture/themes/dialogue/the-slave-route/.
3. Emmanuel Akyeampong, "History, Memory, Slave-Trade and Slavery in Anlo (Ghana)", *Slavery & Abolition* 22 (2001): 1-24; Ana Lucia Araujo, *Public Memory of Slavery. Victims and Perpetrators in the South Atlantic* (Amherst, NY: Cambria Press, 2010); Nassirou Bako-Arifari, "La mémoire de la traite négrière dans le débat politique au Bénin dans les années 1990," *Journal des Africanistes* 70, nos. 1-2(2000): 221- 32; Susan Benson and T. C. McCaskie, "Asen Praso in History and Memory," *Ghana Studies* 7 (2004): 93-113; Ed-

ward Bruner, "Tourism in Ghana. The Representation of Slavery and the Return of the Black Diaspora," *American Anthropologist* 98, no. 2 (1996): 290-304; Paula Ebron, "Tourists as Pilgrims: Commercial Fashioning of Transatlantic Politics," *American Anthropologist* 26, no. 4 (2000): 910-32; Jennifer Hasty, "Rites of Passage, Routes of Redemption: Emancipation Tourism and the Wealth of Culture," *Africa Today* 49, no. 3 (2002): 47-76; Bayo Holsey, *Routes of Remembrance. Refashioning the Slave Trade in Ghana* (Chicago: Chicago University Press, 2007); Katharina Schramm, "Slave Route Projects: Tracing the Heritage of Slavery in Ghana," in *Reclaiming Heritage. Alternative Imaginaries of Memory in West Africa*, eds. Ferdinand De Jong and Michael Rowlands (Walnut Creek, CA: Left Coast Press, 2007), 71-98.

4. Peter F. McLoughin, "Economic Development and the Heritage of Slavery in the Sudan Republic," *Africa* 32, no. 4 (1962): 355-91; Mark Leopold, "Legacies of Slavery in North-West Uganda: The Story of the 'One-Elevens,'" *Africa* 76, no. 2 (2006): 180-99.

5. Wole Soyinka, "Between Truths and Indulgences. Africa's Role in the Slave Trade and Its Consequences," *Transition* 103 (2010):110-17.

6. Seymour Drescher, *Abolition. A History of Slavery and Abolition* (Cambridge: Cambridge University Press, 2009); Adam Hochschild, *Bury the Chains: Prophets and Rebels in the Fight to Free and Empire's Slaves* (New York: Houghton Miflin Harcourt, 2005); David Brion Davis, *The Problem of Slavery in an Age of Revolution* 1770-1823 (Ithaca, NY: Cornell University Press, 1975); Marika Sherwood, *After Abolition. Britain and the Slave Trade since 1807* (London: Tauris, 2007). They were not the first. Denmark abolished the slave trade in 1792. France abolished slavery in 1794 only to reestablish it in 1802. Efforts by a French army to reimpose slavery on St. Domingue led to the establishment of the independence of Haiti. Laurent Dubois, *Avengers of the New World: The Story of the Haitian Revolution* (Cambridge, MA: Belknap Press, 2005); Jeremy Popkin, *You All Are Free: The Haitian Revolution and the Abolition of Slavery* (Cambridge: Cambridge University Press, 2010)

7. Lawrence Jennings, *French Anti-Slavery: The Movement for the Abolition of Slavery in France, 1802-1848* (Cambridge: Cambridge University Press, 2000); Nelly Schmidt, *Victor Schoelcher et l'abolition de l'esclavage* (Paris: Fayard, 1994).

8. A. G. Hopkins, *Economic History of West Africa* (London: Longman's, 1973).

9. Robin Law, ed., *From Slave Trade to Legitimate Commerce: The Commercial Transition in Nineteenth Century West Africa* (Cambridge: Cambridge University Press, 1995).

10. Richard Reid, *Warfare in African History* (New York: Cambridge University Press, 2012), chap. 5.

11. Martin A. Klein, *Slavery and Colonial Rule in French West Africa* (Cambridge: Cambridge University Press, 1998); Paul Lovejoy, *Transformations in Slavery. A History of Slavery in Africa*, 2nd ed. (Cambridge: Cambridge University Press, 2000).

12. Lovejoy and Jan Hogendorn, *Slow Death for Slavery. The Course of Abolition in Northern Nigeria, 1897-1936* (Cambridge: Cambridge University Press, 1993); Frederick Cooper, *From Slaves to Squatters: Plantation Labor and Agriculture in Zanzibar and Coastal Kenya, 1890-1925* (New Haven: Yale University Press, 1980); Klein, *Slavery and Colonial Rule in French West Africa*.

13. Richard Roberts and Suzanne Miers, eds., *The End of Slavery in Africa* (Madison: University of Wisconsin Press, 1988).

14. Alice Bellagamba, "Slavery and Emancipation in the Colonial Archives: British Officials, Slave-Owners, and Slaves in the Protectorate of the Gambia (1890-1936)," *Canadian Journal of African Studies* 39, no. 1 (2005): 5-41.

15. To date, the only book length study is an edited volume that focuses not on a single resistance movement, but rather is a collection of studies by different authors on a range of resistance efforts. Sylviane Diouf, ed., *Fighting the Slave Trade: West African Strategies* (Athens: Ohio University Press, 2003). Many other articles and sections of books, especially those that focus on slavery in Africa, do examine resistance as a theme.

16. Klein, *Slavery and Colonial Rule in French West Africa*; Roberts and Klein, "The Banamba Slave Exodus of 1905 and the Decline of Slavery in the Western Sudan," *Journal of African History* 21 (1980): 375-94.

17. Jan-Georg Deutsch, "The 'Freeing' of Slaves in German East Africa: The Statistical Record, 1890-1914," in *Slavery and Colonial Rule in Africa*, eds., Suzanne Miers and Martin A. Klein (London: Frank Cass, 1999), 109-32; Jan-Georg Deutsch, *Emancipation without Abolition in German East Africa c. 1884-1914* (Oxford: James Currey, 2006).

18. McLoughlin, "Economic Development and the Heritage of Slavery in the Sudan Republic.".

19. Ibrahim K. Sundiata, *From Slaving to Neoslavery: The Bight of Bi-

22

afra and Fernando Po in the Era of Abolition 1827-1930 (Madison: University of Wisconsin Press, 1996); Sundiata, *Brothers and Strangers: Black Zion, Black Slavery 1914-1940* (Durham, NC: Duke University Press, 2004).

20. Cooper, *From Slaves* to *Squatters*, chap. 5.
21. *The Diary of Hamman Yaji: Chronicle of a West African Muslim Ruler*, eds. James Vaughan and Anthony H. M. Kirk-Greene (Bloomington: Indiana University Press, 1995).
22. Ahmadou Sehou, "Some Facets of Slavery in the Lamidats of Adamawa in the Northern Cameroon in the 19th and 20th Centuries," in *African Voices on Slavery and the Slave Trade*, vol. 1, *Sources,* eds. Alice Bellagamba, Sandra Greene, and Martin Klein (Cambridge: Cambridge University Press, 2013).
23. John Iliffe, *Honor in Africa History* (Cambridge: Cambridge University Press, 2005), 202.
24. Helen Duffy, "Hadijatou Mani Koroua v. Niger: Slavery Unveiled by the ECOWAS Court," *Human Rights Law Review* 9, no. 1 (2009): 151-70; Joel Quirk, *The Anti-Slavery Project. From the Slave Trade to Human Trafficking* (Philadelphia: University of Pennsylvania Press, 2011).
25. Myron Echenberg, *Colonial Conscripts: The Tirailleurs Sénégalais in French West Africa 1857-1960* (Portsmouth, NH: Heinemann, 1990).
26. Gregory Mann, *Native Sons: West African Veterans and France in the 20th Century* (Durham, NC: Duke University Press, 2006).
27. Klein, *Slavery and Colonial Rule in French West Africa*, 200-203, 229-31; Sean Hanretta, *Islam and Social Change in French West Africa: History of an Emancipatory Community* (Cambridge: Cambridge University Press. 2009).
28. François Manchuelle, *Willing Migrants: Soninke Labor Diasporas* (Athens: Ohio University Press, 1997); Benedetta Rossi, "Slavery and Migration: Physical and Social Mobility in Ader (Tahoua)," in *Reconfiguring Slavery. West African Trajectories,* ed. Benedetta Rossi (Liverpool: Liverpool University Press, 2009), 182-206. In 2010, Rossi also organized an international workshop on slavery, abolition, and migration at the University of Liverpool and a panel on the same theme at the 53rd annual meeting of the African Studies Association (November 18-21).
29. Mirjam de Bruijn and Lotte Pelckmans, "Facing Dilemmas: Former Fulbe Slaves in Modern Mali," *Canadian Journal of African Studies* 39 (2005):69-95.

30. Alice Bellagamba, "'Silence Is Medicine!' Ending Slavery and Promoting Social Coexistence in Post-Abolition Gambia," in *The Problem of Violence. Local Conflict Settlement in Contemporary Africa,* eds.Georg Klute and Birgit Embalo (Cologne, Germany: Köppe Verlag, 2012), 445-76.
31. Elliott P. Skinner, "Labour Migration and Its Relationship to Socio-Cultural Change in Mossi Society," *Africa* 30, no. 4 (1960): 375-401.
32. Abdoulaye Bara Diop, Société toucouleur et migration (Dakar, Senegal: IFAN: 1965); Manchuelle, *Willing Migrants.*
33. Abderrahmane N'Gaide, "Stéréotypes et imaginaires sociaux en milieu Haalpulaar: Classer, stigmatiser et toiser" *Cahiers d'études Africaines* 43, no. 4 (2003): 707-38; Jean Schmitz, "Islamic Patronage and Republican Emancipation: The Slaves of the Almami in the Senegal River Valley," in *Reconfiguring Slavery: West African Trajectories,* ed. Benedetta Rossi (Liverpool: Liverpool University Press, 2009), 85-115; Jean-Luc Demosant, "Un système informel de retraite basé sur le prestige des notables au village: Etude de cas à Matam (Sénégal)," in *Les relations intergénérationnelles en Afrique: Approche plurielle,* Philippe Antoine (Paris, CEPED: 2008), 121-42.
34. Nicholas Hopkins, "Socialism and Social Change in Rural Mali," *Journal of Modern African Studies* 7, no. 3 (1969): 461-62; Elisabeth Schmidt, "Top Down or Bottom Up? Nationalist Mobilization Reconsidered, with Special Reference to Guinea (French West Africa)," *American Historical Review* 110, no. 4 (2005): 975-1014; Bruce S. Hall, " Bellah Histories of Decolonization, Iklan Paths to Freedom: The Meanings of Race and Slavery in the Late-Colonial Niger Bend (Mali), 1944-1960," *International Journal of African Historical Studies* 44, no.1(2011): 61-87; Felicitas Becker, "Common Themes, Individual Voices: Memories of Slavery Around a Former Slave Plantation in Mingoyo, Tanzania," in *African Voices on Slavery and the Slave Trade,* vol. 1, *Sources,* eds. Alice Bellagamba, Sandra Greene, and Martin Klein (Cambridge: Cambridge University Press, 2013).
35. Roger Botte, "Stigmates sociaux et discrimination religieuses l'ancienne classe servile au Fuuta Jaloo," *Cahiers d'études Africaines* 34 (1994): 109-36; Mamadou Saliou Baldé, "L'esclavage et la guerre sainte au Fouta-Jalon," in *L'esclavage en Afrique precoloniale,* ed. Claude Meillasoux (Paris, Maspero 1975), 203-20. The case of northern Cameroon, where royal slavery has been part of the chieftaincy structure even in postcolonial times, is equally interesting. Issa Saïbou, "Paroles d'esclaves au Nord-Cameroun," *Cahiers d'études*

Africaines 179-180, n.s. 3-4 (2005): 853-78.

36. Jean-François Bayart, "Les chemins de traverse de l'hegemonie coloniale en Afrique de l'ouest Francophone: Anciens esclaves, anciens
combattants, nouveaux musulmans," *Politique Africaine* 105 (2007):
201-40.

37. Kofi Baku, " 'We Shall Not Be Silenced': Claims of Emancipated
Slaves to Property and Consanguinity in the Gold Coast (Ghana)."
Presented at the international conference on Narratives of Slavery,
the Slave Trade and Enslavement in Africa at the University of
Toronto, May 20-23, 2009. See also "Brobbey and Others v. Kwaku,"
Ghana Law Reports, 1995-96, 1 (Accra, Ghana: Council for Law
Reporting, 2004); and a newspaper account of the case, "Installation
of Mamponghene Declared Invalid," *Ashanti Pioneer*, July 17,1991,
pp. 1-4. Concerns about slave status when chieftaincy positions are
to be filled are common in many parts of Ghana. See Sandra E.
Greene, *West African Narratives of Slavery* (Bloomington: Indiana
University Press, 2011), 156-57.

38. Eric Hahonou, "Slavery and Politics: Stigma, Decentralisation and
Political Representation in Niger and Beinin" in *Reconfiguring Slavery: West African Trajectories,* ed. Benedetta Rossi (Liverpool: Liverpool University Press, 2009), 152-81.

39. Mahaman Tidjani Alou, "Démocratie, exclusion sociale et quête de
citoyenneté: Cas de l'association Timidria au Niger," *Journal des
Africanistes* 70, nos. 1-2 (2000): 173-95.

40. Ann MacDougall, "Living the Legacy of Slavery. Beyond Discourse
and Reality," *Cahiers d'études Africaines* 179-80, n.s. 3-4 (2005):
957-86; Zekeria Ould Ahmed Salem, "Bare-foot Activists: Transformations in the Haratine Movement in Mauritania," in *Movers and
Shakers: Social Movements in Africa,* eds. Stephen Ellis and Ineke
van Kessel (Leiden, Netherlands: Brill, 2009), 157-76.

41. Baz Le Cocq, "The Bellah Question: Slave Emancipation, Race, and
Social Categories in Late Twentieth-Century Northern Mali," *Canadian Journal of African Studies* 39 (2005): 42-68.

42. The centre is based in Dakar (http://carte-ucad.org/index.php/presen-
tation).

43. In 2010, the Fon gave one of the editors of this book a tour of the
still new museum and other sites connected to the slave trade. The
most interesting was a bubbling brook, where slaves were washed
before being marched to the coast. In a clearing, there were signs of
sacrifices to the memory of the long-departed victims of the trade.

44. Akosua Adoma Perbi's publications on slavery include A *History of*

Indigenous Slavery in Ghana from the 15th to *the 19th Century* (Legon-Accra, Ghana: Sub-Saharan Publishers, 2007); "The Relationship between the Domestic Slave Trade and the External Slave Trade in Pre-colonial Ghana," *Research Review* (Institute of African Studies) 8, n.s. 1-2 (1992): 64-75; and "Servitude and Chieftaincy in Ghana: The Historical Evidence," in *Chieftaincy in Ghana: Culture, Governance and Development,* eds. Irene K. Odotei and Albert K.Awedobu (Legon-Accra, Ghana: Sub-Saharan Publishers, 2006), 353-78. Kofi Anyidoho's work on the history of slavery in Ghana includes his role as host and executive producer of the series for Ghana television, *African Heritage Series* and appearances in the U. S. television series, *Traces of the Trade*: A *Story from the Deep North*. His interest in the issue of slavery is also quite evident in his poetry. See especially his book *The Place We Call Home* (Banbury, UK: Ayebia Clark, 2011).

45. Yaya Sy, "L'esclavage chez les Soninkés: Du village à Paris," *Journal des Africanistes* 70, nos. 1-2 (2000): 43-69.
46. Robert M. Baum, *Shrines of the Slave Trade: Diola Religion and Society in Precolonial Senegambia* (Oxford: Oxford University Press, 1999).
47. Rosalind Shaw, *Memories of the Slave Trade: Ritual and the Historical Imagination* in *Sierra Leone* (Chicago and London: University of Chicago Press, 2002).
48. Nicolas Argenti, "Things that Don't Come by the Road: Folktales, Fosterage, and Memories of Slavery in the Cameroon Grassfields," *Comparative Studies in Society and History* 52 (2010): 224-54.
49. See, for instance, Monique Chastanet, "Famines, subsistances et enjeux sociopolitiques dans les traditions historiques: Exemples soninkés (Sénégal, Mauritanie, Mali)," in *Entre la parole et l'écrit. Contributions à l'histoire de l'Afrique en hommage à Claude-Hélène Perrot*, eds. Monique Chastanet and Jean-Pierre Chretien (Paris: Karthala, 2008), 76-97.
50. On reconciliation efforts carried out by the government of Benin, see John B. Hatch, *Race and Reconciliation: Redressing Wounds of Injury* (New York: Rowman and Littlefield, 2008), 219-29. On reconciliation efforts planned by the Ghana government in 2007, see Cheryl Finley, "Golden Anniversaries and Bicentennials: The Convergence of Memory, Tourism and National History in Ghana," *Journeys* 77, no. 2 (2006): 15-31.
51. The idea of reconciliation has also manifested itself in the work of African writers. It is important in *Sankofa*, a film by Haile Gerima,

an Ethiopian director living in the United States, which deals with suppressed memories of enslavement and the slave trade. See also Ama Ata Aidoo's plays, *Dilemma of a Ghost* (Accra, Ghana: Longman, 1965), and Isidore Okpewho's novel *Call Me by My Rightful Name* (Trenton, NJ: Africa World Press, 2004).

2. The Struggle for Political Emancipation of Slave Descendants in Contemporary Borgu, Northern Benin

ERIC KOMLAVI HAHONOU

Introduction

In the history of slavery, southern Benin (a fraction of the former kingdom of Dahomey) is part of what Europeans called the Slave Coast between the seventeenth and nineteenth centuries. It has been estimated that over a million slaves were exported to the American continent from Ouidah, which was the principal commercial center in the region and the most important West African slaving port.[1] Slavery was particularly important also in what is today northern Benin, although this part of the country's past is less well known and less discussed than the history of Benin's connections with the Atlantic slave trade. Slaves occupied a central role in the economy as well as in the social and political structures of most northern Benin social groups. This was particularly the case for the precolonial kingdom of Borgu, which covered around 70,000 kilometers stretching from northeastern Benin to northwestern Nigeria.[2] The kingdom of Borgu was dominated by the Baatombu (also known as Bariba) and the Boko (or Boo). Its multiethnic society included Bariba (and Boo) warriors (called Wasangari), as well as cultivators and hunters and Fulbe herders (or Peuls). Each of these groups had slaves—usually called Gando[3]—acquired by capture in wars and raids and by purchase. Slaves worked on the land of their master and performed all kinds of hard

29

work (yam cultivation, cattle herding, wood collection, and other arduous household tasks), while also obeying the will of their owners. They belonged to their master, who could sell them at any time. The Gando were placed at the margins of Baatonu and Boo villages and Fulbe camps. This physical distance is one of the many markers of the social differentiation between Gando and other social groups in these communities. Held in low regard, slaves were not allowed to own cattle, to marry freeborn women, and to behave like a freeborn. Yet slave women could be married by their owners as second or third wives. According to Borgu hierarchical organization, only free men had the right to participate in the political system.[4] Despite a formal set of laws against slavery, the situation of the Gando didn't change much during colonial times and during much of the postcolonial era. In practice, former slaves were performing the same tasks on the fields of their former masters as they performed during the colonial period. The owners could also be paid for the work done by slaves for others. Slavery could thus survive.[5] Former slaves and those descended from slaves were also still placed on the margins of society and excluded from political participation. This continued until the end of Kerekou's revolutionary regime (1974-89). President Mathieu Kerekou's political project was to build a revolutionary multiethnic state (at that time called nationalities) and to fight against all forms of feudalities. Despite formal and symbolic decisions like the appointment of people of slave origins as district officers, the dominant values and norms of the ideology of slavery survived. Until quite recently, slave descendants were hardly recognized as full members of the community.[6]

At present, a major change is happening: people of slave origins are emerging politically in the global context of democratization and decentralization, processes that have affected western Africa. Although it is difficult to say precisely when this process of change began to occur, three major events can be identified in the Gando's recent political emancipation and social recognition. First has been the birth of a collective claim for recognition of the Gando's specific identity and history. At the end of the revolutionary regime, in the 1980s, Gando people joined the Fulbe under the umbrella of an organization called Laawol Fulfulde. In 1987, both the Gando and the Fulbe pastoralist seized this organization as an opportunity to overcome the marginalization they suffered.[7] Whereas official discourses emphasized equality amongst the communities in the nation-state, Gando leaders soon realized they were still seen and treated as inferior by their former masters. The split from Laawol Fulfulde[8] and the creation of various independent Gando organizations in 2000-2001 marked a second step in the birth of Gando collective identity. Semmee Allah (i.e., The Accomplishment of the Will of God) is one of these Gando organizations created in Kalalé by the interviewee (see the following section). Finally, a decade after the Benin transition to democracy (which started in 1990, after the National Conference), the government began in 2002-2003 implementing a program aimed at democratic decentralization. This offered an unprecedented opportunity for Gando to seek political office at the local level. In Borgu, they won municipal elections in 2003, and again in 2008 (e.g., in Kalalé and Nikki). This third event allowed the Gando to emancipate themselves politically and be recognized socially.

This chapter presents an interview with Orou Sè Guéné, a former college professor and Gando charismatic political leader. Gando contemporary struggles for political emancipation are quite a surprise if we consider that fifty years ago Baldus described these people as accepting their inferiority and more recently Hardung saw them as locked in an identity vacuum ("Neither Peul nor Baatombu") and beset by an inferiority complex that together with internal status differences hindered their group cohesion and the emergence of a collective identity.[9] Orou Sè Guéné's education and his personal trajectory are important for understanding the dynamic that has contributed to the collective emancipation of Gando people. Formal public education offered him alternative values that he used to oppose the dominant ideology of slavery.

In this interview, Orou Sè Guéné explains his struggles against stigmatization and discrimination and articulates the ideological foundation for Gando claims. His discourse also introduces the multiple subgroups that today compose the Gando ethnic group (e.g., those acquired by raids and by purchase or child-sorcerers entrusted to Fulbe herders[10]). His narrative allows us to understand how the Gando group has succeeded in resolving its marginality by seeking political office and gaining economic prosperity through hard work.

This interview is part of a research project carried out in northern Benin between 2006 and 2008. Initially, my objective was to compare the social and political effects of democratic decentralization reforms in three West African countries (Benin, Niger, and Mali) rather than focusing specifically on slavery, but I came to see this issue as central to an understanding of today's local politics. Being of slave origin in this West African savanna community was long a handicap for social mobility and a political career. In this respect, the election of a Gando as mayor came as a surprise and created an ideological break.

Orou Sè Guéné was elected as the first mayor of Kalalé municipality in 2003. He was removed from office in 2005, following a motion of no-confidence by a large majority of the municipal council. Orou Sè Guéné explains how he was able to get elected later on as a deputy in the National Parliament of Benin despite his affiliation with an opposition party. I met and interviewed Orou Sè Guéné for the first time in 2006, soon after he was dismissed. This is a second interview with him after he was elected as deputy in 2007. The interview was conducted in French at Orou Sè Guéné's home in Parakou (main city of northern Benin). As with most interviews, Orou Sè Guéné's discourse is not always coherent; he repeats himself and makes efforts to justify himself. I have cut some redundancies and less interesting issues in this translated and slightly polished interview. Yet I have retained a few of these elements in order to give the reader a feel for what ethnographic materials look like. What makes this successful political leader's ideas and trajectory particularly interesting is that the situation of the Gando in northern Benin is not an isolated example. In Mali, Mauritania, and Niger, to take a few West African examples, similar struggles and success stories can also be found. From a social movement perspective, these developments can be understood as collective answers to a situation of marginalization in the context of a global impetus toward democracy.[11]

Interview with Deputy Orou Sè Guéné in Borgu

Q: *Mr. Orou Sè Guéné, today you are a member of National Parliament, and you were the mayor of Kalalé; could you retrace your journey for us and explain in what way Gando identity has played a positive role?*

A: I would like to thank you for inviting me to do this interview. I come from a Gando family. But this is a Gando feudal family.[12] In reality, we are Boo. Our ancestors were warriors and hunters. They founded the village called Boa. Essentially, this village was founded as a camp in a forest with a lot of game. They settled in a region of Fulfulde speakers.... So, our lineage is Boo, but by integrating the Fulfulde language on top of other languages, our ancestors adapted. At the time we were born, our parents already spoke Fulfulde.[13]

What makes us distinct is that our father was recruited at a time of war by the French army in 1943. He participated in defending the territory of our in-laws[14] but African soldiers were paid in valueless money. He was wounded in war and he returned without a pension. Years later France allocated pensions to wounded war vets. He benefited from a very ridiculous pension; it was just a symbol, but he obtained it very early. Considering what he saw in Madagascar and in Europe, he wanted his children to go to school. That is the reason why we went to school from a very young age. I am not his first son. My older brothers had to go, and they went. Our mothers opposed this idea and my father got tired because each time he took my older brothers to school, the mothers went afterward to remove and hide them.... What he did with me was to send me very far away (so that my mother could not remove me from school). I completed my primary school in 1972, which was the same year as the revolution.[15] My "old father"[16] continued to put

33

my other brothers in school because he held onto the idea of us going; and he would stop at nothing. At that time, school was still free, but even so, he encouraged us to go. In 1981, I graduated high school and in 1982, I registered at the University of Abomey Calavi in the Faculty of Technical Sciences. Personally, during my education at several different locations, I noticed a lack of respect for the Gando ethnic group by the other ethnic groups. This personally made an impression on me, so I had to sort this out, and maybe with time, correct it. School had never made a distinction and only took into account the intrinsic values of each child, or rather, his intellectual faculties, his intelligence, and his performance. Therefore we got a shock as soon as we left school.[17] So how could we fix this? The only solution, according to me, was to defeat the others on the education battlefield by asserting our intrinsic worth in school. Therefore, we had to do everything to have school values put in place, all the while fighting against the older values.... While working at the school, I said to myself that this superiority complex must be destroyed to show them that in fact it is meaningless. And I think on that point there, nature has allowed me to do something.... We evolved. And when I got to University, my "old father" was worn-out. I also had to think of the family, like my other brothers and sisters, so that they could continue their education. At any given moment one must not be alone; one must have others to contribute to overcoming fate....[18]

In 1983, I dropped out of university because I took a position in the administration. In 1989, I passed an entrance competition for the teacher's college. I passed. After a three-year education I graduated with a certificate which allows you to teach high school. But that didn't satisfy me. I asked the state to allow me to teach postsecondary courses. But the state said to me that I had to go back to complete more school. I went back to school in 2003. At that time, I had already been elected mayor. I couldn't let it slide, especially since there were not many applicants. The state felt the need to have postsecondary professors, especially since there was a shortage. So I was mayor and I registered and while I was at school in Porto Novo they voted for my dismissal from office. When I heard the news, I asked for a leave from school, which they gave me. I came back and I gathered my councillors. I said, "Well, it is my understanding that you wish to dismiss me; can you tell me what is motivating your conduct?" I had nine of seventeen of my own councillors. Among them, only one had the courage to say, "Mister Mayor, you have not committed one mistake in your management, but we are hungry." I asked him to be clear because if a councillor says he is hungry, it means that the mayor has blocked his rights. He said, "No, on the contrary!" He also said to me to go and get four hundred thousand F CFA for each of my ten councillors. I told them to calculate my two years of salary as mayor and to see that it totaled four million F CFA.[19] I said, "Where can I find four million so that I will not be dismissed? Do you want me to go steal and give it to you!?" I said to them, "Do what you want. As for me, I will be in Porto Novo!" I went back to Porto Novo and I was dismissed from office. So without going into detail, that is the story of my dismissal. In reality, my discharge was planned by the prefect.[20] What was the problem? They [the prefect and the new mayor] are from the same political party and I am not on their side. Therefore for them to win the city, they had to make me leave and to install their group…. That is what drove the prefect, and he in turn pushed the councillors…. The party was FARD Alafia.[21] FARD Alafia was already on the road to extinction. It does not exist anymore. The current mayor (who was from FARD Alafia) was never elected as councillor. A Gando cousin was put at the top of their list….[22] They put him at the top of the list to draw support from people in our ethnic group.[23] The current mayor was only his deputy. However, our Gando cousin agreed to concede his seat to his deputy…. He did it. And incidentally, they threatened him; they sent him elders with some charms[24] to tell him to quit. A couple of months after his election as councillor, he came to tell me that those elders wanted to physically eliminate him with charms. I said to him, "But, you, you are afraid of charms? And you dared to be councillor, you? You mustn't be scared of that!" Then I told him to do whatever he wanted to do and he resigned as councillor. When our cousin quit, his deputy became councillor according to the law. Then, after my dismissal, they organized the elections in the municipal council and he became mayor, just as the prefect wanted.... Yet, the FARD had only one councillor in the city; how can we explain it? This is how we can explain the chaos that has swept across the city. Nobody voted for you and you want to lead these people! That is the situation! When the population learned this, they wanted to revolt. I turned this idea down and explained to the people that we will not fall into this trap; instead we will wait for other electoral periods to retaliate. I said, "But by behaving this way [revolting], it could mean that they will come and lock you up."[25] Yet everyone knows that I don't like it when someone touches me or my people. I said to them, "If this [the election of a new mayor] can bring us happiness, it is good; that is what we seek. We will let him show what he can do." As for me, God gave me the chance. I finished, I got good grades, and I got my diploma. I am going to go back to postsecondary teaching. I said, "If you are with me, I would ask you to do nothing and to remain patient, because patience always pays." So they followed me and nobody said anything.

When the new mayor came into office, things started to get messy.... He considers himself to be one hundred percent Boo, and they are the ones who teased Gando. So when he came into office, the gendarmes and rangers began abusing their power; the custom officers fired upon an innocent crowd. They killed one and left eight others paralyzed for life [during a popular protest march]. That was a complete shock for everyone.

So when it was time to file papers for the parliamentary elections, people told me to apply for the job. I told them that President Yayi Boni took me off his list. At the beginning I was on his cauris list,[26] and I'm not sure what happened, but they almost certainly told Yayi Boni that Mr. Orou Sè Guéné is not popular because he was dismissed. So, they took my name off the list supported by the president.... Me, I'm not accusing the president, but his entourage lied to him. I recognized this. Someone went to see the president to explain how I was dismissed in Kalalé and to say that nobody likes me there [he laughs]. So it's normal; it was set up and I accept it.... Then, Gando people told me that it was not a problem [not to be on the president's list]; they asked me to join any party... they said they wanted to elect a "son of the land." They voted for Yayi Boni [in March 2006]; case closed. Now they had to vote for a "son of the land." Some Bariba also supported me. That's how I went to find a party and I've found one. And paradoxically I have found a party from the South. You see this! And yet you know that political parties in Benin are ethnic stuff. Then, nobody should have voted for this party in our region.[27] How can one explain this paradox: Me, supposedly someone nobody likes. I bring a party from the South, which was established by a Fon [ethnic group of southern Benin], and I win the election in the North! [he laughs].... During the campaign, Yayi Boni himself came to ask everyone to support his Cauris list. Some people asked him what he wanted, because if he wanted them to vote for Cauris he should have positioned Orou Sè Guéné on his list. They then said, "We respect you because you are the president of the Republic, but this time, we want to vote for a son the land." He gave them money, but they told him it wasn't a money issue. They said, "We want to vote for a son of the land. But since you give us money, we accept and take it!" They gave me some money they received from the president so that I could mount my electoral campaign.[28] That is how things happened and you have seen the results! We could have had twice as many votes as the Yayi party [he laughs]. The explanation behind all this is that we didn't have another idea except to see social justice take hold, because to me it is not a fight against a given ethnic group, but that there should be one social justice and that they know that in the eyes of the law everyone is equal. Whatever ethnic group you come from, whatever your faith, in front of the law, we are all equal and as long as I notice imbalance, I will not hesitate to fight against it....

Even Boo supported me because they knew me. I do not let injustices slide no matter what side, whether you are Boo or Bariba, because they are also poor. And people are used to marginalizing them and teasing them. I told them that this doesn't have to happen like this. It's not because the guy is poor; if he is right, one must agree with him. At school, they told us we all must play by the rules of the law, but if someone is wrong we have to arrest him.

In reality, it's because I started to flaunt my origins. If I hid myself, this would not have been possible.... I did my secondary school at Nikki.[29] Ever since school, I have always told myself that we must show everyone that Gando are not beings with less intelligence than everyone else. I never hid my origins. We must show what Gando are capable of. In reality, if those who were in the same classrooms as me are not hypocrites, they know who I am. The proof is that I was the only one who reached a university level among all those involved in my classrooms. First this!... There was after all the superiority complex, but that depends on the education of common people.[30] And I don't let myself do it. If you tease me because I am Gando, I will whip you. And I had this opportunity, and when we were at odds with each other, victory was on my side ninety percent of the time. So it doesn't mean anything to me and I am proud to be Gando. When someone comes to me proudly with his Bariba title, I tell him that "history has shown us that when a group of people is stronger than another, they take them as slaves. Thus, it is not any given ethnic group that is an ethnic group of slaves...." Since there are no internal tribal wars anymore there are no more slaves. Therefore it doesn't make any sense to take someone as a slave. It's your intellect that determines whether you are a slave or not. The only battlefield where we can struggle today is school. The new social norms to evaluate the value of a man are at school. To prove this, I had children from a Nikki king who drew my water and swept my room. I said, "Despite your princely title, me who is your slave, it is you who has become my slave. You are sweeping my house, you do my washing, and if you don't do it, I discipline you because I am your professor. I educate you! I am the one to tell you what to do...." Under these conditions, who is the slave? And who is the master? At this moment, the slave becomes the master. I am proud to be Gando. The values I learned at school are what motivate my conduct. History has already given a lot of information on the topic of slavery, even the triangular commerce over four centuries. Between us blacks, nobody should be so proud that he claims to be superior to someone else as far as there is nothing to prove it. There's no ethnic group who can say that they weren't taken to the Americas as slaves, to be sold and mistreated. Because they reckon that Gando are Fulbe slaves, yet Bariba and Boo consider Fulbe as secondary beings, meaning beings under their protection. Therefore Fulbe slaves are their slaves as well. That is the kind of idea which upholds their conduct. But they forget that Gando warlords had their own set of slaves.[31] They admit it.... They [the Bariba] voluntarily admitted it, even now. Me, when I was conducting those activities, it was to make everybody equal under the eyes of the law because there are new norms of appreciation for the social value of each individual.... When I was the director of the establishment, my watchman was a prince. However, I sent him to run my errands.[32] I felt bad when I saw him running around. But where is the master; where is the slave?

Q: *Was this defense of the Fulbe and Gando not also the result of Laawol Fulfulde's work?*

A: I'm going to tell you, concerning Laawol Fulfulde. Effectively every Bariba knows that a Pullo (sing. of Fulbe) is not a slave, but a secondary being, meaning someone who is under their protection. And yet, before the arrival of the Fulbe, the Bariba only knew bush-meat because the Bariba were not herders. The Fulbe introduced milk to the Bariba. Instead of going hunting, the Bariba preferred to go back home and eat the meat that the Fulbe offered them. Yet when you have a stranger who gives you food, you have to watch over this stranger so that he continues to give you food. As was the case during the period of the raids, the Fulbe also had to have a king who protected them from all that. So, the Fulbe were obligated to do it....[33] In our region, the Fulbe were a minority and they accepted the decisions made by their hosts, who were traditional chiefs. They pledged to give everything to the king: beef, milk, meat, etcetera. And, the kings don't ask for anything more. All the while, these people were considered to be inferior beings because they were seeking protection. Therefore, they do not stand on the same foot of equality. This is what sparked off the Laawol Fulfulde Movement. Actually, this movement was an organization of Fulfulde-speakers, red Fulbe and Gando.[34] We initiated this structure and the first president was M. Rouga Ousseini. And I was a member of the National Committee. What split the group up were perverse ideas of masters and slaves. From this moment onward, we, as intellectuals, should not accept such ideas. When, for example, the president of the movement thinks that when he speaks about a given subject a certain group of people has no right to speak...this doesn't make sense to me. He shouldn't impose his ideas on us. This procedure doesn't work. In the case of the Kandi congress,[35] they spoke of Laawol Fulfulde which was in pursuit of *sudu baba*, which means the specific traditions of the Fulbe. I told them that there were two groups present, including us, who do not have Fulbe ancestry. Based on this fact, I argued that it was better to broaden the idea so that the Gando could also assert their culture. We were not in agreement with Rouga Ousseini and I said I was not ready to take over this idea. I said, "Because you are Red Fulbe, this is not just about your interests. There are not just Red Fulbe who are here. Where are you going to put us? You guys are a minority? Are we going to pick up your traditions and drop our own?" And it is there that I realized that there were still people who were subject to slavery in the real sense of the term. In 1987, there were groups who were still subject to slavery, especially at Karimama and Banikoara. Then I gave some advice to these people. I said, "Why don't you want to send your children to school? Why is it that up until now you continue to be victims of slavery? Because you were born slaves! This happened to your parents, but not to you! Why can't you build your houses outside the master's compound?" And an old man told me that because of this his children left, but he wanted to respect traditions. I said to him, "Your kids are right. The world has changed since 1848!" I told him, "So because your parents were some of those guys' slaves, and they gave birth to you, you automatically become the slave of their sons!" And right up until now, it still happens! There are also some Gando who have broken from their Pullo family and have built their own houses, but they always say they are from a Fulbe family. How I understand it, they say they are from a Pullo family, but they are camouflaging themselves. They don't want to say that their ancestors were bought and this is why they can't go. And they cannot marry a Pullo. In Fulbe families, Gando women play the domestic role, and these women are not paid.

Q: *You speak about slaves. It seems that there are several categories of slaves.*

A: A person is called a Pullo slave (*esclave Peul*) if he or she was sold in one form or another to a Pullo. In the Fulfulde language we call him Madjiro Pullo. This was true in ancient times. In those days, wars raged and the prince brought his prisoners home. A prince who did not have anything could take one of his captives to the Pullo, who was under the protection of the king, and ask to be given a young bull in exchange for a slave. The slave could work the land and manage the Pullo's animals. When the Pullo bought such a slave, he attached him by a rope to a tree in his compound. Just like when you buy an animal, you tie it up before letting it go. So, this is what we call the slave of the Pullo, Madjiro Pullo. This kind of Gando can be found numerous in the Fulbe and Bariba milieu.

There is also a second category of slaves. Among the Bariba, before the arrival of the Fulbe in this area, people were concerned about anomalies in childbirth, such as breech births, meaning children who come out feet first, and also children born with teeth. For the Boo or Bariba, these types of children are considered dangerous. It is believed that such a child can lay waste to the entire family. It is a witch-child. They are different from the Madjiro Pullo. That is the reason why they refused to be called slaves. Before the arrival of the Fulbe, such children were physically eliminated. Infanticide characterized Boo and Bariba societies. When the Fulbe arrived, they didn't want to hurt their hosts because they knew that it was just a superstition. In order to find a solution, the Fulbe said

41

that putting them with their animal herd would crush the witch-spirit and the child would return to normal and no longer bother its parents, but they will instead bother the animals. The manner in which the Fulbe treat their animals means that the spirit would no longer be able to do anything bad. Since some people did not want to kill their children, they gave them to the Fulbe who raised them with their herds. Therefore the children grew up in difficult conditions and were not considered as the children of the Fulbe. The conflicts between Fulbe children and Gando children were such that at a certain time, Gando children decided to leave. As a result, certain parents came back to get their children when they were all grown up. By way of thanking them, the [Boo or Bariba] parents gave the Fulbe presents [cloth, etc.] for having cured their children. However while the sons left the Fulbe camp where they endured such bad treatment, they didn't rejoin their parents who had abandoned them. Therefore, they formed the Gando village located between the Fulbe camp and their paternal village. The name is significant: Gando means "There are good places to live in," or "It is better to live elsewhere."[36] And since these were people who lived in these difficult conditions, they quickly prospered. As these were not people who were sold, they didn't consider themselves to be Fulbe slaves. The Fulbe had only raised them, but they hadn't bought them! …

So there are different categories of Gando, which depends on the way they came to the Fulbe. They enthrone the king.… There are even true Gando princes who could aspire to the supreme magistracy. This is case with Sero Tassou who was a Gando and was king before the current king of Nikki.[37]

Toward Bori, there is another typical case; a king's son stayed at a Fulbe camp because his upper teeth came in first. When he grew up, the king wanted him back. But he said, "No!" He didn't go back and he automatically became Gando. Therefore the term *Gando* does not designate an ethnic group, but rather it is a mixture; it is a Bariba or Boo subgroup....

To come back to Laawol Fulfulde, I was the one who had the idea of probing Gando history more deeply. They didn't want to, so I said to them, "If this is the way it has to be, we are breaking up the group and I am taking care of the Gando subgroup." And that's when Father Paul Quillet [a French priest who helped to create the Fulfulde alphabet of northern Benin and to give birth to the Laawol Fulfulde linguistic movement] said, "That's fair!" and they authorized me to do it. Then, they were no longer interested in it [the history and culture of the Gando people] and that is why we separated eight years later. The structure didn't work in a regular way and congresses were not held regularly. Many Gando were no longer concerned with what Laawol Fulfulde was doing. That is why the Idi Waadi Movement was created at Nikki. It is a Gando cultural movement created to affirm their uniqueness. Laawol Fulfulde could not properly defend the Gando because we did not have the same objectives. This aspect of slavery must cease. A little bit after, Semme Allah was born in Kalalé, the Djannati was born in Kandi, and N'djeti Allah was born in Gogounou. These Gando movements got together in Ina in 2001 to put a federal office in place, of which I was the general secretary. It is a federation of four Gando movements.

When they created the structure, they came to see me because they knew that things weren't going well between Laawol Fulfulde and me. They told me that the people wanted me to come. I then said that since the people wanted me to be there, I said to myself, "I must return in order to fix the problems of the Gando ethnic group, even though I was no longer part of the Laawol Fulfulde. …" And I have to tell you that it was against the will of Mama Sambo Souley, the lord who made rain and sunny days.[38] He is from the family that controls Laawol Fulfulde. Therefore, their behavior motivated the separation. First, they didn't realize it, and they didn't want to leave even during the congress; they were unmovable.... Their problem is they suck the blood out of other people. They behave like vampires. You have to call a spade a spade. They profited from the Gando who were in Kalalé and even other weak Fulbe. They profited from the situation to lock up their brothers. They knew the gendarmes of the brigade. The commander of the *brigade de gendarmerie* did not hesitate to undress people and lock them up without due process! If a person said he only had fifty thousand F CFA, they told him that it wasn't enough and that he must pay five hundred thousand F CFA. After the person was released, they come and hand in fifty thousand F CFA to the gendarme and keep four hundred fifty thousand F CFA for themselves. Because even the gendarme ignores that a negotiation was made. So, this is how they swindle poor people.

Q: *Someone who can take out five hundred thousand F CFA is not what I would call poor…. Don't people say that the Gando are better positioned economically than other groups?*

A: Of course, the Gando dominate economically because they are used to harsh treatment and difficult working conditions. The Fulbe and Bariba cannot compete in agricultural work…. But the fact that not many Gando have gone to school [means] their "kin"[39] have all the political power, and they use it to keep them poor. Because finally, every small problem ends up at the brigade [police office]. And there [at the brigade] they have all this anxiety because they cannot do anything against the state. It's a machine and they cannot do anything because they haven't understood that they have the same rights as those who pretend to be their "kin" (i.e., the Boo and the Baatombu), or the Fulbe, who pretend to be their saviors and who are their masters. So they have their duties, but they ignore their rights. Other people exploit them and that's what we are trying to highlight. It is necessary that the state lets us make everyone understand that. The state gives us the right to organize ourselves. Each movement is free to develop itself. The law allows for it. So, you guys, individually, you cannot prevent us from creating our movement. But in fact the Gando are better positioned, economically speaking, by work, by school…. Now, schooling is getting more widespread among us. It has been hidden for a long time. They need politicians to represent them. Provided that emancipation through school continues … and since we are the teachers, we must defend their causes, increase public awareness, and help those we can help, especially the most intelligent among them. We

44

have to do everything we can to break through to a higher level.[40] There are many ways. There are scholarships that must be negotiated at the ministerial level. And there are also cases where we are obliged to pay out of our own pockets.[41] But in the long term, it is the negotiation of scholarships so that these "locked" people can also benefit from the state and struggle in order to emerge, to graduate with degrees, and so that we can find jobs for them. It's important that some are able to succeed[42] and to encourage others to go to school....

So, the main weapon of Gando movements is to approach the Gando and to stimulate massive school enrollments because this is the only way to get out of this rut. It is important for adults to become literate. That is the function of these movements. And the desire of the Gando to become literate and to become educated, which you have noticed, is the work of these structures. Even rural Gando are creating their own community schools and they are paying for them until the state takes charge of them.[43] Laawol Fulfulde does nothing except court cases and money embezzlement....

In my opinion, certain corrupt agents of the state need to be suppressed. We must end impunity. If it is a case that deals with the *brigade*, I used to approach the commander directly and present duplicate copies to the prosecutor, and sometimes even to the minister of defense so that if someone who's going to the toilets sees me coming, they would prefer to sit on their own crap, right? [he laughs]. Because when I see something that is not normal, I speak up. If you see me being corrupt, you also have to write it up. Me, I am a teacher, but someone has to provide the proof. But I ask myself, what can I embezzle?[44] Still, I make sure that in my duties I act correctly, I arrive on time, and I do my duty. A director of a high school cannot annoy me.... For the college exams, I had the highest percent of graduated pupils.[45] What do you want to blame me for? So, I make sure that no one can reproach me. That way I can talk in front of anyone. If you saw me do something illegal and you have proof, you can write against me and I will be submitted to the penalties of the law....

In the long term, it is a question about raising awareness. Because you have to grapple with an evil right down to its core. If we send a lot of Gando kids to school, it's so that they understand and they can defend themselves because we won't be alive forever. At a given moment, we can get worn-out and they will be the ones to take over. So you have to inculcate the idea of defending ourselves, of defending our relatives. That's why we have created Gando movements. Whereas the parents send their kids to school, they tell them to follow the example of so-and-so. In reality, every APE[46] [permanent agent of the state] has heard of me and they have to be careful if they want to abuse their power or embezzle. I said, "If I take you on, I won't say anything to you, but I will take you to your parents to fix the problem. If you ask me what my ties are to the person I am representing, I will say that he is my uncle. Can you prove the opposite? Better yet, if you have a machine that can measure kinship ties, measure away!" The guy [the APE] is cornered, and the poor guy can be set free. We must fix the problem, that's all. My only weapon is my ballpoint pen,[47] because I went to school, but you have to fight the evil at its roots at any given moment to fix this affair. And I don't hesitate to write against a prosecutor or prefect. The prefects know that I've fixed a lot of things together with the minister. They know it. Even though now I am a deputy, my power is even greater. I can ask Yayi Boni to make you step down; consequently, this is more powerful. I have no more reason to write about it. They have an interest in complying. This is why people now prefer to choose a *son of the land* to better defend them. That is why they have invested in my electoral campaign.

Q: *But doesn't this attitude make trouble for you? People, I mean, couldn't they use other means, for example, occult?*[48]

A: I don't care about witchcraft. I'm not afraid of anything because in order to be a victim of witchcraft, you have to offend the sorcerer. But if you don't offend him, you are safe! Anyway, experience shows that the witch doctors are more powerful when you offend them. When you provoke them, they come back to haunt you. And when that happens, you better take good care of yourself. But they themselves are well aware of the fact that in those situations I'll challenge anyone, except God.... Today, I don't base my fights on any given movement. I have today [as a deputy] the means to react without getting worried. Before, they threatened me with prison. Today, parliamentary immunity allows me to be safe and that's why I can challenge anyone. It's not because you are here. We could have given them billions, but they were going to vote for me. I went to a Boo village, and they said to me, "Hey you, we know that you are poor; we don't need your money. We want you. The others are going to come and give us their money, and when we choose them, that's where it ends. They are going to quit and leave us with our problems. But you, you are always going to be with us." I haven't asked for someone to support me. If they support me, when the time comes, I will do my duties. At this time, we haven't started yet. I come here; I am seeing what happens. Currently, if a gendarme or a ranger abuses their power, I'm going to warn their superior. I'm going to even go see the minister to ask him to deal with the case, because that is what is necessary [his mobile phone rings and interrupts the interview].

Q: *Beside the battles you personally lead, what does your organization do?*

A: At the level of the organization, our means are limited, thus so are our activities. It is a question first of encouraging all children old enough to go to school. We have sparked off a craze. But today the priorities are community infrastructures, which the state must put in place in order to receive this horde of children, and well-trained teachers who teach these children.[49] That's one aspect. The other is literacy. This is one of our basic principles to invite adults to acquire knowledge in their own language. This will allow them to have a broader perspective about the vision of our world. This being so, our objective is attainable. That being done, it will be difficult for a permanent state civil servant or private actors to cheat them or to take of advantage of their ignorance. On the other hand,

47

these are generations that are coming. Through the ideas they will get in the schools, these generations will not behave in the same way. In this slow way, once we train these people, it will also make it more difficult to take advantage of them, as it is being done with their illiterate parents today. We are convinced that up until now we have only done a tiny part of what needs to be done, but this could spread like a wildfire. But that's not enough. We know today that certain people are still hesitant to send their kids to school. We know that traditions carry a lot of weight, but I say and I continue to insist that if there is a project to provide educational supplies, places to host these children [in the cities where they will study], … we could convince that particular group, not by forcing them, but by convincing them with clear explanations and success stories so that they send an impressive number [to school]. Because in reality, if people refuse to send them, it's only because they are ashamed. They don't have anything and they know that school is a terrible investment. And as they have nothing, nothing to invest with, they prefer not to send their kids to school because they have to put a lot into something [school] where the results are uncertain. Children can fail, and above all girls can get pregnant.[50] But if we are certain that things are done right and that each child gets his chance…. Today nobody expects that that girl [pointing out a young girl in the court] would do her *maîtrise*.[51] Now she is preparing for her master's degree. No one expected a Gando woman to do that. Therefore we must follow her example. So if we really have such projects, it would be really good.[52] On the other hand, we need support of the state to promote a few Gando intellectuals within the public administration [by recruitment of well-educated Gando students]. That's also my reason for being in the national assembly. It's my duty to use my connections with the government so that my Gando brothers can find a place somewhere. This will serve as an example for those who want to send their children to school. We must not end up with children who did school but returned to their village to do nothing, exasperating their parents.[53] The parents say, "This kid went to school, but it didn't work. He's back and he is an encumbrance!" So these projects have to help us insert them back into society. This will facilitate the task at the base level, so that before 2015 every child who can be educated will be educated.[54] It's a right and every child can enjoy that right. We have to be able to reach that goal for both the Gando and Fulbe without distinction. But it's when a Pullo becomes dangerous that we consider him to be an enemy of the people, and as such, I am ready to fight against him. This even happens among the Gando; it doesn't just happen among the Fulbe.... We have some enemies among the Gando. Even our uncle played this role until he left it after he saw that it wasn't profitable. That was his son who came to greet us earlier. He was one my greatest adversaries, but he noticed that this didn't give him any results. On the contrary, this only pushed him away from the people. Otherwise, normally, they are the ones who have to be elected. These are our elders. He's our father's cousin. So we had to support him.[55] But because of his behavior, the public lost confidence in him. It is not possible to send people like this over there. He understood and he returned.

Notes

1. Robin Law, *Ouidah: The Social History of a West-African Slaving Port, 1727-1892* (Athens, Ohio, and Oxford: Ohio University Press and James Currey, 2004).
2. Ibid.; see also Elisabeth Boesen, Christine Hardung, and Richard Kuba, eds., *Regards sur le Borgou: Pouvoir et altérité dans une région Ouest-Africaine* (Paris and Montréal: L'Harmattan, 1998).
3. *Gando* is a general term that covers a variety of statuses in different languages (Boo, Baatonu, and Fulfulde). To put it simply, one can distinguish slaves who were caught from those who were bought or those who were fostered as child sorcerers to the Fulbe. Bernd Baldus, "Responses to Dependency in a Servile Group: The Machube of Northern Benin," in *Slavery in Africa: Historical and Anthropological Perspectives*, eds. Igor Kopytoff and Suzanne Miers (Madison: University of Wisconsin Press, 1977), 435-58; Hardung, "'Ni vraiment Peul, ni vraiment Baatombu.' Le conflit identitaire des Gando," in *Trajectoires peules au Benin: Six études anthropologiques*, eds. Thomas Bierschenk and P. Y. Le Meur (Paris: Karthala, 1997), 109-38. Finally, a fourth category is composed of the people of free origin who lived among the Gando and adopted their language

(like the deputy).

4. Jacques Lombard, *Structures de type féodal en Afrique noire: Etude des dynamiques internes et des relations sociales chez les Bariba du Dahomey* (Paris and The Hague: Mouton, 1965).

5. Baldus, "Responses to Dependency in a Servile Group."

6. Eric Hahonou, "Past and Present African Citizenships: Lessons from Benin," *Citizenship Studies* 15, no. 1 (2011): 75-92.

7. Thomas Bierschenk, "Rituels politiques et construction de l'identité ethnique des Peuls du Benin," *Cahiers des Sciences Humaines* 31 (1995): 457-84.

8. Laawol Fulfulde means "the road of the Fulfulde." Martine Guichard and Thomas Bierschenk translate it as "the way of the Fulbe" or "Fulbe's lifestyle." Guichard, "'L'Ethnicisation' de la société peule du Borgou (Benin)," *Cahiers d'études Africaines* 30 (1990): 14-44; Bierschenk, "Rituels politiques"; Thomas Bierschenk, "Introduction," in *Trajectiores peules au Bénin*, eds. Thomas Bierschenk and P. Y. Le Meur (Paris: Karthala, 1997), 5-19. This translation refers to the notion of Pulaaku, that is, Fulbe's rules of conduct. However, Fulfulde literally refers to a language that is the language of the Fulbe as well as the language of most Gando. Whereas Laawol could be translated as "way" or "road," it could as well refer to a potentiality. The movement sought a fuller integration of all Fulfulde-speaking people into the nation-state of Benin.

9. Baldus, "Responses to Dependency in a Servile Group"; Hardung, "Ni vraiment Peul, ni vraiment Baatombu."

10. For a more comprehensive understanding of the categories among Gando, see Baldus, "Responses to Dependency in a Servile Group," and Hardung, "Ni vraiment Peul, ni vraiment Baatombu."

11. Eric Hahonou and Lotte Pelckmans, "West African Antislavery Movements: Citizenship Struggles and the Legacies of Slavery," *Vienna Journal of African Studies, Stichprobe* 20 (2011): 141-62.

12. By feudal family the deputy is saying that his ancestors were free hunters and warriors and not slaves. This seems surprising since the Gando are generally considered to be people with slave origins. The interviewee has probably read Jacques Lombard who described Borgou's political structure as feudal in his book *Structures de type féodal en Afrique noire. Etude des dynamiques internes et des relations sociales chez les Bariba du Dahomey* (Paris and The Hague: Mouton, 1965). The allusion to the feudal kingdom of Borgou demonstrates the cultural background of the interviewee.

13. As slaves or dependants of the Fulbe, Gando of this area mostly spoke the Fulfulde language. In other areas of Borgou Gando spoke

mostly Baatonu (the language of the Baatombu).

14. Here, the "in-laws" designates the French former colonialists.

15. In 1972, a group of army officers led by Mathieu Kerekou seized power. Kerekou dominated the politics of Benin for twenty-seven years, though in his last years, he was returned to office in multiparty elections. Chris Allen, "Restructuring an Authoritarian State: 'Democratic Renewal' in Benin," *Review of African Political Economy* 54 (1992): 42–58; Dov Ronen, "People's Republic of Benin: The Military, Marxist Ideology and the Politics of Ethnicity," in *The Military in African Politics,* ed. John Harbeson (New York: Praeger, 1978).

16. In French, *mon vieux* is a respectful way to speak about one's father without pronouncing his name.

17. While at school each child was treated according to his ability. Mockery of, and discrimination against, Gando children was very common outside of school in the villages or cities where the pupils lived. Hardung, "Everyday Life of Slaves in Northern Dahomey: The Process of Remembering," *Journal of African Cultural Studies* 15 (2002): 35-44.

18. Overcoming fate (in French, *vaincre la fatalité*) refers to the fact that the Gando are continuously belittled by other ethnic groups.

19. The amount 4,000,000 F CFA is approximately $7,400. In Benin this sum is excessive because the official minimum monthly salary is around $55.00.

20. In Benin, the prefect is an appointed official who represents the state at a district level. Prefects have the authority to veto decisions made by municipal governments.

21. FARD Alafia (in French, Front d'Action pour le Renouveau et le Développement; *alafia* means health) is a political party founded in the mid-1990s to support former President Kerekou. The Action Front for Renewal and Development was especially strong in northern Benin (Atacora and Borgou departments). The party almost disappeared after 2003 when the leaders joined in a larger coalition called UBF (Union pour le Bénin du Futur). The FARD Alafia only had one seat in the municipal council of Kalalé.

22. In Benin, all candidates for municipal elections and their deputies are registered on the electoral list of a political party. Municipal councillors are elected according to the proportion of votes received for each list.

23. In this electoral district, the Gando are a large majority. They represent more than 60 percent of the electorate. People often vote for a candidate from their ethnic group. According to the law of Benin, when a candidate resigns from a political office he must be replaced

by his deputy. Hahonou, "Past and Present African Citizenships: Lessons from Benin."

24. Magic charms (in French, *grigris*) are related to witchcraft. They are believed to be powerful enough to kill people. Witchcraft is a common weapon. People are often concerned to protect themselves against it.

25. The deputy means that in case of popular demonstrations against the newly elected mayor, the police could arrest all the "troublemakers" on grounds of "act of public disorder."

26. For the legislative elections of March 2007, President Yayi Boni promoted a list of political elites in order to get popular support and to assure himself a political majority in the National Assembly. Most mayors from the North were inscribed on this list, called *cauris* (cowries). The cauris are small seashells that were used as money in precolonial Dahomey. It is a symbol of wealth. Considering the huge electoral support that Yayi Boni got from the North in March 2006, and the general reluctance in Benin to be classified as an opponent, being promoted as a candidate on his list one year after his election gave a high probability of being elected as a parliament member. In that respect, it was surprising that Orou Sè Guéné was elected even after being dropped from the president's list. That was due to his popularity among the Gando. Hahonou, "Slavery and Politics: Stigma, Decentralisation, and Political Representation in Niger and Benin," in *Reconfiguring Slavery: West African Trajectories*, ed. Benedetta Rossi (Liverpool: Liverpool University Press, 2009), 152-81; Cédric Mayrargue, "Yayi Boni, un president inattendu? Construction de la figure du candidat et dynamiques electorales au Benin," *Politique Africaine* 102 (2006): 155-72.

27. In Benin, as in many West African coastal countries (from the Ivory Coast to Nigeria and Cameroon), there is a division between North and South. This is mostly due to the fact that the colonial conquest started from the South, and the colonial power used southern people to rule other territories. Later on, a large number of civil servants were recruited from the South. Therefore, northern people are rather hostile to southerners who were seen as strangers and representatives of a foreign power.

28. In Benin, electoral candidates usually give money and goods to potential supporters in order to win their votes. The deputy explained something rather unusual in Benin because contrary to political custom his supporters gave him part of the money which they received from other candidates, most notably from candidates supported by the president. The money his supporters gave him allowed him to

pay for his campaign fees, fuel, vehicles, the distribution of gifts, and so forth.

29. Nikki is the capital city of beninese Borgu, where the king of Borgu and his court reside. The king is known to possess slaves who serve him. Nikki is also an administrative center where the general high school is situated. Most important, Nikki has symbolic value for the aristocracy. It is well known in Borgu that an appointed civil servant of Gando origins ruled Nikki in the 1990s but was later replaced by a prince from Nikki. In his introductory discourse, the newly appointed sub-prefect said, "Nikki cannot be ruled by a slave!"

30. Bariba and Boo princes have a superiority complex, but the Gando suffer from an inferiority complex because of the low social status of their group.

31. He means to say the Boo in his family.

32. In the local context, sending someone to run errands implies a social distinction between those who give orders (masters) and those who carry them out (slaves).

33. This refers to the giving of meat and milk to their Bariba protectors (king, princes, or other Wasangari warlords).

34. The speaker is using the color red to refer to nobles—in contrast to black, which denotes a servile status.

35. This was the first congress of the Laawol Fulfulde Movement in December 1987.

36. According to Baldus, "Responses to Dependency in a Servile Group," in precolonial times, the term *Gando* designated the camp where the slaves of the Wasangari were held (p. 438).

37. The case of Sero Tassou is interesting, because this king claimed to belong to the Gando people. Though the deputy does not develop this, it provides evidence that Gando are not slaves.

38. Mama Sambo Souley was also a rich Pullo from an aristocratic family who possessed several slaves and dependants. He was an influencial politician in Kerekou's regime. Together with other Fulbe members of the Laawol Fulfulde movement, he refused to allow the Gando any role in the decision making within the organization.

39. Here the term *kin* refers to the Boo and Bariba groups.

40. He is arguing that the Gando should continue their education and succeed at the university level in order to succeed socially, economically, and politically.

41. When it is not possible to obtain grants from the state, students or their families often have to pay their own expenses.

42. If some Gando were to succeed through education, it would provide an alternative model of success and would encourage people to send

their children to schools.

43. Once the Benin state recognizes a village school built by villagers, it pays out of the national budget all associated expenses, notably teacher's salaries.

44. The deputy was accused of the embezzlement of 50 million F CFA during his term as mayor (about $100,000). This was one of the arguments used against him by his opponents.

45. Here, to justify his work, Orou Sè Guéné compares the success of his pupils in examinations with those of his colleagues.

46. The term *APE*, in French, Agent Permanent de l'État, generally refers to civil servants and government officials. However, the use of this term here specifically refers to those who wear uniforms, meaning gendarmes, police, customs officers, and park rangers.

47. Orou Sè Guéné refers to ballpoint pens as the intellectual's weapon. The pen has the ability to denounce the APE's abuse of power and go after senior officials. The judicial process requires written claims which illiterate peasants cannot produce.

48. In Benin, witchcraft is usually employed in most conflicts from the family level to the highest level of national politics. Concerning the specific use of witchcraft, curses, and blessings in the Gando-Fulbe milieu, see Hardung, "Curse and Blessing: On Post-slavery Modes of Perception and Agency in Benin," in *Reconfiguring Slavery: West African Trajectories,* ed. Benedetta Rossi (Liverpool: Liverpool University Press, 2009), 116-39.

49. When a school is created by villagers, teachers are generally recruited from among former pupils, who often lack the qualifications to teach.

50. The children who fail are considered failures by their families. They can't find jobs in towns. In the cities and at school they have forgotten the values of hard work. They won't work in the fields like their illiterate brothers and sisters. The young girls can also be seduced by teachers or young men and come back home pregnant. These children are also considered spoiled.

51. In Benin, following the former French system, the *maîtrise* is the level obtained at the end of the fourth year at the university. It comes one year before the master's degree. It is also interesting to note here that the girl he is speaking about is his younger sister. Together with two other women, she was elected as a municipal councillor in Kalalé in 2008.

52. The informant is making these comments because he knows that I am connected to a potential international donor capable of supporting the education of Gando.

53. Educated children who go back to their parents are sometimes a bur-

den. After the government implemented structural adjustment policies, the state could no longer hire university graduates. These educated unemployed return home without being able to economically
contribute to their families. They are also unable to pay back their
parents, who invested in their education and financed their studies.

54. This is one of the Millennium Challenge Goals that the government
of Benin wants to achieve before 2015.

55. As is common in African political cultures, in Benin, elders are preferred as political representatives.

3. On Remembering Slavery in Northern Igbo Proverbial Discourse

DAMIAN U. OPATA

A person enslaved to a freeborn individual among the northern Igbo of southeastern Nigeria was called *ohu* or *oru.* The enslaved were also identified using particular expressions: *ndi aka nwe or ndi enwe enwe,* "people owned by others." In some areas, they may have even been referred to as *ndi obia*, "strangers," but as "owned people," they were all regarded as property. They were denied many social rights and were treated as less than equals of the so-called freeborn. Because slave status was thought to last forever, northern Igbo slave holders did all they could, using every public occasion, every opportune time, to remind their slaves, their former slaves, and the children of former slaves that they did not belong, that they had no intention of allowing them to belong and that they could never join the mainstream, of their communities. Slavery was designed to be permanent and the descendants of former slaves, no matter their changed circumstances, were supposed to live with their lowly status.

Despite the fact that officially slaves no longer exist, the status of those of slave origin in twentieth-century Nigeria is still a fraught issue. There can be no doubt about this. How have the linguistic habits of the Igbo mirrored this fact? To this day, the northern Igbo still refer to descendants of former slavers as *ndi ohuor ndi oru*, although discussions about slavery are particularly sensitive. One must be very careful in choosing one's words depending on who is part of the conversation. An example: in 1989, a student at a Nigerian university, who I shall call Madeline, participated in an exchange in which students were abusing one another, using various slurs. One student employed the pejorative term, *ndi wawa* (allegedly backward people) to refer to the group to which Madeline belonged. In response, Madeline remarked that only certain Igbo, including *ndi ohu* (slaves), used that epithet. This was her way of indicating that she was the social superior of those who took pride in casting aspersions on others. Before she could react, she was both verbally and physical assaulted by another person at the session who accused Madeline of still calling her people slaves. The fury with which this student attacked Madeline forced her to flee from the room. This did not calm the offended woman, however. Immediately, the woman found Madeline's bedroom and proceeded to use a knife to cut into pieces her precious plastic water bucket. This still did not assuage her anger. The woman then rushed to her own room and returned with a bucketful of water which she then poured onto Madeline's bed, clothes, and books. This incident reveals the extent to which sensitivity about slave origins—in this case triggered by the use of the term *ohu* continues to influence social interactions among the northern Igbo.

Subsequently, Madeline came to realize that her attacker was an Igbo descendant of ex-slaves. This type of reaction characterizes many discourses involving the allegedly free borns and descendants of ex-slaves. This also makes people very sensitive about what they say in an audience in which people do not know well the social origin of others.

Proverbs are part of every people's cultural repertoire. In the case of the northern Igbo, their proverbs both narrate and memorize slavery. As John A. Robinson has aptly remarked, "the intimate association between memory and narrative arises from [the] urge to use the past to instruct present and future generations.[1] Life memories tell us something about remembering and the rememberers. Northern Igbo proverbs discuss slavery, but today, public discourse about the institution has been largely characterized by silence. Proverbs about slavery are used quite selectively. But I agree that only when the linguistic memory about slavery is erased or modified can the social discrimination against the descendants of slaves begin to disappear.

Because of the muted discourse about slavery among the Igbo, some of the twenty proverbs presented here have been drawn from a number of delicately handled interviews, but most come from published collections of proverbs.[2] These proverbs describe the status of slaves, the care needed to prevent slaves from escaping, and the expectations of slaves during the heyday of slavery.

The Permanently Degraded Status of Slaves

1. *Ichi Fada anaghi ehiche oru, o ria Enigwe o gbara ndi ibe ya oru.*

Translation: Being an ordained priest does not end slavery; when a person gets to heaven, he will become a slave to others.

Exegesis: According to this proverb, Christianity cannot wipe away the social stigma of slavery. Even if an *ohu* is ordained a priest in the Roman Catholic Church, the person is still an *ohu*. Further, if the person goes to heaven after death, the person will become a slave to others (fellow freeborn priests). Slavery does not recognize space and temporality; it extends even to heaven. God sanctions it.

2. *Nwa ohu siri: ndi ihe ozo ga-emekwama yak aria onodu ya noo?*

Translation: The slave said: what worse fate can befall me?

Exegesis: The permanently degraded status of the enslaved is captured in this saying in which the enslaved is supposedly given a voice, stating that no condition is worse than slavery. This is reminiscent of Gerard Manley Hopkins's poem "No worst, there is none."

3. *Nwa ohu anaghi agbaka onye gbatara ya.*

Translation: The slave is never greater than his or her enslaver.

4. *Onye enwe enwe adigh enwe onwe ya.*

Translation: One who is owned (a slave) does not own him or herself (i.e., is never independent).[3]

5. *Onye obia adigh echi eze na-ala ndi ozo.*

Translation: A slave (stranger) is never crowned a king among the freeborn (titled men).

6. *Ohu gbara arọ, ọ bukarima ohu.*

Translation: A slave gets more enslaved with time.
Exegesis of Proverbs 3, 4, 5, and 6: These four proverbs assert that the enslaved is permanently enslaved to the master. He or she can never rise above his social status.

7. *Nwa ohu si na ya mara ihe ya ga-ekwu kama ọ buru na ya ekwue, a ga-egbu nne ya; ma obu tufue ya onwe ya, si na ya mere aru.*

Translation: A slave says that he knows what to say, but if he says it, either his mother would be thrown away or he himself would be killed and it would be affirmed that they committed an abomination.
Exegesis: The slave is to be denied the opportunity to express his or her opinion even when he or she believes that there are pertinent things to be said.

8. *Oru di ka onye ogbi tara onugbu.*

Translation: A slave never bares his or her mind.
Exegesis: Speaking can become a source of danger.

The Terrorizing and Humiliating of Slaves

9. *Ohu na-ele ebe ana eke ohu ibe ya itinye na-ili marakwa na O bu ka o ga-adi ya.*

Translation: A slave who looks on while a fellow slave is bound and thrown into the grave should know that the same fate awaits him or her.

10. *Ohu huru ka eji mbazu eli ihe ya achi ochi chetalwa ubochi nke ya.*

Translation: A slave, who laughs at the sight of a shallow grave dug with sticks for another slave, should remember that his time will come.

Exegesis of Proverbs 9 and 10: These two proverbs illustrate the terror and humiliation that slaves faced. The Igbo were and still are known for elaborate funerals for the deceased. The slave, however, could do nothing to give a colleague a decent burial. In other words, the slave remained an outcast from the land of the living and the dead. Buchi Emecheta's fictionalized account of traditional Igbo life before contact with the West, in her novel *Joys of Motherhood*,[4] presents a grim account of a slave who twice attempted to jump out of a grave to plead for mercy, but was clubbed back into the grave. The account represents a past reality. Among the northern Igbo, this practice was called *itunyu oku ama*, "putting out the fire after taking the *ama* title." The ritual involved burying a slave alive. The eleventh proverb illustrates the mean manner in which a slave who has escaped burial with his master would still be interned with little regard.

11. *Isi di ala anaghi ato na mba.*

Translation: A citizen (freeborn) is never buried in a foreign land.

Exegesis: This proverb further highlights the distinction

between a slave and a non-slave even when it does not mention the word slave. It implies that a slave can be buried anywhere; that a slave has no recognized nativity, that indeed, a slave should not expect certain funeral rites because to be buried in one's native place entails the right to the rites specific to that place. A person who can be buried anywhere has no right to expect such respect. Burial of a freeborn in their home village established a connection with the land which has been one of the material bases for the distinction between slaves and freeborns. The Igbo believe that the family (*umunna*) includes ancestors, current living individuals, and the not yet born. The ability to have an *umunna* wasn't traditionally available to slaves. Hence, it didn't matter where they were buried.

Comparing Slaves with Their Masters and the Freeborn

12. *Nwanyi siri na ndi mmadu ga-na-anwuri nay a aburo ohu, kama ha ga-adi na ekwu na ya joro njo.*

Translation: *Nwamu* (the descendant of a freeborn) said that people should be happy she is not a slave and thus not complain about her ugliness.

Exegesis: The proverb states that an ugly girl is happy she is not a slave. But it says more than this. The girl wants people to recognize the fact of her free status and to understand that being ugly is nothing compared to the status of being a slave.

13. *Mmiri no-ama ohu, na-ama onye kpo ya.*

Translation: The rain that beats a slave beats the enslaver.

14. *Mmiri na-ama ohu di abuo: mmiri na onye kpo ya.*

Translation: The rain that beats a slave is twofold: the rain itself and the enslaver.

Exegesis of Proverbs 13 and 14: These two proverbs illustrate the different messages proverbs can convey on the same subject. Proverb 10 states that the rain that beats the enslaved also beats the enslaver, but it can mean that the same experience can indicate two different things to two people. Proverb 14 infuses the term *rain* with a dual meaning. Here, the rain is a trope for the enslaver and thus the enslaved operates under the yoke of two different burdens: the rain itself and the enslaver.

The Desired Characteristics of the Enslaver

15. *Ogbaa inyama mmadu, anya mee mee, obi na-azu, obi na-azu.*

Translation: He who enslaves another, red eye, red eye, heart to the back, heart to the back.

16. *Onye afogori na-ego adighi anogide.*

Translation: A slave bought by a fool does not remain a slave for so long.

17. *Nwaloke siri Idenyi na-eji ako ere ohu.*

Translation: Nwaloke told Idenyi that it is with tact that a slave is sold.

Exegesis of Proverbs 15, 16, and 17: In these proverbs, slavery is treated as a risky business, requiring specific traits on the part of the enslavers. Capturing a slave demands that the enslaver be "manly," willing to engage in wicked acts. Proverb 16 says those who buy slaves, however, must understand that the slaves can take advantage of their masters. Accordingly, foolish buyers will very quickly lose their slaves. Because slaves do have sense and can be quite wise, the last proverb, Proverb 17, advises the master to sell a slave cautiously. Such a sale brings to the slave yet another humiliating experience that could lead to a great resentment on the part of the slave. Caution is required.

Characteristics of the Enslaved

18. *Ohu eregi onu, onye jeko na-ala nna ya.*

Translation: The slave who fails to tell lies: who is going to his or her fatherland?

Exegesis: This proverb suggests that a slave can say anything, particularly about his or her past. There is no person who would be interested in traveling to the slave's homeland to verify the person's statement. The implication is that a slave has no ancestral home, no past, and is of questionable, if not unknown, identity.

19. *Ajuo oru ihe ejiri mma ya na-aka oku, o si na o bu ichi echi choo yam ma.*

Translation: Ask a slave why she has a scar on the hand, the person will answer that it is a beauty mark.

Exegesis: The scar on the hand of a slave is a sign of ownership, a sign well known to the master. Ordinarily, among the Igbo, scarifications are a mark of beauty and clan identity. During the period when slavery was common, such marks protected the person from being enslaved by someone from the same clan. A slave enjoys none of this, neither the protection of clan membership nor the aesthetics of scarification. This proverb indicates that slaves cannot be trusted to tell the truth, that they will misrepresent reality to blunt the stigma of their slave status.

20. *Nwamu tukwasiri ohu ishi, mbosi o ga-acho isi ya, oma fu ya.*

Translation: A freeborn who rests his head on a slave will never find it when he looks for it.

Exegesis: A slave should never be trusted.

The northern Igbo experience with slavery captured in the proverbs examined in this study is rarely deployed by those who are concerned about offending others. Such individuals would cite them only when the descendants of former slaves are out of earshot. Even then, they would offer them with caution, for fear of hurting others. In the past, the majority of slaveholders and the freeborn would have recited these proverbs without hesitation. Since words can wound, so must the enslaved and their descendants have been deeply hurt. Times may be different today, but the Igbo still refer to the descendants of former slaves as *ndi ohu/ ndi oru,* that is, as "slaves." There is no prefix such as ex- or post- attached to the name. In other words, slavery may have disappeared, but people are still referred to as slaves. As long as the Igbo continue to refer to the descendants of the formerly enslaved by such terms, so long as the memories of slavery are continually nurtured through the recitation of proverbs, discriminatory practices against this group will also continue. It is high time the Igbo abandoned this abominable past.

Notes

1. John A. Robinson, "Autobiographical Memory: Historical Prologue," in *Autobiographical Memory,* ed. David C. Rubin (Cambridge: Cambridge University Press, 1986), 19.
2. Solomon Amadiume, *Ilu Ndi Igbo: A Study of Igo Proverbs,* 2 vols. (Enugu, Nigeria: Fourth Dimension Publishing Company, 1995); G. E. Igwe, *Onye Turu Ikoro Wa Ya Eze* (Ibadan, Nigeria: University Press, 1986); F. C. Ogbalu, *Ilu Igbo: The Book of Igbo Proverbs* (Onitsha, Nigeria: University Publishing Company, 1965).
3. The northern Igbo do not talk about former slaves; they only speak of slaves even in reference to the present generation, who are only descendants of slaves.
4. Buchi Emecheta, *Joys of Motherhood* (London: Allison and Busby, 1979).

4. To Cut the Rope from One's Neck? Manumission Documents of Slave Descendants from Central Malian Fulɓe Society

LOTTE PELCKMANS[1]

In my home village those who butcher meat on the market are ennobled slave descendants, they no longer have a rope around their neck. They have become like their masters.
—Beidary Tamboura, interview, Bamako, 2006

Fulɓe people often use the image of a rope around one's neck to discuss social hierarchies and legacies of slavery.[2] Beidary is a Fulɓe slave descendant[3] from the central Malian region in Douentza Province. According to him, the butchers of his home village (butchery is a job typically associated with slave labor) have rejected the rope of slavery. But why does he say they have become "like their masters"? In order to understand this, this chapter presents two Islamic manumission documents issued in the 1990s to two slave descendants, whom I fictively call Diougal Issiaka and Bilal Allayidi.[4] I obtained these documents by consulting two imams in two Fulfulde villages near Douentza. Diougal Issiaka's and Bilal Allayidi's families were willing to show their manumission documents. Both men passed away some time ago.

Similar to other Sahelian societies, slavery in central Malian Fulɓe society has been a long-standing system of control over people.[5] Today the descendants of slaves are considered free but since slave status is hereditary, their freedom remains defined by the specific sociocultural context in which they live. This often means that slave descendants do not enjoy full citizenship in terms of access to certain positions in the mosque and village politics. Their hereditary status is translated into ritual and labor obligations and their slave past continues to stigmatize them.

Most slave societies offered specific avenues of redemption or social climbing to their slaves. Islam, so central to the Sahelian Fulɓe society described here, offered the possibility of ransoming and of manumission or redemption. Ransoming is done by kin or acquaintances who buy the freedom of someone enslaved after capture.[6] The difference with manumission is that the ransomed slave returns to his original freeborn status and home society. Redemption can be defined as all actions taken by a slave in an effort to get released. So this would include those manumitted by the secular law of first, the colonial state, and the postcolonial state.[7] Martin A. Klein and others described a situation in French West Africa, in which slaves could walk away from slavery because the state would not support the master's attempt to keep control of his slave.[8] For those who obtained redemption through the described legal Islamic procedure, I prefer to use the term *self-manumission*.[9]

Most studies focus on self-manumission of slaves in colonial times.[10] The need for ransoming completely disappeared with the ending of enslavement during colonial rule.[11] Manumission, however, remained possible and self-manumission was actually encouraged by the French colonial administrators.[12] This documents presented in this chapter contextualize postcolonial self-manumissions as one of many strategies that slave descendants even today use to overcome the stigma attached to slavery. As I will demonstrate, the manumission documents of Bilal Allayidi and Diougal Issiaka bear witness to the attempts of a small number of slave descendants to climb the social ladder within the sociocultural boundaries of their community. Current use of manumission documents in Fulɓe societies seems rare. I have encountered references to the practice today only in northern Cameroon.[13]

Only a minority of slave descendants in the central Malian Haayre region are concerned with manumission today.[14] The attached documents were written in the 1990s, by different imams in two neighboring villages. In the first section, I will focus on the procedure of liberation and content of these documents, both in their local specificities as well as in relation to perspectives on manumission in Islamic legislation more generally. Subsequently I address the central question of why liberation, for a minority of mainly rich and elderly slave descendants, is a culturally recognized strategy of obtaining social mobility within their home community. In a last section I explain why the majority of slave descendants do not engage in liberation. They have other strategies for obtaining social recognition. Unlike those who freed themselves, they were able to rid themselves of the stigma not by challenging existing social boundaries, but by bypassing and ignoring them.

Manumission as Legal Redemption in an Islamic Context

It is generally acknowledged that legal abolition by the French colonizers[15] and later also the national Malian Constitution from the 1960s,[16] did not result in the actual emancipation of former slave populations. Although slave descendants in Fulɓe society have been declared legally free, slavery has continued to exist psychologically and socially.[17] State law is only weakly implemented in Mali and tribunal courts are difficult to reach due to physical distance, particularly in distant regions like Haayre. As of 2006, there was only one tribunal per 141,176 persons in Mali.[18] The dominant religious legal framework is at odds with national state law which, as a result of political decentralization, has gained ground in the past decade. The religious judiciary system remained important because the reach of modern law was limited. French colonizers also issued liberation certificates,[19] but unlike manumission documents, French certificates did not establish a legal agreement between the three parties central to the Islamic contract: the master, slave, and God and thus lacked sociocultural validity and moral prestige.[20] The documents central to this chapter should be understood in the religious context of Islamic ideology and legislation.[21]

Slavery has long been regulated by Islamic texts and the legal pre-scriptions of Muslim scholars in the region.[22] In fact, Malikite law juridically distinguishes between only two categories of persons: those free and those not free.[23]

Since manumission always depends on the approval of the po-litical and religious elites, these elites can manipulate access to manumission for their own benefit. The paradox is that by accept-ing payments for self-manumission, the religious elite promote re-demption. However, in so doing, they, at the same time, reinforce their own position by gaining material profits and formalizing moral boundaries based on inequality.

There are a variety of modalities of legal enfranchisement in Muslim law ranging from ransoming[24] to self-manumission (Doc-ument I). As opposed to ransoming, manumission does not result in full enfranchisement[25] or to a return to one's former status and home society. According to Islamic legislation, manumission turns the slave into a client with subservient instead of freeborn status in the former owner's society.[26] Other scholars[27] explain how a manumission contract legally turns the master-slave relation into a patron-client relation, called *mawla* in Arabic. Claude Meillas-soux concludes that manumission "in reality is only designed to serve the master's interests. A slave was redeemed to make of him a devoted servant, whose privileges attached him to his master; or he was redeemed because he was too old to be kept on."[28]

So manumission is the formalizing of a new relation of domi-nation (patron-client) replacing an older one (master-slave). By self-manumission the client confirms his deference to his patron and/or God. In turn, he is ideally rewarded with a more privileged position vis-à-vis other slave descendants. The most important en-visaged privilege was access to the *hajj* and access to several other important pillars central to Islam, such as slaughtering one's per-sonal sacrificial animal on the occasion of the Tabaski festival, almsgiving, and the right to wear a white veil for women after they have been to Mecca. Other privileges included more freedom of movement,[29] access to other freed women, and entitlements to a freeborn patronym. Furthermore, since most legal procedures are based on Islamic rather than state law,[30] inheritance has become another important reason for some slave descendants to self-manumit today. A woman will, for example, manumit herself if her husband's first wife did so as well. If she does not, she will not be entitled to inherit from him.

The attached manumission documents are written in Fulfulde using the Arabic alphabet (*adjami*) by Islamic Fulɓe scholars in order to "certify" the liberation of a slave according to Islamic law. The central question is why Diougal Issiaka and Bilal Allayidi who, according to national legislation, were no longer considered slaves, wanted to manumit themselves according to local Islamic legal procedures.

Children of the Rope

Part of the answer lies in how religion is internalized in Fulɓe identity.[31] Islam and nobility in the Haayre region over time became entangled over time and expressed in honor codes.[32] Access to honor was reserved for people of freeborn status, based on piety and freeborn ancestry. Since slave descendants lack freeborn ancestry, they are denied access to honorable behavior (*ndimaaku*) through stigmatizing insults, proverbs, and stereotypes that remind them of their slave ancestry. An example of such an insult is a freeborn person saying: "I refuse to discuss [this] with a child of the rope."[33] This expression demonstrates the arrogance espoused by a freeborn who does not want to lower himself by arguing with a "child of the rope," in other words, a person of slave descent. Such negative expressions reinforce moral boundaries between freeborn and slave descendants.

The stigma of slavery can in specific contexts be read from slave descendants' family names.[34] One advantage of self-manumission is that it entitles the descendant of a slave to be renamed, often by taking on his master's first and family name.[35] In this sense, manumission comes close to renewed social birth, which is also apparent from the manumission ceremony, which reflects elements of the baptism ceremony. Apart from a new name, the manumitted slave descendant could receive a new outfit (clothes and shoes) again investing his new status with more dignity. Lastly, the master sometimes gives the manumitted slave land to build his own house. This demonstrates how, in actual practice, manumission allows slave descendants to renegotiate their position to some extent. They nevertheless remain excluded from specific aspects of honor in the community of noble freeborn. The continued distinction is reinforced by Fulfulde terminology: the freed slave is called *dimdînaado*,[36] while the freeborn person is called *diimo*. Up to the present, manumitted slaves are not included in freeborn lineages by marriage and do not have access to high political or religious functions. Also in terms of property, some discrimination remains because a freeborn master inherits from a childless freed slave (*dimdînaado*), but not vice versa.[37] The rope once used to impede slaves from running off became a stigmatizing symbol that reproduces the social boundaries between status groups.

Documenting Legal Redemption in Mali

Various occasions for the legal (self-) manumission of slaves are described in the *hadith*, "the sayings and doings of the prophet" and the *fiqh*, "Islamic legal books." Manumission can be done on the initiative of the master who, for example, can opt for rewarding a loyal slave through manumission. The majority of Islamic legal procedures focus on reasons for masters to manumit their slaves. However, there is one option for self-manumission, in which the slave himself pays for his freedom.[38] In the Haayre region, the majority of current manumissions are paid for by slave descendants themselves.[39] So over time the price of manumission was transferred from descendants of masters to descendants of slaves. Self-manumission Document I of Diougal Issiaka specifies that he paid two calves and thirty-six hundred units of something.[40] Diougal Issiaka explains how he discussed the price, typically consisting of animals and money, with his former master.[41] Belco, an intellectual of slave descent,[42] describes these payments as "moral bribery" by a dominant elite "abusing religious arguments."[43]

Manumission Document II describes the renewal of Bilal Al-layidi's former document. The document states that this is "for the sake of Allah and his Prophet to the parents of Bilal." Although the document does not clearly mention it, Bilal was manumitted by his master because he and his parents have always been very loyal. A co-villager stated that Bilal Allayidi's master exceptionally "had the courage" to free Bilal Allayidi. But there is another explanation. According to Islamic legislation, Bilal Allayidi officially "needed" his manumission in order to be allowed to marry his wife Dikel. Dikel is the daughter of a manumitted slave-woman with a noble pastoralist master. Because of her mother's manumission, Dikel also enjoys manumitted status. Thus for Bilal Allayidi to marry Dikel, he first had to manumit himself; otherwise their marriage would be unacceptable. Bilal Allayidi's manumission was issued in the 1960s. His family explains how, in 1992, he asked the imam to copy his former document (issued in 1984) as it was in a deplorable condition. Informants believe that if the paper goes missing, one becomes owned (*jeyaado*) again. It is plausible that French colonial administration, by issuing liberty certificates stimulated the perceived importance of manumission documents for the older generation of slave descendants. During the past decade of his life,[44] Bilal's seniority made him chief of the slave descendants (called *amiiri maccuɓe*) in his home village. He enjoyed a special status and on the occasion of Tabaski he was the only one among the slave descendants of the ruling elite to have his own sacrificial animal slaughtered.

The procedure for liberating (*rimɗineede*)[45] someone works as follows: on the day of liberation, the slave descendant, his former master, and witnesses gather.[46] An Islamic scholar, preferably the imam, writes the manumission document.[47] Various books stipulate the formulations that should be used on the manumission document.[48] In the Haayre region convention has it that the reason for liberation (*asahaada*), the name of the freed person (*dimɗinaado*), the date (day, month, and year), and the names of the witnesses are mentioned. The witnesses must include a minimum of four freeborn persons, which is the case in both Documents I and II. Since

Issiaka Diougal self-manumitted, the price he paid is mentioned in Document I.

The fact that a document was deemed necessary as a guarantee for liberty shows that it did not suffice to be *known* as freed in order to be recognized as such. The freed person keeps the manumission document, which is important upon marriage (to another freed slave descendant) or in case of conflict (e.g., over land or inheritance). Manumission Document II is a "renewal" of liberation. It describes how the imam authorizes his son to copy the manumission document of Bilal Allaydi. Copying documents is a common thing to do in order to avoid deterioration. Commonly there are two copies: one kept by the imam, the other kept by the manumitted person or family.

Those Manumitted: Social Mobility in the Religious Home Community

The possibility of manumission is a good illustration of how the ideology of slavery for a long time was closely intertwined with religious arguments and legislation. In this section I focus on those who self-manumitted and I demonstrate how they incorporated the ideology of slavery into their actions. They believe in manumission as an enfranchising or as they have called it, an ennobling strategy.[49]

Age seems to be an important factor in explaining who engages in liberation today. According to local interpretations of Islam, slaves are restricted in where they can sit in the mosque and what role they can play in Muslim rituals and prayer. Only manumitted slaves can become "true" Muslims.[50] The older generations internalized ideas of their unequal status in the hierarchy and for a long time remained within the confines of the village community. Slave descendants in their sixties remember how they worked as child slaves. The old men, Allay, who is a slave descendant in a neighboring village, and Diougal Issiaka, were child slaves working at the royal court and in the imam's family, respectively.

Allay was not fortunate in his quest for honor. The desire to

74

make the pilgrimage after being liberated was widespread among slave descendants in the Sahel.[51] When Allay, who always dreamed of going on a pilgrimage to Mecca, proposed to manumit himself, the imam and his former master refused. Instead they advised Allay to give the money (manumission price) to his former master, the mayor, who was going on pilgrimage about that time. Allay was told that God would reward him for doing so as a demonstration of his loyalty to his former master. So finally he gave his money to contribute to his master's pilgrimage. When I met Allay some years later (in 2005) he had become too old to leave for pilgrimage, but he assured me he still considered self-manumission worthwhile in order to travel on horseback instead of on foot in his afterlife.

For both Diougal Issiaka (Document I) and for Allay, the main motivation for liberating themselves was to obtain full access to the Muslim community without the restrictions related to their slave status. Besides that, liberation grants more social prestige within one's social status group. Diougal Issiaka, the freed slave descendant central to Document I, is currently the *muezzin* of the village mosque. He takes pride in actively demonstrating his piety. Paying for his liberation was a precondition for him to be able to do so.

Apart from the eldest generation of slave descendants, some wealthy slave descendants are eager to manumit themselves as well. The imam who issued Document I says that most self-manumissions are initiated today by rich slave descendants. Since they became wealthier than their former masters' families, they no longer benefit from their historical bond. They no longer rely on the social security that the hierarchical relation used to guarantee. Liberation allows them to "climb" in status vis-à-vis other slave descendants by establishing their proper endogamous group: they only marry among themselves. I have already described how his marriage with a freed woman was an important motive for Bilal Allayidi's manumission (Document II).

Contesting Manumission

Slave descendants' opinions on manumission vary. There are those who consider themselves free according to Islamic law and those who consider themselves free according to state law. Few manumission documents are issued today. Those who consider themselves free according to state law describe those resorting to manumission as still being caught in "mental slavery." As one informant has it: "Slavery is finished, but mental slavery still exists." It is mostly youths and migrants who look down upon those who manumit themselves back home and consider them as stuck in "the middle ages" and naive. They reproach those manumitting themselves for believing that the only way to really be free is in the eyes of God, as opposed to liberating themselves in their own mind.

However, apart from migrants and youths, villagers themselves have varying opinions on those who self-manumit. The rich descendants of slaves who manumit themselves after resettlement in their home community are particularly criticized for their motives. Fanta Tamboura explains:[52] "We insult those rich descendants of slaves [Riimayɓe] who self-manumit by reminding them of how they never will become 'really' noble or freeborn. We gossip about them only 'pretending' to have become freeborn. I would never liberate myself, I am proud of who I am. If you free yourself, you are neither this nor that kind of person." Such social critiques and witchcraft accusations effectively deter some rich migrants from engaging in manumission altogether. The assertion of this woman also shows that there is honor in knowing yourself and in accepting your social position.

Those who believe in manumission reproach those who don't for adhering to the wrong frame of reference and rules. In the eyes of this small group of demonstrably pious slave descendants, God does not approve of the prayers, pilgrimage, and other religious obligations of those who did not manumit. Some, however, don't believe in self-manumission and insist that the former master should take the initiative. Often these are older widowed women like Fanta Tamboura who benefit from their relation with their former master because they are regularly offered paid jobs. Fanta Tamboura criticizes self-manumission: "According to my religion, if you don't obey your master,[53] you go to hell. This is why people are scared to change their identity. Only if your master blesses or damns you, you are sure that God does so too. It is only if your master frees you that God agrees. This is the religious path, but some are too blinded by the money, which makes them ignore their religion." Fanta Tamboura does not agree with those who self-manumit, because for her this goes against God's will. Although the rope is not there in material practice, this demonstrates how it is inscribed in some people's minds and moral ideas.

Alternative Strategies for Social Mobility and Countering Social Stigma

Only a small minority of, often older, people hope to renegotiate their position through self-manumission. Over time the younger generations obtained access to a much broader array of alternatives for social climbing and emancipation. Currently, slave descendants make money through seasonal or long-term international migration. Their wealth and absence automatically makes them less dependent on the freeborn elite in their home community.[54] Many never return to their hometowns but settle elsewhere in cities and other countries. This facilitates their getting rid of their social stigma. It allows them to bypass the social control of their village community and marry (noble) women from other ethnic (status) groups.[55] Others changed ethnic affiliation altogether, for example, by replacing their stigmatizing descent reflected in their surnames with more prestigious surnames. Hardly any young slave descendant today dreams of manumission in order to conduct pilgrimage in the way Allay and Diougal Issiaka (Document I) did. Most of them identify with different interpretations of Islam, which allow them to conduct the *hajj* without resorting to manumission first. For this generation it is seems that mobility is the main precondition for emancipating themselves from "mental slavery."[56]

Paradoxically those slave descendants who obtained enfranchisement in the fullest sense of the word are impossible to trace. They cannot be named, traced through documents, or even referred to as such. Anonymity is the only way to obscure any reference to one's former status and past. Manumission is not all that helpful in obscuring the stigma of the rope. Rather it reframes the slave stigma by slightly improving the relative inclusion of slave descendants in the freeborn community.

Conclusion:
Manumission as Renegotiation from Within

Manumission documents are issued by Islamic scholars to slave descendants. I described why a minority of older slave descendants tried to obtain social mobility within the existing hierarchies of their community. They freed themselves in order to obtain full recognition in a close-knit religious community. Manumission for them is a culturally accepted strategy of inclusion and social mobility from within. To be freed does not equal being free. Those who engage in manumission today are freed, but not free. They are still likely to be stigmatized as "children of the rope." Manumission does not result in full enfranchisement. If anything, self-purchased freedom is not directed toward gain in an economic-material realm but rather is about social recognition in a cultural context where religious identification is central. Besides obtaining religious inclusion and cultural prestige, self-manumissions are about renegotiating social distances based on memories of slavery *from within*. For the younger generations, strategies to distance oneself from memories of slavery are obtained *from outside*. For them social distance is created through geographic mobility. This makes it easier to bypass rather than renegotiate patron-client relations based on a slave past.

Translation of Two Manumission Documents

In the following sections, the reader finds a translation of the manumission documents referred to in this chapter. The documents are in Arabic written with the Fulfulde alphabet (called *Adjami*). I express my warm thanks to Saajo Bah and Inge Butter for their assistance in translating these texts. Please note that the words between brackets are explanations or fake names (in order to respect the privacy of the people involved).

CERTIFICATE I: LIBERATION OF [DIOUGAL] ISSIAKA

In the name of Allah, Most Gracious Most Merciful

Let the reader of this writing know that [Diougal] son of Ishaaq son of Sana Ibraahiim has today become a free man, on the 3th of the month of Muharram 1420 of the Hijri calendar [1999].

The children of Muhammad son of Abdulaye Qaadir son of Yero Mahmuud [who were his masters] have freed him for 3600 and two calves.

Surely [Diougal] son of Ishaaq has purely become a free man, there is no doubt in his freedom.

Witnesses: Amiirii Booni Ibraahiima [Ibrahim Dicko, actual chief of Booni], Amiirii Booni, Amiiri Booni's Nassourou [assistant], Hamma Samere and Buuba Kisi.

Peace.

Writer: Alhajji Muhammadu in the town of [Wuro Ngeru]

CERTIFICATE II: RENEWAL OF CERTIFICATE OF [BILAL]ALLA YIDI

Let the reader of this writing know that this paper certifies the renewal of the freedom of [Bilal]Alla Yidi who is known as [Bilal] Alla Yidi, in the presence of (witnesses to this are:) Amiiru Dalla who is known as Yerowal, Alhajji MBouli, Alfaa Hammadaa and Sammba Sam.

Hamare Sory has freed his slave, [Bilal] Alla Yidi, for the sake of Allah and his Prophet to the parents of [Bilal] Alla Yidi.

The writer of this certificate is Muhammad Ben Tokara Moodi under the authorization of Alfaa Hammadaa, on the 24th of the month of Dhu Al-Hijjah, 1413 Hijri [1992] which we have seen on Wednesday.

Peace.

Notes

1. I thank Martin Van Vliet, Eric Komlavi Hahonou, Jennifer Lofkrantz, Yacine Daddi Adoun, Adam Mahamat, Walter Nkwi, Jan Bart Gewald, and Rivke Jaffe and colleagues for their invaluable comments and additions on earlier drafts. I thank Anneke Breedveld for her corrections to the spelling of Fulfulde concepts (central Malian Haayre dialect) and Saajo Bah for the translation of the documents.
2. In Fulfulde: "*A tayyi* (cut) *ɓoggol* (rope) *e daande ma* (neck)": You cut the rope from your neck.
3. In this text I use the terms *slave descendants* (*Riimaybe* in local Fulfulde dialect) to describe an extremely heterogeneous group of people who shared the common denominator of being recognized by a majority as those whose parents and/or ancestors at some point in time were enslaved. I use the term "former master" (*Kalfaado* in local Fulfulde dialect) for an extremely heterogeneous group who shared the common denominator of being categorized by the majority as freeborn members of society (*Riimbe* in local Fulfulde dialect). To be freeborn means to be able to own slaves oneself.
4. Thanks to a grant from NWO-WOTRO, I conducted field work for a period of six months in Central Mali (2001-2), Bamako (2005-6 and 2007), and Paris (2004-5).
5. Mirjam E. De Bruijn and Han Van Dijk, *Arid Ways: Cultural Understanding of Insecurity in FulBe Society, Central Mali* (Amsterdam: Thela, 1995); Caroline Angenent et al., eds., *Les rois des tambours au Haayre: Récitée par Aamadu Baa Digi, griot des Fulbe à Dalla* (Leiden, Netherlands: Brill, 2003).
6. See Jennifer Lofkrantz, "Ransoming Policies and Practices in the Western and Central *Bilad al-sudan* (c 1800-1910" (Ph.D. diss., York University, Toronto, 2008), 116. Paul E. Lovejoy argues that "a system of ransoming effectively enabled those who could afford it to achieve their redemption should they be unlucky and have been enslaved," see Lovejoy, "The Slave Trade as Enforced Migration in the Central Sudan of West Africa," in *Removing Peoples: Forced Removal in the Modern World*, eds. R. Bessel and C. Haake (London: German Historical Institute, 2009), 145-64, esp. 162-63. Lofkrantz, in her thesis on ransoming in the Sokoto caliphate, analyzes this line of argument in extensive detail.
7. The term *redemption* is used by Lovejoy, "The Context of Enslavement in West Africa: Ahmed Baba and the Ethics of Slavery," in *Slaves, Subjects and Subversives: Blacks in Colonial Latin America*, ed. Jane Landers (Albuquerque: University of New Mexico Press,

2006); Lovejoy, "Slave Trade as Enforced Migration in the Central Sudan of West Africa"; Lofkranz, "Ransoming Policies and Practices in the Western and Central Bilad al-sudan"; Kwabena Akurang-Parry, "Slavery and Abolition in the Gold Coast: Colonial Modes of Emancipation," *Ghana Studies* 1 (1998): 11-34.

8. Martin A. Klein, *Slavery and Colonial Rule in French West Africa* (Cambridge: Cambridge University Press, 1998).

9. Self-manumission is comparable to what has been coined *murgu* by Lovejoy and Jan Hogendorn, in which the slave pays a predetermined amount to become a landowning client. See Hogendorn and Lovejoy, *Slow Death for Slavery: The Course of Abolition in Northern Nigeria 1897-1936* (Cambridge: Cambridge University Press, 1989).

10. Klein describes how self-manumission was related to slave resistance and contradicted French colonial abolitionist legislation. Klein, "Studying the History of Those Who Would Rather Forget: Oral History and the Experience of Slavery," *History in Africa* 36 (1989): 209-11.

11. Hogendorn and Lovejoy, *Slow Death for Slavery*, describe it as a means of compensating owners for the loss of slave labor in the British colonies.

12. Lofkrantz, "Ransoming Policies and Practices in the Western and Central Bilad al-Sudan," 3.

13. See Cameroonian scholars Ahmadou Sehou, Issa Saibou, and Adam Mahamat. Ahmadou Sehou, "Some Facets of Slavery in the Lamidats of Adamawa in the North Cameroon in the 19th and 20th Centuries," in *African Voices on Slavery and the Slave Trade*, eds. Alice Bellagamba, Sandra Greene, and Martin Klein (Cambridge: Cambridge University Press, 2013); Issa Saibou, "Paroles d'esclaves au Nord-Cameroun," *Cahiers d'études Africaines* 179-180, n.s. 3-4 (2005): 853-78; Adam Mahamat, "Esclavage et servitude dans les abords sud du lac tchad (XVIe début XXIe siècle)" (Ph.D. diss., Université de Ngaoundere, 2009).

14. Claude Meillassoux counted 53 manumitted versus 1,040 slaves born in captivity in the Malian region of Gumbu. Meillassoux, *Anthropology of Slavery: The Womb of Iron and Gold* (London: Athlone Press, 1991 [1983]), 12. While manumission was relatively "scarce," ransoming was more frequent. Lofkrantz, "Ransoming Policies and Practices in the Western and Central Bilad al-sudan"; Lovejoy, "The Slave Trade as Enforced Migration in the Central Sudan of West Africa."

15. Klein, *Slavery and Colonial Rule in French West Africa*.

16. Baz Lecocq, "The 'Bellah' Question: Slave Emancipation, Race and

Social Categories in Late Twentieth-Century Northern Mali," *Canadian Journal of African Studies* 39 (2005):42-68, esp. 53-57.

17. Roger Botte, "De l'esclavage et du daltonisme dans les sciences sociales: Avant-propos," *Journal des Africanistes* 70 (2000): 7-42.

18. Naffet Keita, "Genre et droit au Mali: La problématique de l'accès des femmes á la décision," in *Luttes politiques et résistances féminines en Afrique. Néo-libéralisme et conditions de la femme*, ed. F. Sarr (Dakar, Senegal: Panafrika Silex, 2007), 151-91, esp. 162.

19. The French issued freedom certificates after a three-month residence in a so-called liberty village. Klein, "Slave Resistance and Slave Emancipation in Coastal Guinea," in *The End of Slavery in Africa*, eds. Suzanne Miers and Richard Roberts (Madison: University of Wisconsin Press, 1988), 203-19; Denise Bouche, *Les villages de liberté en Afrique noire Française, 1887-1910* (Paris: Mouton, 1968); E. Ann McDougall, "The Practice of *Rachat* in French West Africa," in *Buying Freedom: The Ethics and Economics of Slave Redemption*, eds. K. A. Appiah and M. Bunzl (Princeton: Princeton University Press, 2007), 158-78.

20. Yacine Daddi Addoun, "Pour que dieu émancipe les patrons: Manumission des esclaves et salut des maitres en Algérie," Seminar paper, York University, Toronto, 2005. McDougall, in "The Practice of Rachat in French West Africa," argues that French liberty certificates did not have the same sociocultural validity because they lacked both material advantage and "moral prestige."

21. Descriptions of such formulations are described in Islamic jurisprudence (Fiqh). For more on Islamic fiqh, see, for example, Mohammed N. Mahieddin, "Le fiqh islamique et la formation du droit en Algérie," *The Maghreb Review* 13, n.s. 1-2 (1988): 42-48. On the centrality of documents in Islamic legislation, see Yacine Daddi Addoun, "Translation and Commentary on Some Documents from CEDRAB (Centre de documentation et de recherches Ahmed Baba) at Timbuktu," Seminar paper, York University, Toronto, 1998.

22. Lovejoy describes Ahmed Baaba's writings on the "ethics of slavery in Islam." Lovejoy, "The Context of Enslavement in West-Africa: Ahmed Baba and the Ethics of Slavery," in *Slaves, Subjects and Subversives: Blacks in Colonial Latin America*, ed. Jane Landers (Albuquerque: University of New Mexico Press, 2006), 9-38. Lofkrantz describes various scholars in nineteeth-century Sokoto engaging in debates about ransoming in the legal tradition of West African Islam. Lofkrantz, "Ransoming Policies and Practices in the Western and Central Bilad al-sudan," 27-43.

23. Jean Hurault, "Les noms attribues aux non-libres dans le lamidat de

Banyo," *Journal des africanistes* 64 (1994): 91-107, esp. 91, and R. Brunschvig, "Abd," in H. A. Rosskeen, ed. *The Encyclopaedia of Islam* (Leiden: Brill, 1960).

24. Lofkrantz, "Ransoming Policies and Practices in the Western and Central Bilad al-sudan."

25. Meillassoux defines full enfranchisement as the process through which the slave acquires all the prerogatives of the freeborn, including the honor attached to his status, and thus, his origins are effaced. Meillassoux, *Anthropology of Slavery*, 119-20. Although manumission changed the slaves' condition, it did not change the slaves' status. It was partial enfranchisement.

26. Lofkrantz, "Ransoming Policies and Practices in the Western and Central Bilad al-sudan," 1. Suzanne Miers and Igor Kopytoff thus call Islamic manumission "incomplete": "The freed slave and his descendants became, in perpetuity, the clients of their former master." *Slavery in Africa: Historical and Anthropological Perspectives*, eds. Suzanne Miers and Igor Kopytoff (Madison: University of Wisconsin Press, 1977), 27.

27. Yacine Daddi Addoun, "Pour que dieu émancipe les patrons."

28. Meillassoux, *Anthropology of Slavery*, 12.

29. Xavier Yacono, "Un affranchissement d'esclaves à Alger en 1847," *Revue d'histoire maghrebine* 1 (1974): 77-80.

30. Access to religious legislation remained much easier than access to national secular law for many rural villagers in Mali. Tensions over Islam in the neoliberal era of the Malian nation are addressed in *Islam and Muslim Politics in Africa*, eds. Benjamin Soares and René Otayek (New York: Palgrave Macmillan, 2007). At present, tensions are rising over the secular constitution and national family legislation, Keita, "Genre et droit." The first draft of a new family code was rejected for being too secular: http://www.irinnews.org/Report.aspx?ReportId=85960.

31. On the central entanglement of Islam and the ideology of slavery in Fulɓe society, see Roger Botte, "Pouvoir du livre, pouvoir des hommes: La religion comme critère de distinction, " *Journal des Africanistes* 60 (1990): 37-51; Botte, "Stigmates sociaux et discriminations religieuses: L'ancienne classe servile au Fuuta Jaloo," *Cahiers d'études Africaines* 34, n.s. 133-35 (1994), 109-36; Jean Schmitz, "Islam et 'esclavage' ou l'impossible 'négritude' des Africains musulmans," *Africulture* 67 (2006): 110-15.

32. The honor code is called *ndimaaku* in Fulfulde. For a discussion of the notions of *ndimaaku* and *ndimu*, see Anneke Breedveld and Mirjam E. De Bruijn, "L'image des Fulbe: Analyse critique de la con-

struction du concept de Pulaaku," *Cahiers d'études Africaines* 36 (1996): 791-821.

33. In Fulfulde language: "Mi haɓɓataa e ɓi ɓoggol" (*ɓi* = child/ *ɓoggol* = rope).

34. For more about naming, see Lotte Pelckmans, "Surnames as a Passport to Social Mobility," in *New Perspectives on African Slavery, Slave Trade, and Abolition,* eds. Alice Bellagamba, Sandra Greene, and Martin Klein (Trenton, NJ: Africa World Press, forthcoming).

35. See, for example, Jean Schmitz, "Islamic Patronage and Republican Emancipation: The Slaves of the Almaami in the Senegal River Valley," in *Reconfiguring Slavery: West African Trajectories*, ed. Benedetta Rossi (Liverpool: Liverpool University Press, 2009), 85-115, esp. 96; Stephen Baier, *Economic History of Central Niger* (Oxford: Clarendon, 1980), 83 quoted in Bruce Hall, "Mapping the River in Black and White: Trajectories of Race in the Niger Bend, Northern Mali" (Ph. D. diss., University of Illinois, Urbana-Champaign, 2005), 13. Hurault, "Les noms attribues aux non-libres dans le lamidat de Banyo," 100 and 106, indicates that only upon manumission could the slave's name be changed by his master.

36. In Fulfulde *dimɗinaaɗo (*sing.*)*: "the one who has been liberated"; *Rimɗinaaɗe* (pl.): "those who have been made noble/free."

37. It was possible for freed slaves to make testaments. Yacine Daddi Addoun, "Manumission," 15.

38. Both Yacine Daddi Addoun and Ahmadou Sehou mention different forms, reasons, and terminology for the various forms of self-manumission in Arab and Fulfulde respectively; see Yacine Daddi Addoun, "Pour que dieu émancipe les patrons"; Ahmadou Sehou, "Nègres au pays des Noirs: Statuts, representations et situation des esclaves dans les lamidats de l' Adamaoua (Nord-Cameroun), XIXe-XXe siècle." Paper presented at the conference "Constructions historiques de la notion de race et hiérarchies sociales, " Dakar, 2008.

39. Lofkrantz, "Ransoming Policies and Practices in the Western and Central Bilal al-sudan," 3 gives a possible explanation for this by arguing that "colonial reforms … took the power to allow for redemption away from the owners and put it into the hands of the slaves."

40. Manumission Document I spells out that 3,600 units of something are given. The unmentioned unit is most likely francs, which in Fulfulde counting has to be multiplied by 5 = 18,000 francs CFA today, equaling about 27 euros. Klein mentions the same amount being paid for self-manumission by a Senegalese slave descendant in 1975. Klein, "He Who Is Without Family Will Be the Subject of Many Exactions: A Case from Senegal," in *African Voices on Slavery and the*

Slave Trade, vol. 1, *Sources,* eds. Alice Bellagamba, Sandra Greene, and Martin Klein (Cambridge: Cambridge University Press, 2013).

41. Prices are high and comparable to the amount paid for women in marriage. Other examples of prices for liberations in the Haayre region in the 1990s are: 1 bull + 10,000 francs CFA; 3 goats + 10 000 francs CFA + 5 cotton bands; and 1 bull + 30 000 francs CFA. The money is for paying cola nuts to be distributed among the witnesses of the liberation.

42. Belco Tamboura, an intellectual of slave descent from Mopti region, currently living in Bamako, Interviews, 2007.

43. The Cameroonian scholars Issa Saibou, Ahmadou Sehou, and Adam Mahamat depict the payments for liberation asked by freeborn Fulɓe in northern Cameroun as outright swindling. Issa Saibou, "Paroles d'esclaves au Nord-Cameroon," 869 and 873; Ahmadou Sehou, "Negres au pays des noirs" and "Lamido Iyawa Adamou de Banyo (Nord-Cameroun): Chef traditionnel, parlementaire et esclavagiste (1902-1966)," paper presented at the conference, "Tales of Slavery," Toronto, 2009; Adam Mahamat, "Esclavage et servitude dans les aborts sud du lac tchad."

44. Bilal became blind and died in 2007.

45. In local Fulfulde dialect the liberation procedure is called *Rimɗineede* (inf.): "to be made noble/free." Some use the verb *joppude* = to let go, to drop. An informant described how a master let go of his slave through manumission, saying *kanko joppan*, literally: he drops it, but here meaning that "he [master] let go of him [slave]."

46. The place of gathering is ideally the mosque but can also be the imam's or chief's compound.

47. This manumission document is literally called "paper of confidence" and is considered a legal contract (called Wassigatu/Almouktaba).

48. Yacine Daddi Addoun, "Pour que dieu émancipe les patrons," refers to various formularies used for Islamic contracts.

49. In French, many informants translate "manumission" as *anoblissement*.

50. M. E. De Bruijn and H. Van Dijk, "Drought and Coping Strategies in Fulbe Society in the Hayre (Central Mali): A Historical Perspective," *Cahiers d'études Africaines* 34, n.s. 133-135 (1994): 85-108, esp. 99-103.

51. Klein, *Slavery and Colonial Rule in French West Indies*, 246-47. In 1968, the first slave descendants to liberate themselves in Dalla (central Mali, Haayre region) left for Mecca on foot. From 1978, they went by airplane. All were manumitted before leaving.

52. Fanta Tamboura (b. circa 1950) in Joona. Interview in Bamako, 2007.

53. In Fulfulde, Fanta uses the word *kalfaaɗo* to designate "master."
54. In my thesis, I analyze to what extent mobility of slave descendants contributes to their emancipation; see Lotte Pelckmans, *Travelling Hierarchies: Moving In and Out of Slave Status in a Central Malian FulБe Network* (Leiden, Netherlands: African Studies Center, 2011). Florence Boyer describes how physical distance of slave descendants in Niger allows them more "mental" freedom from existing hierarchical relations. Boyer, "L'esclavage chez les Touregs de Bankilare au miroir des migrations circulaires," *Cahiers d'études Africaines* 45 (2005): 771-804.
55. Benedetta Rossi, "Introduction: Rethinking Slavery in West-Africa," in *Reconfiguring Slavery: West African Trajectories*, ed. Benedetta Rossi (Liverpool: Liverpool University Press, 2009), 1-25, esp. 4.
56. Other strategies, often involving mobility, which became available to [Fulбe] slave descendants in the Sahel are French education, Islamic schooling, and emigration. J. H. Jezequel, "Histoire des bancs, parcours d'élèves: Pour une histoire configurationnelle de la scolarisation à l'époque coloniale," *Cahiers d'études Africaines* 33 (2003): 409-33; Abderamane N'Gaide, "Conquête de la liberté, mutations politiques, sociales et religieuses en haute Casamance: Les anciens Maccube du Fuladu (région de Kolda, Sénégal)," in Roger Botte, Jean Boutrais, and Jean Schmitz, eds., *Figures Peules* (Paris: Karthala, 1999), 141-64. On Islamic schooling, see Jeremy Berndt, "Closer Than Your Jugular Vein: Muslim Intellectuals in a Malian Village, 1900-1960s" (Ph.D. diss., Northwestern University, 2008); Jean Schmitz, "Patronage." On the impact of decentralization policies, see Mirjam De Bruijn and Lotte Pelckmans, "Facing Dilemmas: Former Fulбe Slaves in Modern Mali," *Canadian Journal of African Studies* 39 (2005): 69-96; Olivier Leservoisier, "Nous voulons notre part!'": Les ambivalences du mouvement d'émancipation des Saafaalбe Hormankooбe de Djéol (Mauritanie)," *Cahiers d'études Africaines* 179-180, n.s. 133-35 (2005): 987-1014; Eric K. Hahonou, "Past and Present African Citizenships of Slave Descent: Lessons from Benin," *Citizenship Studies* 15 (2011); Aurelien Mauxion, "Rice Farming Intensification and Political Enterprise in Northern Mali," *Politique Africaine* 110 (2008): 153-169. On emigration more generally, see Francois Manchuelle, *Willing Migrants: Soninke Labour Diasporas, 1848-1960* (Athens: Ohio University Press, 1997); Boyer, "L'esclavage chez les Touregs de Bankilare au miroir des migrations circulaires;" Rossi, "Introduction."

5. Memories of Slavery
in a Former Slave-Trading Community:
The Aro of the Bight of Biafra

G. UGO NWOKEJI

Discussions about oral traditions often seek their point of departure in what traditions mean, whether they have a place in historical research generally, what their strengths and weaknesses are, and so forth. In the absence of fresh answers offered to these old questions in recent years, here, I sketch the problems and dynamics of collecting narratives of slavery among a specific group—the descendants of the Aro, the leading slave traders of inland Bight of Biafra. I illustrate these issues with my conversations with six Aro respondents in five wide-ranging interviews focusing on slavery and the slave trade. I also sketch my approach to collecting the traditions, and what I learned regarding how the late twentieth-century Aro viewed history as a system of knowledge generally, and the history of slaving in particular.

The Aro were the dominant slave-trading group in inland Bight of Biafra. The Bight of Biafra comprises the lower segment of the Gulf of Guinea, from the Rio Nun in the Niger Delta in modern Nigeria, to Cape Lopez in modern Gabon. The ports of this region accounted for 13 percent of all captives shipped from Africa to the Americas between 1551 and 1850. The Nigerian section of the region, where Aro operations were concentrated, accounted for more than 90 percent of all captives exported to the Americas from Bight of Biafra ports. The region's slave trade exhibited two salient patterns. First, the region sent the highest proportion of females into the Atlantic slave trade. This was due to unique structural and cultural reasons— warfare that tended to kill men and capture women and children, a division of labor that placed men rather than women at the center of agricultural production, and the virtual absence of the trans-Saharan slave trade that absorbed women elsewhere in West Africa. The second salient pattern was in the trajectory of the region's slave trade. Although the slave trade expanded appreciably in virtually all African regions during the eighteenth century in response to the sugar revolution in the Americas, this expansion was particularly dramatic in the Bight of Biafra. While the region's share of captive exports from all African regions was 5.5 percentage points during the first half of the century, the corresponding figure for the second half of the century was 16.6 percentage points (see Table 1).

TABLE 1

Estimated Volume of Biafran Captive Exports,
1551-1850, by Twenty-Five-Year Period

Period	Bight of Biafra	All Africa	Biafran Percentage of African Total
1551-1575	3,383	61,007	5.5
1576-1600	2,996	152,373	2.0
1601-1625	2,921	352,843	0.8
1626-1650	33,540	315,050	10.6
1651-1675	80,780	488,064	16.5
1676-1700	69,080	719,674	9.6
1701-1725	66,833	1,088,909	6.1
1726-1750	182,066	1,471,725	12.4
1751-1775	319,709	1,925,314	16.6
1776-1800	336,008	2,008,670	16.7
1801-1825	264,834	1,876,992	14.1
1826-1850	230,328	1,770,979	13.0
Grand Totals	**1,592,478**	**12,231,600**	**13.0**

Source: G. Ugo Nwokeji, *The Slave Trade and Culture in the Bight of Biafra: An African Society in the Atlantic World* (New York: Cambridge University Press, 2010). Numbers with decimal points are not precise because of rounding.

The big surge began in the 1740s. Between 1741 and 1800, the region exported an annual mean of 13,800, reaching a peak of 20,000 during the 1780s. Apart from West-Central Africa, the Bight of Biafra sent the highest numbers of captives to the Americas during the eighteenth century and the peoples who we know today as Igbo were the single largest African ethnolinguistic group arriving in the Americas during that century.

The expansion of the Bight of Biafra slave trade was linked with the expansion of the Aro merchant group. The surge of the 1740s coincided with the expansion of the Aro from their Arochukwu homeland northwestward into the central Igboland, the most densely populated region in West Africa, where the Aro established diaspora settlements that acted as trading centers. One of these settlements was Arondizuogu, the home of four of the five respondents cited in the attached interview excerpts. The impact of Aro expansion was felt on the coast, where the centrally located port of Bonny overtook the easterly located Old Calabar, which had handled the largest number of slave exports up to the 1730s. By the mid-eighteenth century, the Bight of Biafra ports of Bonny and Old Calabar had become the busiest ports in West Africa north of the Equator (see Table 2). Not only did more captives pass through both ports than other West African ports, the rate at which the captives were loaded onto ships was also fastest there. The average number of captives loaded onto a slave ship per day in Bonny and Old Calabar were 5.5 and 3.7, respectively, while the busiest port of the first half of the century, Whydah in Dahomey (today's Benin Republic), had fallen behind with 3.2 captives. The Aro are descended from the culturally and linguistically variegated original settlers of the town of Arochukwu and the many immigrants whom the Aro have incorporated since the seventeenth century when the Aro began their expansion in connection with their slave-trading activities. Aro settlements outside homeland Arochukwu had, by the nineteenth century, numbered more than 150, overwhelmingly among the Igbo, whom the vast majority of the Aro identify with today. To this day, the Aro refer to the Aro in the diaspora settlements as Aro-Uzo (Aro Abroad), and the Aro in homeland

89

Arochukwu as Aro-Uno (Homeland Aro). Aro ability to maintain a strong trading network through their unity, massive incorporation of the non-Aro, mobilization, and deployment of specialized non-Aro warrior clans, and their control of region-wide institutions—including the powerful Ekpe cult and the feared Ibiniukpabi oracle—gave the Aro enormous influence in the region.[1] The oracle, which British colonizers of the twentieth century called Long Juju, served as the de facto supreme court of the entire region. As agents of the oracle, Aro settlers in various part of the region took their non-Aro hosts to the oracle in Arochukwu for the adjudication of legal cases and disputes.[2]

TABLE 2
Daily Average Number of Captives
Loaded per Vessel, 1751-1800

Imputed Principal Port of Slave Purchase	Average No. of Captives Embarked per Vessel per Day	No. of Vessels in Sample	Number Embarked
Gambia	1.7	56	66,459
Anomabu, Adja, Agga	2.7	81	122,820
Whydah	3.2	87	109,010
Bonny	5.5	65	279,898
Calabar	3.7	53	131,144

Source: G. Ugo Nwokeji, *The Slave Trade and Culture in the Bight of Biafra: An African Society in the Atlantic World* (New York: Cambridge University Press, 2010). Numbers with decimal points are not precise because of rounding.

Aro narratives of slaving display an ambiguous understanding of history. Earnest Aro expressions about the possibility of accurate historical reconstruction are at odds with the resistance, hesitations, selectiveness, and equivocations the history field-worker observes among them. Everyone that I spoke to—not just interviewed—conceptualized history as a distinct and knowable body of knowledge. People had no qualms referring me to other people they believed knew Aro history, often remarking on the depth of a person's honesty and/or the depth of the supposed experts' knowledge. Respondents often lamented that, had I done my research a few years earlier when this or that man or the occasional woman was living, they "would have told [me] all about it." Names of particular individuals were mentioned frequently. The social backgrounds of these persons varied widely, but they were united in their acclaimed knowledge of "history." This kind of recognition implies that a historian could have interviewed one person and found all historical knowledge of the Aro. History for the Aro people is, above all else, a body of knowledge and truth, which should be protected from falsehood. Perhaps persuaded by this apparent Aro certitude about the existence of their historical past, a colonial anthropological report of 1927 noted that the Aro had "an undimmed recollection of their past history." Another officer in 1935 observed that Arondizuogu did not have any legends. Both reports relied on Aro oral traditions collected in the course of British efforts to uncover Aro origins, the "basis of Aro power," and the structure of their organization. From this perspective, therefore, slavery and the slave trade were somewhat tangential, and Aro respondents were not generally required to dwell on slaving. If Aro respondents cooperated with the British and the traditions showed remarkable consistency in representing the fundamentals of Aro history as the foregoing reports suggest, this was often not the case with my experience interviewing the Aro about slaving.

Problems and Method

Much of the fieldwork for this study was done in 1995-96 in the course of researching the slave trade in the Bight of Biafra. The vast majority of the people I interviewed were Aro. I have since had numerous conversations with many other Aro respondents. As an Aro myself, I already knew some of these respondents, although sometimes by reputation only. It was, however, obvious to me from the spread of the Aro network, their conflicts with various groups, the vastly heterogeneous origins of Aro people themselves, and their controversial enterprise in the slave trade that traditions collected only from among the Aro would present only a partial perspective. Thus, I also studied hundreds of other traditions collected by other researchers, in particular, Elizabeth Isichei, David Northrup, and the various authors of undergraduate theses in Nigerian universities.[3] I complemented these sources with genealogy, the study of the Aro homage system (Ihu),[4] artifacts, architectural structures, migration and settlement patterns, and, of course, written sources, where available, in an effort to make sense of the narratives I collected and to give them some chronological orientation.

I got to the field armed with a set of questions relating to migrations, trade, aspects of social relations, slavery, and the slave trade in particular. I referred to my male Aro respondents with the reverential title Mazi [5] and the women as Mama. Invariably, however, I began by asking respondents about themselves before delving into the questions, generally proceeding from "softball" enquiries to touchier ones. I adjusted my method as the process progressed. Sometimes the respondent would anticipate a question I intended to ask at a later stage of conversation, would bring up interesting insights on a topic apparently unrelated to the one at hand or would bring up a topic I was completely unaware of. Whenever any of these happened, I followed up before returning to the script. At other times, I returned in later stages of the conversations to subjects the respondent was reticent discussing the first time.

The conversations were often battles of wits. If a researcher thinks that he is in the field to tease out information from respondents and to get the respondents to package the information in particular ways (e.g., specificity and time-sensitivity), the latter—when they are talking at all—similarly seek to use the researcher to broadcast the respondents' perspectives of their history, sometimes commanding the researcher what to "write down" and what not to write down. These commands entrap the researcher in the tension between research ethics and analytic rigor. In spite of my urging that respondents try as much as possible to cite concrete examples of the issues they discussed and to indicate when events occurred, they rarely did so, leaving me to devise remedial strategies in my conceptualizations, data collection, and analysis. Many not only resisted my attempts to hedge them in with my prescriptions about how to answer my questions, they also taught me a lot about their history. Sometimes, respondents gave vague answers and expected me to draw the correct inference. Often, multiple inferences could be drawn from one vague statement. When I asked for specificity, some respondents hinted that I was ignorant, which was often—at least as I understood it in the context of the body language—a ploy to embarrass me out of probing further. Respondents frequently asked me, with exaggerated impatience, "Do you now understand?" Often, I would say, "I understand, but … " Sometimes, I would repeat what they had told me and show how it did not answer the questions I asked. On other occasions, I would have to rephrase the question or simply ignore their answer.

Express refusal to answer questions was not uncommon. This was particularly the case asked when I asked respondents to specify whose ancestors were slaves. These respondents often insisted that answering those questions was inimical to present relations. Some respondents preferred to refer me to particular individuals to address sensitive questions. In some cases, the reason for not discussing given issues was that a particular respondent was afraid of misrepresenting history; at least I was given that impression. Women often hesitated to discuss matters concerning their husbands' lineages, always pointing out that *a biaru m abia* (I came [from elsewhere]). Depending on circumstances, this response grew out of apprehensions over the prospect of appearing impertinent to the male elders of her husband's lineage, or it was simply an inoffensive way of withholding information. Several male respondents decided to involve other individuals in their interviews.

Group interviews were not part of my original plan for fieldwork, but circumstances forced them on me. Such circumstances arose when a potential respondent decided to include lineage members—often their seniors—for unstated reasons. In other instances, people intruded in the interviews—sometimes by accident, other times deliberately. Group interviews generally failed to yield much reliable information. In one interview in an Arondizuogu lineage-group, one lineage-level *amadi* (noble) intruded when I was interviewing a man of humbler origins. After listening for a while, the intruder began to forcefully urge my respondent to stop answering my questions. The intruder charged that I was asking questions like a "trained person," asserting that my method was uncannily similar to that of dynamic radio anchor and Arondizuogu native, the late Chima Eze. It should be observed that I knew little about the family origin of this respondent beforehand, but his submission to the intruder's authority came across to me as reluctance on the respondent's part to appear to speak for a lineage group in which he is a marginal member. Even though I was not seeking a spokesperson for the lineage group, he nevertheless feared the intruder might understand it that way.

The intruder's presence ruined the remainder of the interview. Unfortunately, I could not return to this respondent because the incident occurred toward the end of my fieldwork. But this encounter also speaks to present-day class relations. Despite his humble origins in terms of lineage status, the respondent would have been more confident in conversing with me had he been wealthier and/or more educated than the intruder, in which case, he could have felt confident speaking for himself at least (if not for the lineage group), and the intruder would have shown more respect to my respondent. This means that low ancestral pedigree is exacerbated by poverty and ameliorated by affluence. In another lineage-group, one intruder insisted that I should first see their "chief" and other elders. Because this respondent had, in the course of our casual conversation, begun to say things I considered of sufficient value to write down, he was defensive when the chief arrived, explaining to the chief that we were discussing procedural matters and "minor issues," that he had already advised my company and me on how best to approach the elders. By hesitating or refusing to answer particular questions, insisting on having other parties present (although this was sometimes not much of a choice on their part) and sometimes by throwing questions at me, my respondents often redefined the terms of the interviewing process.

Slaving, Resistance, Manumission, and Abolition

I would now like to illustrate some of the foregoing observations with actual encounters I had with respondents during fieldwork. The specific aspects of these conversations highlighted here relate to the slave trade, slave work and treatment, manumission, slave status and ideology, slave resistance, as well as slave and slave master responses to British efforts to end slavery.

SLAVERY AND THE SLAVE TRADE

Respondent 2 was freely answering my question, but when I sought specifics about the slave trade, she started out with the disclaimer: "You know, I was merely told about these things. I was not there, you see." I had a running battle to get Respondent 4 to speak about the slave trade, who at first tied the travels of his ancestors to trade in camwood. When asked to elaborate on his ancestors' trading operations, he merely sketched the route of the camwood trade. When pressed for other things traded, he mentioned cloth and "other things." When asked what the "other things" were, he mentioned gunpowder and smoking pipes. I reiterated I was asking about trade goods in the days before the British conquest of the Aro and not after that period. Yet, Respondent 4 asserted, "This is what I am telling you about." I decided to ask specifically about captives, at which point he admitted that captives were sold, "but [that] the Europeans came and abolished it." I informed the respondent that I was asking about the time before the Europeans arrived and sought to know where his ancestors bought people from and where they sold them. Respondent 4 would still not give me a meaningful answer, only offering, "For instance, they bought from here and sold there. That is how it was." To get Respondent 4 to give me a specific answer, I sought to know if the captives were drawn from "any places more than the others." The respondent mentioned "the area of Benue," a reference to the Middle Belt groups of Igala, Tiv, Idoma, and other groups in today's state of Benue, north of the Igbo. By giving this answer, the respondent clearly meant to sell

95

me "a dummy." Many of the captives the Aro sold were drawn from the Middle Belt, but the vast majority was drawn from Igbo communities. Respondent 4 opened up and became graphic in his narrative only when I referred to specific places where Aron-dizuogu people were drawn from.

Unlike Respondent 4, Respondent 5 answered the question, "What kind of things did the people trade in?" in a straightforward way. But when I pressed for specifics, though he began with: "You know, I was merely told about these things. I was not there, you see," he nevertheless became detailed and specific from this point on.

Oftentimes, one question led unexpectedly to different issues unanticipated beforehand. For example, in conversation with Respondent 5 about Aro reaction to British efforts to end slavery, my respondents told me in some detail about intra-Aro enslavement, which I had thought was negligible, if it existed at all. Yet, when I probed this matter with Respondents 3 (group interview), they offered a view that appeared to contradict this notion.

SLAVE WORK AND TREATMENT

Similarly, I received different responses from different respondents regarding how much an enslaved person worked for his master. Respondents 3 told me that masters did not work and that enslaved people and clients worked for him one in eight days. Since masters did not supposedly work themselves, it seemed to me implausible that an enslaved person worked only one in eight days. Thus, I asked the respondents repeatedly to confirm that they actually meant just one day in eight days. They suggested that because masters usually had many slaves, masters did not depend on just one slave for their labor needs. I still wanted to know if a slave worked only one in eight days right from the first day of their bondage. To my persistence, one of Respondents 3 retorted, "Do you want to be a selfish man?" My respondents were probably projecting their modern sensibilities onto the slavery era, but I sensed they also sought to embarrass me out of finding out about the harshness of slavery by making it appear I was a "wicked man" to conjure a harsher work regimen for slaves than was reasonable. Not ashamed about my questions, I rephrased my question again, this time informing my respondents that I had some information about the subject. This approach failed to work this time; instead, my respondents ridiculed the contrary information I had. I gave up, concluding that Respondents 3 either actually believed their testimony to be true or were determined not to give me the right answer. My impression, however, is that one of the respondents, acutely aware that my research would be read abroad, was determined to paint Aro society in as good a light as possible. As you will see in the attached transcripts, it was he who challenged me when I asked for his ancestry and who sought to discourage me from asking where a particular enslaved person came from.

To the same question—how much did slaves work for their masters?—other respondents gave me more nuanced answers. Respondent 2 said it was two days out of the four-day *izu* (Oye and Awho) from the beginning of the planting season to the beginning of yam harvest, approximately March-September.[6] This meant four in eight days rather than one in eight days claimed by Respondent 3. If the enslaved person worked for the master all-year round, this regime would translate to 50 percent of the slave's work time. But when the work was rendered only during planting to harvesting season, approximately March to September, this would translate to 25 percent of the time. It is safe to say that the master could summon the slave at any other time, and could start the planting season earlier and end harvesting later, depending on weather conditions. For his part, Respondent 5 related what seems to me a more realistic model when he clarified that working two of the four-day *izu* was for enslaved people already well-established rather than newly acquired slaves, who did not work for themselves and depended on their masters for their upkeep. Respondent 1 also stressed there was always a difference between a person's child and their slave, but that in given instances they were treated the same way. Examples of how they were treated in the same way, according to Respondent 1, include the need for the master's offspring to prove his mettle or "the hardworking subject" may overshadow him, merely giving the master's son *ihu, "*homage." A master could also sell into slavery or exchange his own offspring who proved stubborn or indolent.

The diversity of responses to the same question can be attributed to differences in perspective. The respondents were referring to different Aro communities, different masters, and different times, with some elders referring to situations they witnessed, which was during the early part of the twentieth century, when slavery was already ending. The respondents almost never described any changes the slave work regimen may have undergone over time. Also, while the work described was often within an agrarian setting, the Aro did not participate in agriculture in a significant way before the 1880s. The tendency to describe situations in later periods as if they also applied to earlier periods is a common feature of oral traditions known as "telescoping."[7]

MANUMISSION, STATUS, AND IDEOLOGY

As Respondent 5 observed, there were, and are, contending views about at what point a person was deemed to be free. While ex-slaves understood themselves to be free of slave status, the slave owners often referred to the formerly enslaved as slaves even after they had been redeemed. In addition, different respondents (whether descendants of the enslaved or enslavers) could express divergent opinions on the same subject. Respondent 1 said most emphatically that once enslaved, a person and his descendants were always under the person (and his descendants) who owned them. I took him to task. If this was the case in his own lineage-group where he was part of the charter group, does it then mean that he himself was owned by the descendants of the Aro founder of the settlement through whom his ancestor came? My respondent answered that before his ancestor "dropped the bag of slavery" (burden of slavery) he had redeemed himself by giving the founder of the settlement (Izuogu) another enslaved person. He said that this act did not free them from perpetual obligation to the descendants of Izuogu, but merely gave them a niche in the hierarchy. On the other hand, Respondent 3 asserted that a person was no longer a slave after the seventh generation. The contradiction in these responses is more apparent than real. While the apparently pro-slavery Respondent 1's view is that redemption was possible in the lifetime of an enslaved person, apparently anti-slavery Respondent 3 would have a person mandatorily meet the seven-generation threshold.

RESISTANCE AND ABOLITION

When asked whether he could give specific instances of slave flight or rebellion in his lineage-group, a direct descendant of the group founder began by saying that he could not tell what he "did not witness or what [his] father did not tell [him]," but added that some persons owned by his forefathers ran away or returned to their natal homes. When prompted, he mentioned a 1952 incident involving a man who did just this, who had come into his society earlier in the century as a slave. At a later point in the interview, he stated, when asked, that masters took special measures to forestall flight. At a later point still, when I asked if enslaved people seized the opportunity of the British colonial presence to flee, his first reaction was that because slavery had ended with British displacement of the Portuguese and the Aro, it was no longer possible to hold slaves. When I persisted, specifying the fate of "newly acquired people," this respondent answered, "Those of them who were pampered well enough to stay, did. Those who could flee did so." At one juncture, after giving a graphic answer about the role of slavery in the lineage-structure, my respondent seemed to rue the disclosures in a way that suggested remorse or shame for the Aro slave-dealing past: "God forgive me. This sort of thing should not be told to children."

In general, respondents were most forthcoming and most consistent in regard to manumission; they were more willing to discuss the slave trade than slavery, although even at that they often sought to shy away from discussing specifics, and most respondents gave the impression that slave resistance was virtually impossible.

Conclusion

One gets the impression that the Aro rarely incorporated into their families enslaved people and their descendants through the extension of fictive kinship status, as seems to be the case in most other African societies. A combination of factors embedded in Aro history and institutions often rendered fictive kinship both unnecessary and untenable. Many of the most notable figures in the history of Aro trade and expansion, including founders of important diaspora settlements, were of slave descent. Such individuals earned widespread respect; their achievements were emphasized and celebrated, and their slave origins and the non-Aro societies from which they came were both acknowledged. Where so many people descended from once enslaved persons, who themselves almost always achieved significant autonomy in their lifetimes and many became notables, and all acknowledged and often maintained relations with their non-Aro natal societies, it was often unnecessary to claim fictive kinship affiliations. Also, the fact that both the well-born and freeborn performed the *ihu* "homage," people of slave descent did not feel singled out for humiliation. This rite routinized ties among individual males in a hierarchical order defined by social origins, age, and kinship affiliation. The system articulated a hierarchy of hegemonies. Rarely, if at all, would an Aro deny the provenance of his or her ancestors. Also, the Aro public recitations of genealogy (*eye*) created an atmosphere that precluded an individual from misrepresenting his ancestry without being challenged, shamed, sanctioned or ridiculed as a fool lacking the basic principle of self-identity. With changing times and the resulting decline of *ihu* and the near demise of *eye*, things have become a bit muddled, and efforts to suppress the slavery past have sometimes forced people to explain the complex relationships in more socially acceptable ways. Yet, the vast majority of Aro people eschew fictive kinship claims, and those eager to whitewash the relationships instead use terms of immigration to describe slavery. On the basis of these factors, Aro claims of blood relationships are often reliable.

Despite Aro respondents' unwillingness to discuss the specifics of slavery and the slave trade, Aro oral traditions show the people to be acutely aware of their slaving past. Under normal circumstances, many respondents would have conversed with me without reservations about the slavery past. We were, however, on a different platform when I showed up as a "researcher," armed with a tape recorder and a notebook.

Excerpts from Transcripts

These are excerpts from interviews with five respondents of slave ancestry. The first four are from Arondizuogu, a major Aro trading center founded in the 1730s, in central Igboland. Respondent 2 is a woman. The fifth respondent is from Arochukwu, the original Aro community. All of the respondents had ancestors who became free at some time in the past. This means that their lineages are still subordinate to the lineage of the person who once owned their ancestor, to whom the most senior person of the junior lineage presented ihu. *All, however, are now* amadi [freeborn or noble].

Slavery and the Slave Trade

RESPONDENT 3

Q: *Tell me, did kidnapping take place here before the British came?*

A: What are you talking about? Robbery had been in existence from the beginning of time. Where do you think that the "black Negroes" originated?[8] They were sold on a barter basis.

Q: *Did the kidnappers have special skills or did they just exert physical strength?*

A: Listen. Assume that you and me are about to embark on a mission. At the market, one person may innocuously point at the other and take money for him. Right there, the person would be chained. He could be killed if he resisted.

Q: *From where did they get most of their slaves?*

A: From Anambra.[9] A person may have seven children and in

THE BITTER LEGACY

order to feed them, he might sell one. My father's brother was sold, that is, Duke's maternal grandfather, Kanunta. He was sold. He said, "So this is the way that I have been treated—like a chicken?" It was due to poverty. The ultimate responsibility was with the head of the family. If I needed to solve a problem, I would sell one of my children.

Q: *They bought people from Nkanu.*[10] *To whom did they sell?*

A: To get this issue right, you need to determine the trade in which the Aro were engaged. They retained the more handy and obedient ones. It was the ones that were retained that have now prospered. They grew to acquire persons on their own accord.

Q: *What I am asking is: If a person from this place was about to sell his own child to solve a problem or that child cut the upper teeth first, where would he sell the child?*

A: The Aro did not maintain that kind of taboo [i.e., a taboo on raising children who had cut their upper teeth first]. The Aro were stricter about twins. It was a serious taboo.[11] The Aro sold their slaves to the Portuguese. The slave trade stopped in 1807.

Q: *But people continued to sell slaves after abolition in 1807. Where did they sell their slaves, especially when they stopped selling to white people?*

A: When the British banned it, the Portuguese continued to buy. Will cheating or roguery ever be eradicated from this world? People continued to sell in order to accumulate money.

[Another man intervenes] There are some people to whom our people sold and they in turn sold to the Portuguese. These were the people of Opobo.[12] Our people got tobacco in return. [Respondent continues] Jaja of Opobo, where did he come from? Was it not Nkwere, and they now call him Jaja. He owned thousands of slaves called *nde-be-Jaja* [people of Jaja].

RESPONDENT 4

Q: *Could you please tell us more about this trade?*

A: They would buy wares from Calabar for instance and sell in Bende.[13] They bought camwood in Bende, exchanging it with what they brought from Calabar. The cycle started all over again.

Q: *What specific things did they buy and what specific things did they sell?*

A: They traded things like *akwa miri* [a kind of cloth] and many other things.

Q: *What main things did they trade in?*

A: They traded in gunpowder and smoking pipe, a lot.

Q: *What we are asking about is trade goods in the days before the British conquest of the Aro and not after that period.*[14]

A: This is what I am telling you about.

Q: *Did they not trade in human beings?*

A: They did, but the Europeans came and abolished it.

Q: *During the period before the Europeans' arrival, where did they buy people from and where did they sell them?*

A: For instance, they bought from here and sold there. That is how it was.

Q: *Did they buy from any places more than the others?*

A: Yes. They went to the area of Benue [state].

Q: *What about the area now known as Anambra state? It appears that most Ndizuogu people came from that area.*

A: It is true, in those places, up-country.

RESPONDENT 5

Q: *You said that Ndizuogu was a "center of trade." What kind of things did the people trade in?*

A: It was mainly slaves. They also sold *ukara* cloth and other items.[15]

Q: *From where did they usually buy slaves then?*

A: You know, I was merely told about these things. I was not there, you see. Some slave gangs were procured from trading trips. Others were captured in wars and sold to the Aro. Many slaves originated in disputes.

Q: *Apart from warfare, how else were slaves procured or sold away?*

A: There was the phenomenon of people being seized. For instance, Iheme was seized, though he came from a reasonably well-to-do family.[16] Others were simply seized and sold to get food for the rest of the family. In other instances, a group of persons conspired to seize a person from a family in order to harm that family. They seized the person and got rid of him. This was what happened to Iheme.

RESPONDENT 3

Q: *Could an immigrant arrive here without being under anyone?*
A: In whose place would you be? There would not be any space for you.

Slave Work and Treatment

RESPONDENT 1

Q: *Mazi, did the slave and his master's children do the same kind of work?*
A: Why not? Both slaves and master's children would be taken to a farm to work. It was a survival of the fittest situation. If you were lazy because your father was the ruler, the hardworking "subject" might become richer, a situation that might necessitate the saying *aro iche, mkpona iche*[17] ("Nobody could dispossess the subject"). [The slaves's] responsibility to you was to pay you homage when it was time to do so.
Q: *Was the slave worked harder than the* amadi*?*
A: It happened before, but not anymore. The slave was given a hard job and the *amadi* a soft one.
Q: *Is this a true illustration of the saying that ohu avwu nwa* [a slave is not offspring]*?*
A: In a way, but the main meaning of *ohu avwu nwa* is that the slave would never displace an *amadi*.
Q: *Because the slave could not be trusted?*
A: You could exchange him for somebody else if he became stubborn.... Among the Aro, a stubborn child could be exchanged

for somebody else. But, the person so secured was almost never your own child.

RESPONDENT 2

Q: *Was there any other thing that you did for Okoro's household?*[18]

A: During [the annual festival of] Ikeji, men brought *ihu*, eight yams or a choice piece of meat, to those superior to them.[19] But in extended families, people received *ihu* from their own junior kin.

Q: *Must it be accompanied by eight yams, not just meat?*

A: Yes. It was not only meat.

Q: *Did the* ihu *giver also work for the* ihu *receiver?*

A: Yes, they worked for the receiver as well, but that does not happen anymore. They worked for two days.

Q: *Up until when did they work?*

A: They worked until nde-Akaeme's Ogidi [own individual annual] festival, when everyone went back to his house.[20]

Q: *Did the person begin all over the following annual cycle. Was there not a period when the person stopped working?*

A: That is what is being said, after sometime, no one would work anymore.

Q: *Before the British came, did* the *people* [i.e., slave descendent households that were junior kin] *who did such work continue to do so until they died or did they stop after sometime and become independent?*

A: Yes, they stopped at a time and became independent

Q: *Would a slave stop working for his master after a specific term of service say, after six or seven years, and start working for himself?*

A: Yes.

Q: *How would it be known that a person had qualified for this liberty?*

A: If he was a man, he would have set up his own house and had children. He would be focusing on his own work.

RESPONDENT 3

Q: *My next question is: What did a person's slave do for him, apart from simply giving* ihu*?*

A: A person's slaves did the work. The masters were free from work. It was the persons of his household who did this work. They worked for the master one day in eight. This means that, if a person had five slaves, the five of them came together once in eight days to work for him.

Q: *Just one day in eight?*

A: Yes.

Q: *You mean that that was all the slave owner got?*

A: Is it not much? Was it only one person who did the work?

Q: *Do you mean that if I go all the* way *to Ogidi, for instance, to acquire a person, he would come here and work for me only one day out of eight days—right from the first day?*

A: Do want to be a selfish man? How could the person find the time to do his own work?

[Another man interjects] Are you saying that one day in eight is not enough?

Q: *Why I am asking is that some persons tell me that the slave worked for the master two days in the four-day* uzu *market cycle.*

A: It was a woman whom a man fed all the time who did that sort of work and not a man who must fend for himself.

Q: *Were there slave women?*

A: Do you mean could a woman own slaves?

Q: *Whether a woman could be a slave and whether* a woman *could own slaves.*

A: A woman was not a slave, unless you are talking about a woman in marriage to a man. A woman could have slaves. Rich women married and some married many. The offspring of the woman's slave had a situation inferior to that of the children of the paterfamilias.[21] Their inheritance was limited to their mother's owner's property.

Q: *Do you mean that if a woman acquired a female slave, such a slave is referred to as her wife?*

A: No. She should not be called her wife. She was a slave and her children would be under the direction of her owner's children. Mr. Nwokeji, you have good questions, but this society has changed much. Many things have also changed for public relations and political reasons.

RESPONDENT 5

Q: *How often did a slave work for his master?*
A: I think it was two days out of the four-day *izu*. This practice was already established in the place. He worked for himself on the remaining two days. A newly acquired slave that was not a trade slave, worked full time for his master. He did not work for himself. In this case, his master still fed him.

Q: *Were master-slave relations usually a harsh experience for the slave?*
A: It depended on the behavior of the slave. Some slaves had their masters' confidence more than real sons of the masters. A master could go out to acquire an intelligent and enterprising slave if he found these qualities to be lacking in his own sons. He often believed in this slave more than in his sons. In this kind of case, it was difficult to distinguish the slave from the free-born. This did not happen in all instances. One person was bought in the olden days, but the person who bought him soon sold him to another person. This second buyer found that the slave was a highly skilled horn player. This second buyer therefore gave the slave a good position within his household. Then the first buyer died. On the second buyer's way to the funeral, the expert horn player commented through his instrument that the deceased [his first master] would not have sold him had he, the deceased, known that he, the slave, was an expert horn player.

Q: *What kind of work did a slave do for his master?*
A: It depended on the occupation of his master. A slave could be a skilled trader. In such a case, his master would give him capital or part of his wares to trade independently.

Manumission, Status, and Ideology

RESPONDENT 1

Q: *At what stage did a slave become* amadi*?*

A: I repeat, *ohu avwu nwa* [i.e., the slave is different from the offspring]. *Aro iche, mkpona iche:* this saying denotes that a true Aro person was different from a non-Aro, irrespective of wealth or other criteria. When the Aro are discussing and they say, *e me gbaa* [in the final analysis], they have concluded the issue. I have given you three sayings. I will explain each if you want.

RESPONDENT 5

Q: *At what stage did a slave become free?*

A: This is a controversial issue. To many, a person was free once he had redeemed himself with a slave. To others, come what may, a slave is always a slave. This second position is wrong. Iheme, for instance, gave a slave to Izuogu to redeem himself.

Q: *Is there any other way for a slave to become free, apart from giving his master a slave?*

A: I do not know of any other way.

RESPONDENT 3

Q: *At what time did a slave become free?*

A: Thank you. In our Aro-Uno, you would not hear anyone use the term *ohu* [slave]. What you would hear is *nwanna* [paternal blood relative]. There, a person married his blood relation, but here it is the seventh generation. I checked it yesterday. After the seventh generation, a person would no longer be *ohu*. He would become *amadi*.

Q: *But the person continued to give* ihu*?*

A: Yes, but it has become merely "honorary."

Resistance and Abolition

RESPONDENT 1

Q: *Did some slaves rebel or get violent out of a distaste for their condition?*

A: There was nothing like that then. What obtained was flight if a slave did not like his condition. If he made trouble in the morning, he would be missing by the evening.

Q: *Are there instances of flight or rebellion in this place?*

A: I cannot tell. I am over sixty-five. I cannot tell what I did not witness or what my father did not tell me. Some persons owned by our forefathers ran away, ran back home.

Q: *Can you not give examples?*

A: I do not really know, but there was a man whom my father's mother trained and for whom she found a wife. We took him as a relative, but in about 1952, he said that he had found his home town. He left and took his wife and children with him.

Q: *Did masters take any special precautionary measures with regard to a newly acquired slave to ensure that he did not flee or rebel?*

A: Yes, something was done. A master would give a new person a "test" if he did not plan to sell him. This test entailed sending the new slave on errands in the company of longer-serving slaves. When it was confirmed that he was not planning to run and would be humble, the master would invite his kinsmen and inform them of his intention to retain this slave whom he had found to be good-natured and humble. Then the slave was made to swear an oath against sabotaging his master, or stealing the wares entrusted in the slave's care, or consort with the master's wives, and so forth. A kola nut was then broken and the slave was given a piece to eat. The eating of this kola nut concluded the covenant.

Q: *Did some people in this society oppose slavery?*

A: It did not happen in our place. The only time ending slavery became an issue was when the white people came.

RESPONDENT 5

Q: *Did slaves like their condition?*

A: It depended on the particular situation. I knew one Aron-dizuogu man who was proud of his slave status. He openly avowed this pride of being an Aro slave, as opposed to being a non-Aro slave. There was also this case of an Anambra Aro man who came to Arochukwu to fulfil Ekpe initiation rites for members of his family, both sons and his head slave. His head slave swaggered and danced happily singing *onye amaghi na o ga eru ya, o ruvwe ye!* [he who expected nothing belongs]. So, he was happy to have joined the Ekpe and to be head slave. On the other hand, a slave may lack any freedom and would not gain the favor of his master to take him into the Ekpe society or like favors. Generally, however, a slave who had been set up in a separate homestead, with the requisite facilities, was happy.

Q: *Since individuals, both masters and slaves, differed in character, were there not instances when a slave would rebel or become violent, disregarding whatever favors or confidence that his master may have given him?*

A: Such cases occurred, but the slave had to try to redeem himself, usually by buying another slave for his master.

Q: *Could he simply run away?*

A: Unless the person ran away to an unknown place, the person to whom he ran would not likely welcome him.

Q: *Could a kidnapped person not run back home since his/her kin would be looking for him/her?*

A: The owner would look for him/her certainly. If his/her people wanted her back, they had to pay back the owner, may be with another slave.

Reactions to British Efforts to End Slaveholding

RESPONDENT 1

Q: *How did people, slave and master, react to the British attempt to end slavery and pawnship?*[22]

A: You see by the time the British arrived here, they had already expelled the Portuguese and American slavers on the coast and conquered the Aro. How then could our people continue to buy slaves? To whom would they sell? Pawnship continued, but in secret. A debtor would give a child to his creditor and ask the creditor to marry her if he liked her at maturity. Otherwise, the debtor would repay the creditor when the girl was mature enough to marry. The creditor would do so with the dowry paid on the girl.

Q: *If a creditor was given the liberty to marry off the girl when she was mature, would this understanding give him a conjugal access to the girl?*

A: A self-respecting *amadi* would not stoop so low. He would exercise much more self-control than that.

Q: *How did slaves respond to the British attempt to end slavery? Did they flee?*

A: Why should they when they had lived with their master for a long time. Probably, the person's situation was beyond the first generation. To where would he run?

Q: *What about newly acquired persons?*

A: Those of them who were pampered well enough to stay, did. Those who could flee did so.

Q: *So, the masters began to pamper their slaves when the British began to end slavery?*

A: Yes, of course. That was the way of having him to remain your servant. After all, you could not do the work that he was doing for you.

RESPONDENT 3

Q: *When the British arrived here and abolished slavery and pawnship, how did people receive this law?*

A: Did you ever hear that the British invaded Ndizuogu?

Q: *How did the people here, the slave masters, receive the British law ending slavery?*

A: The Aro expedition took place in 1902. Thereafter, the British heard that there was another Aro group. They then came down here, saying that the Aro would be doing the same kinds of things that they did at Aro-Uno [homeland Aro].

Q: *Did the British prosecute or imprison anyone here for enslavement?*

A: One man was imprisoned. It was politically motivated of course. It was a minor incident. I think that he had a woman and the British hung on to that in order to do him in. No other person was imprisoned.

Q: *How did slaves receive the British law ending slavery?*

A: There is no one who left, except one man called Kanu Nwangovwi. He was bald and had a dark complexion. He and some others embezzled Felix Igbo's money. He was the only one that I witnessed to have left. Kanu Igbo owned him and he was called Kanunta. He left recently, after the Second World War. He married Wilfred and Emmanuel's sister. She still lives here. No one here that we know left, but we cannot account for Iheukwu Okoli whether he is dead or alive.

Q: *Did some of the people sold away return after abolition?*

A: You should realize that our people did not sell away our people. Emphasis was on addition. Why then would you sell? The people that you see here came from Anambra. They did not generally go back because there was plenty of food here.

Q: *During the time that pawnship prevailed, did a pawn become free after working for a term?*

A: No, not at all. The person remained a pawn until the money was paid back. This practice was ended in a courtroom right in Ndizuogu. One Isuochi man borrowed seven shillings from Mgbowko Adanwa and became a pawn.[23] When he reneged on his work, the creditor sued him. She [the creditor] calculated the money equivalent of the labor not supplied and asked for restitution. The court asked the creditor to calculate the days and the equivalent sum for the days that the debtor worked. This was done, based on six pence per day. Rather than grant the creditor her plea, the court asked the creditor to pay the debtor for all the labor that he had performed.

Q: *When did this happen?*

A: It was during the first customary court that nde-Izugou had—1936 or 1937.

Q: *After the end of slavery, how did slave users cope?*

A: Abakaliki and Nkanu people came to work here.[24]

RESPONDENT 5

Q: *How did both slaves and the masters respond to the British attempt to end slavery?*

A: Slaveholders were not happy. They could not do anything if their slave decided to go. A slave of my father decided to go back to his original home in Isimkpu [an Arochukwu lineage-group]. Nobody prevented him.

Q: *You mean that an Isimkpu person was enslaved in this Amankwu?*[25]

A: Yes. At the time when the British had arrived and abolished slavery, it became possible for rivals to welcome and do favors for one another's slaves to reduce their competitors' influence while increasing their own. This former slave of my father became a court messenger. I sometimes spent some of my holidays with him when I was in government school.

Q: *Could an Aro diaspora person be enslaved in Arochukwu and could an Arochukwu person be enslaved in the diaspora?*

A: Yes.

Q: *How did the slave masters cope with labor demands?*

A: They looked for unpaid voluntary labor and they hired laborers as well. Many Aro people established plantations. People from other towns came to sell their labor, including tree climbing. Up to now, Aro people do not climb trees. The people from these other places cut their palm fruits.

Notes

1. Ekpe was a secret society that transcended ethnic boundaries in the Bight of Biafra and was important in regulating the slave trade and resolving any conflicts that arose. Only the most privileged persons were members of Ekpe.
2. For a detailed version of the foregoing summary, see G. Ugo Nwokeji, *The Slave Trade and Culture in the Bight of Biafra: An African Society in the Atlantic World* (New York: Cambridge University Press, 2010).
3. See Elizabeth Isichei, ed., *Igbo Worlds: An Anthology of Oral Histories and Historical Descriptions* (Philadelphia: Institute for the Study of Human Issues, 1978); David Northrup, *A Collection of Interviews Conducted in Southeastern Nigeria in 1972-1973* (unpublished, n.d.) and numerous undergraduate history theses completed in Nigerian universities.
4. *Ihu* was the Aro homage system, in which every adult Aro male gave to his senior male particular parts of a beast (often a goat, but it could also be a sheep or cow) they killed during the annual festivals, funerals, and other rites of passage. The animal could not be a bird or any type of reptile. The senior male could be a man's father, eldest brother (if his father had died), and the father or eldest brother gave the Ihu from the beast he killed to the next male higher up in seniority. The next person higher up in seniority could be an uncle, a master, or the oldest heir to a deceased master. If the person (or his ancestor) giving Ihu was an immigrant, he gave the Ihu to the patron or the living heir of the patron that brought him into Aro society. Ihu consisted of seven specific meat parts, including the rib cage, spleen, and a piece of the liver. The meat parts may be (and this was often the case) accompanied by kola nuts, yams, and drinks. Given the frequency of the occasions in which Ihu had to be performed, it served to maintain individual and group hierarchies on a regular basis.
5. *Mazi* is an honorific for male Aro elders or seniors, very much like Spanish *señor*. It is said to have been reserved only for the Aro consul or designated leader in a "foreign" station during the earliest days of Aro expansion. The original meaning of this title has been watered down to the extent that it has now been adopted in the Igbo language

as a translation of the English Mr. However, the Aro continue to attach real importance to the title and generally refrain from using it to refer to non-Aro. I addressed all my male Aro respondents as Mazi.

6. Izu is a four-day market cycle. It is sometimes referred to as a market week. Each day in the cycle a different town holds its market.

7. David Henige, "Oral Tradition and Chronology," *Journal of African History* 12 (1971): 373-76.

8. This is a reference to people of African descent in the Americas, particularly in the United States.

9. In the days of slavery, Anamabra referred to a tributary of the Niger and a town located at the Anambra-Niger estuary. The name of the river was later adopted for one of the Igbo states created in 1975. The respondent is referring to the present Anambra state. This state is home to the historic Nri. Scholars of the slave trade have referred to much of this area as the "Nri-Awka" region, to describe the area from which the Aro preferred to draw immigrants (free and slave) into their society. This was a densely populated region from which the majority of the Igbo captives sent to the Americas were taken.

10. Nkanu is the generic Aro reference for people from the towns of the Anambra area. It is not to be confused with the real town of Nkanu in northern Igboland.

11. The twin taboo in precolonial Igboland was so strong that twins were thrown into the "bad bush" at birth. Even though the Aro did not practice some other Igbo taboos, such as rejecting children who cut their upper teeth first or the *osu* outcastes whom other Igbo did not interact with at any level, the Aro took the twin taboo extremely seriously. There is evidence that the Aro in the diaspora had begun to abandon this practice by the early nineteenth century, although the taboo continues to be strong in Arochukwu until this day. Twins are not allowed near sacred places. During my fieldwork, I was allowed to enter the Arochukwu mansion of a major slave trader which had become a national monument in 1972, only after the keeper verified that I was not a twin.

12. Opobo was formed in 1869, by a breakaway Bonny ex-slave, Jaja, who had grown rich and powerful trading in palm oil. It became the most important port in the Bight of Biafra during the era of palm oil exports that succeeded overseas slave exports.

13. All mentions of Calabar refer to Old Calabar, which is the present-day city of Calabar in southeastern Nigeria. Bende was a major market town.

14. The British conquered Arochukwu during a 1901-2 military campaign.

15. *Ukara* cloth is a kind of patterned cloth produced by the Abaliki of northwest Igboland and worn in members of the Ekpe secret society. It was also worn in masquerades: http://www.hamillgallery.com/IGBO/IgboTextiles/UkaraCloth/UkaraCloth.html.
16. Iheme was the powerful lieutenant of Izuogu, the founder of the major Aro diaspora settlement of Arondizuogu in the 1730s. His lineage-group within Arondizuogu today is probably larger than all other Arondizuogu lineage-groups combined. His case, as those of Jaja and many others, shows how people of slave origins could rise in status in the societies of the Bight of Biafra.
17. This phrase can be paraphrased to mean that a full-fledged Aro is different from a recent immigrant or recently emancipated former slave and their offspring.
18. *Isi ite* refers to the practice of all the families in an extended family cooking and eating together at the altar of their common ancestor during festivals. This informant is a woman, who is referring to obligations her husband fulfilled to Okoro, who owned her husband's father. She is referring to a time when she was newly married into that family in the late 1920s.
19. Ikeji is the preeminent annual festival of the Aro. Within Aro society, every adult male gave homage called *ohu* to his immediate superior. This involved either yams or choice pieces of meat from an animal he had slaughtered.
20. Ogidi is the annual festival of one Arondizuogu lineage-group, but Ikeji was for all Aro.
21. This informant is speaking of a relationship sometimes referred to as "woman-woman marriage," but it was really a woman owning a female slave. In Aro and Igbo society, there was no social space for a female slave, except in the case of a female slave owned by a woman. I believe that this relationship assumed the idiom of marriage in the early colonial period when the British tried to end slavery. That is why this informant conflated slave with wife. Women rarely owned many female slaves.
22. Pawnship is the use of a human being to secure a loan. The person used as security, the pawn, worked for the creditor until the loan was paid off or for such a length of time that both the borrower and the creditor agreed would be sufficient to offset the loan. See Felix Ekechi, "Pawnship in Igbo Society," in *Pawnship, Slavery and Colonialism in Africa*, eds. Paul Lovejoy and Toyin Falola (Trenton, NJ: Africa World Press, 2003), 165-86.
23. Isuochi is a town near Arondizuogu.

24. Abakaliki is a town in northeastern Igboland. Nkanu is an area in northern Igboland. The city of Enugu is located on land claimed by the Nkanu.

25. Amankwu and Isimkpu are two of the nineteen quarters of Arochukwu town. Each diaspora settlement was regarded as an extension of the Arochukwu quarter where its founder came from, and the people of that settlement were automatically deemed to be full and equal members of that Arochukwu quarter. An individual's status within Arochukwu was unaffected by whether the person was primarily domiciled in Arochukwu or in the diaspora.

6. Tabula and Pa Jacob, Two Twentieth-Century Slave Narratives from Cameroon

ZACHARIE SAHA

Editorial note: When Dr. Saha submitted these narratives to the editors of this volume, we were quite startled by Tabula's story. We were surprised at his being sold or tricked into slavery as late as the First World War, and that he remained in servitude until 1968. The only important book on Fernando Po did not go beyond 1930 and did not address our questions.[1] Fortunately, at a conference in Berlin, we met a Spanish graduate student, Enrique Martino, who was doing research on forced labor in Spanish Africa. According to Martino, the agents of planters were actively recruiting labor in southern Cameroon in the 1920s, and they were being moved to Fernando Po from 1925. Until the 1940s, they were known for deception and trickery tantamount to kidnapping. The recruiters were paid commissions for every worker delivered with no questions about how they were delivered. In the 1930s, when there were about four thousand Cameroonians in Spanish Guinea, France complained at the League of Nations about illegal recruitment. Both the French and the British saw the Spanish labor regime as a "neo-slavery." With labor in short supply, the Spanish authorities rarely responded to requests for repatriation. For plantation workers, little changed. Those working on plantations far from the city of Santa Isabel were in complete isolation. They could only return home with signed permission of the planters and, in fact, were often forbidden to leave the plantation. The population of Fernando Po

*was 80 percent to 90 percent male. Though there were some trav-
eling prostitutes, Tabula's isolation on an overwhelmingly male island explains why he never had a relationship with a woman.
Another problem for Tabula was probably that there were few
Bamileke in the interior, which meant that there were no informal
chains of communication with home areas. The Spanish planters
left in 1969, though some plantations operated for a few years
longer.*

"It is only today that I know that my hands belong to me. Before,
they were not mine. Whites made use of them. Now that they belong to me, I no longer have the strength to use them."[2] These were
the words of Tabula when, on July 25 1981, he was brought back
to his native village of Lensap in the Grassfields, an area of southern Cameroon, which was an important source of slaves for the Atlantic slave trade, and after the decline of slave exports, for the
plantation economy of areas near the coast. This second type of
slave trade was an internal trade, which remained active well into
the twentieth century. This involved child trafficking, which is described in the story of Pa Jacob—the other slave whose recollections I present in this chapter. On his return, Tabula was received
in triumph by His Majesty Gilbert Tela Nembot of Baleng, the local
chief. As an adolescent, he had been seized from his family and
severely exploited as a plantation laborer, actually a slave, until
the declining years of his life. It is quite probable that the men who
subjugated and exploited both Tabula and Pa Jacob would deny
that either was enslaved, and present them either as contract laborers or as migrants. But the testimonies that both Tabula and Pa
Jacob gave about their lives meet any definition of slavery.

Tabula

Tabula was born in the last decade of the nineteenth century. He
did not remember his mother, who died when he was very young.
His older brother also died when he was still crawling. His mis-
fortunes began when his father sent him with a gift of plantain for

the chief of Lensap. From the chief's palace, he was deceived into going to Dschang. We can date this because Dschang was founded as a German post in 1906 or 1907. Though established on the coast from 1885, the Germans reached the Grassfields of central Cameroon only in 1903.[3] Along with other unfortunates, Tabula was sent to Dschang by the chief in a group led by recruiters of servile labor. They were not whites. According to Tabula's account, he first saw white men in Dschang. This was probably shortly after 1907.[4] After four nights in Dschang, they traveled by night to Victoria, near the base of Mount Cameroon, an area where plantation agriculture was being developed. There he worked for some time on a European coconut plantation, apparently as a water-carrier, after which he was told he was being recruited as a soldier.[5] But as he explains in his narrative, he soon understood that he had been deceived again. His subsequent life was to know various changes, all of them unhappy. In vain, he tried to escape. An uncle, who was enslaved with him, escaped from the plantation after decapitating a white foreman. Tabula was then sold to Spanish planters from the island of Fernando Po, an island situated just off the Cameroonian coast. He worked on cocoa plantations there and changed masters several times.[6]

In 1968, Equatorial Guinea became independent under the leadership of Francisco Macias Nguema. Though Macias Nguema became a brutal dictator, he started by freeing the slaves, including many Cameroonians. Tabula was one of these. He saw one of his deepest desires realized in becoming a free man. He still remained unhappy, however, because he wanted to return to Lensap, the village of his ancestors. In addition, he lived poorly in a shack put together from materials others threw away and had a very precarious existence. He had little to eat and had neither family life nor any emotional relationship. Returning to his native village remained his obsession.

Like many other recently freed persons, Tabula headed to the capital of Malabo. Guinean independence was the beginning of a new life, that of a slave without chains. After the departure of the Spanish, he performed the most menial tasks, working for a while as a night watchman at a Malabo nightclub. Then he became a street sweeper. In this job, he worked from 6:00 a.m. to 1:00 p.m., but it provided neither enough to eat nor means to take care of his health. The only moments of happiness were when he gathered with old friends and former slaves. They used to meet at the Tahiti Bar, which was owned by Joseph Keugne, who was also from West Cameroon. In 1979, Francisco Macias Nguema was overthrown by his nephew, Theodoro Obiang Nguema Mbasogo. The new president appealed to foreign investors to help rebuild a country ravaged by corruption and brutality. Among those who came was a young Cameroonian businessperson, Jean Tawembé. By chance, Tawembé was at the Tahiti Bar, where he was surprised to hear an old man order a beer in Bamileke. Curious to see one of his countrymen in a strange country, he sought out Tabula and his companions and was amazed to listen to their miserable stories of enslavement.

According to witnesses, Tabula had always insisted to his companions that he would return some day to his native village of Lensap. He frequently spoke of the younger brother who was only four years old when he was enslaved. A number of his friends gave him locks of hair or stones, which he was to bring with him when he returned home.[7] When he was brought back to Baleng in Cameroon, he was welcomed by Chief Tela Nembot Gilbert, who gave him the title of Fo Me'npouh, which means "chief of the slaves." His benefactor, Jean Tawembé, received the title of Ndé, which means "noble." He also reconnected with the younger brother, who had been an infant when he was enslaved. The act of enobling Tabula and his benefactor, Jean Tawembé, had profound significance in Bamileke society. It was a rite of reconciliation and reparation, which recognized that a profound wrong had been done to Tabula. Enslavement and sale were legal in the societies of the Grassfields, but only for blood crimes, adultery, sorcery, or treason.[8] Tabula was guilty of none of these crimes. The chief thus sought forgiveness from the victim and his ancestral spirits. This was both a political and religious act, which tried to protect peace among the living, with ancestors, and with God. The chief who enobled Tabula was a descendant of the chief who had sent him into slavery. He was not criminally responsible, but he was morally responsible and responsible to the ancestors for what had happened to Tabula. In Bamileke belief, he and the community could be cursed by the wrong committed by their forefather, in this case, by the act of enslavement and sale. Similar rites of reconciliation, in which the descendants of slavers ask forgiveness from the descendents of slaves, have been common in the Cameroon Grassfields.

In itself, the ritual of ennoblement did not remove the curse. Tabula was brought back home on July 25, 1981, but he died less than a year later, on May 22, 1982. It was deemed necessary to organize funerals for Tabula and his companions who had been enslaved. The Tabula Foundation and the Association Esclavage-Mémoire et Abolition have for several years been organizing such events.[9] The funeral organized for Tabula was not only to pay homage to the deceased, but through religious rites to make him an ancestral spirit capable of mediating between God and men. The deceased becomes through these rites divine and immortal.

Tabula's Story. Collected by Jean Tawembé and Rearranged by Zacharie Saha[10]

PART ONE. ENSLAVEMENT AND PLANTATION LABOR

At the beginning, Tabula's account is rather difficult to understand as his memory collapses together different episodes of his early life, and the narrative thread is far from being coherent. It should be borne in mind he recollected these events at a very old age. A long time had elapsed since he had left his home-village. The first part refers to his transfer from Cameroon to the Island of Fernando Po; then his thoughts shift back to events that took place in the period he spent in the plantation near Victoria. Then, he talks about the Fernando Po plantation again. There is violence in these reminiscences, and a clear reference to the kind of culture plantation laborers developed far from home. Tabula, for instance, mentions the use of dreams as a means of keeping in touch with his home

123

village;, he describes different forms of magic used by him and his fellow mates and their attachment to Bamileke religious practices in spite of their conversion to Christianity.

One Sunday morning, at Bimbia [southern Cameroon], a ship approached the shore and docked. They lined us up and presented us to the commandant, who was there to recruit soldiers.[11] The selection commenced soon afterward. It was necessary to march like a real soldier. Several persons were called without anyone noticing me. I prayed then and instead of steps, which seemed difficult for me, I began to jump.[12] The commandant appreciated my effort. We then learned that there was not enough military equipment and that only a part could be distributed. To this end, a new selection had to be made under the cocoa trees. My hopes were broken and I soon realized that we had been sold again. Kom, a sturdy Bayangam man, who had stolen a helmet at the Victoria plantations, also saw his dreams of becoming a soldier shattered.[13] To get revenge, he raped the niece of Monsieur Perico, who had come from Spain. He was then beaten to death and buried in the fields. His younger brother, Mogo Martin, inherited the helmet.

Three years went by. A new group of recruits joined us…. In this group, three gangster friends with impressive broad shoulders transformed the camp into a ring, refusing to distribute property such as money and jewels acquired through theft. In fact, two of the three, Nembouet and Kamlah, were formerly burglars in the pay of a local chief. They had been recruited to steal things from within neighboring chiefships. In spite of several brilliant thefts, the two accomplices received no reward from their employer. They then showed their discontent by robbing from him. Stopped when fleeing by the chief's guards, they were not punished because their victim feared to be denounced. To the great surprise of the people, an order was given to a local notable to take them to Dschang, where they were enlisted in the army…

Once they arrived on our plantations at Bata the two thieves found themselves again involved in burglary; they stole *biklé*, a kind of iron money owned by a slave from South Cameroon, who had buried it under a coconut tree. While waiting for a solution to the division of property at issue, I was asked to take care of it. To find the *bikié*..., Kamlah and his friends supposedly used the *tchagang*, a fetish in a ram's horn that could find objects of value even when they were hidden. The following night, when many other slaves were sold for an unknown destination under the pretext that they had been recruited by a commandant, I became the heir of a small fortune that had been entrusted to me. One night in 1925, we were embarked on a ship because the commandant announced that our military equipment was on the island of Annobon. Once there, we were told that the airplane that was bringing the material that would make us soldiers had been destroyed by fire. We were once more in the fields.

I often informed my fellow slaves of deaths that struck my family at Lengsap in Baleng. My amulets told me about them through dreams. The first death on the island was of Papa Kamwa; he was buried in the slave cemetery and a funeral was held according to the rituals of our Bamileke people. Some slaves had rejected Christianity, which did not agree with our funeral rites; this is why they mocked me when I became a Christian. One day, a very old slave, feeling that he was near death, rubbed a stone on his head and gave it to me because I never stopped speaking of my hope to see sooner or later the land of my ancestors. He left me instructions that after his death, I was to rub his body with the stone, and after my return, I was to put the stone in the wild. It would symbolize his return. Another made me promise that I would cut his hair and keep it in my baggage.

The slaves took advantage of the departure of the whites at Independence to pillage homes and stores. I seized a pair of high leather boots from my last master, Senor Mariano. I negotiated with the accomplices for a second pair of boots. Others took sacks of cacao which were quickly reclaimed by the president's soldiers. All the churches were transformed into stores. We were then abandoned to ourselves: no more care, no more food, no more cloths. Famine decimated many of us for a long, long time.

PART TWO. AFTER EMANCIPATION

*The departure of the colonizers from Equatorial Guinea left Tabula
and his mates alone. They headed toward the capital city, where
they hoped to find jobs. Poverty and lack of social networks made
their lives extremely miserable. Thanks to the help of a woman,
who hosted, fed him, and even provided him with the only sexual
experience of his life, Tabula carved out a niche to survive until
the opportunity to return to Cameroon he had long yearned for
manifested itself suddenly.*

This hut is mine since the departure of Mama Abena in February
1974. We met in 1970.[14] I was a night watchman at the nightclub
Anana. She came to see me one Sunday and suggested that we go
to Mass the following week, and after that to her house, where she
would feed me. I was very happy with her offer. After arriving at
her hut on that day, the good lady had me take a bath and then gave
me a good meal. I ate well for the first time since the departure of
the whites. She then asked me to sleep with her. I could not because
I am a deep sleeper and risked being late for my work. She was
unhappy and suggested that I seek work as a street sweeper so I
could stay with her.

Mama Abena suggested that I get a Cameroonian consular card;
she showed me hers, and explained how it was procured. I asked
why Cameroonian. She said, "You are Cameroonian. You need a
card." "No, I responded. "I am from Lensap near Sente." She
replied that was in Cameroon. I agreed to cut the conversation
short.

She found me work at the city hall at Ayotomiento. I worked
from 6 h. to 13 h. and for the rest of the day I rested.

The first night I spent with Mama Abena, she touched me down
there where I piss. I was happy. She asked me to mount her stom-
ach and then we did it. It was the first time in my life. Several days
later, my testicles swelled and descended almost to my knees. She
took me to the hospital. I was cured, but became afraid of resuming
such things.

I am very happy to find myself before the court of the chief. I was surprised that the chief is so young. The chief who was here at the time was old with big eyes. If I remember correctly, he was called Fo Nembouet Konguiet.[15]

Pa Jacob

In 2009, I went to Bamendjina in the northwest region of the Cameroon Grassfields with one of my students, Michelle Tchuenkam. Bamendjina is the site of the city of Mbouda, a military and administrative center built during the revolt that troubled the first years of Cameroonian independence. It was in the past the location of an important slave market. I wanted to ask the chief, Jean-Marie Tanefo, for authorization to do research on this slave market and on traditional domestic slavery. I looked particularly for informants who had living memories of slavery. We learned that Pa Jacob, one of the last slaves freed in Bamendjina, was still alive and that as a free man, he was able to live a dignified life. The chief invited him to come to the palace, where he told about his life.

At the time of the interview, Pa Jacob was a peaceful farmer of about eighty years old and the father of several children. He had been enslaved in colonial times, in a period in which slaves were no long being exported from Africa but when there was still an internal market for slaves, and for slave children in particular. Wealthy and powerful men needed workers or servants, or they simply wanted to increase the numbers of their dependents. A large entourage was a clear mark of their social superiority. In geographic terms, Pa Jacob was never as far from his people as Tabula. He hailed from Mock'Mbuim, about 80 kilometers from Bamendjina in the former Anglophone West Cameroons, where he lived as a slave. Mock'Mbuim means "bushfire." It was in a very roughly accidented area on the route which led from Bamileke country to Calabar. This relative proximity masks the profound gap which enslavement established between the young Jacob and his native community. Pa Jacob was enslaved as an infant and was raised by one of his master's wives. He does not remember his parents or how he became a slave. As a child he was often sent to get water or to collect wood for making fires. As he grew older, he worked alongside sons of his master. In addition to this work, he sometimes worked on European plantations. He lived in his own hut in his master's compound. Before the Second World War, he got married, but several days after the marriage, his wife fled. He then lived for several decades alone. Then, one of the wives of his late master gave him another wife, with whom he still lives and with whom he has had children.

Pa Jacob's Story

I was born in the time of the Germans. I was bought at Bamouck in the southwest part of the country. When I was very young, one of my relatives sold me to Papa Ndambi, who was a slave merchant. I do not remember my father's name. I spent most of my life working on plantations.

Q: *When were you married?*
A: I have been married for five years and am the father of three children. I have been freed for a long time and today possess my own field nearby. When I was freed, people helped me to construct a house.
Q: *When did your master die?*
A: My master died after the solar eclipse.[16]
Q: *Can you return to your village of origin to perform rites?*[17]
A: I cannot do it. And over there, no one knows where I am at present.
Q: *Do you know people of your condition who live in Bamend-jina?*
A: Yes. There were several, but they are already deceased. I cannot even remember their names.
Q: *What were you allowed to do in slavery and what could you not do?*
A: I worked on the coffee plantation of a white man at Mbouda.

I did not have the right to marry. I got married only five years ago, a long time after I was freed. Before that, I had not known a woman sexually. I did not have the right to property. I gave my master everything I had including what I earned on the plantation.

Q: *What did you receive in exchange?*

A: My master gave me a wife, but this wife came and then fled. My first wife fled before we could consummate the marriage.

Q: *When did the first marriage take place?*

A: It took place before independence. I did not sleep in my master's house. I slept instead at the home of my wet nurse.[18]

Notes

1. Ibrahim Sundiata, *From Slavery to Neo-Slavery: The Bight of Biafra in the Era of Abolition 1827-1930* (Madison: University of Wisconsin Press, 1966).
2. Fondation Tabula, Brochure, "Histoire réelle," 3.
3. On German colonial rule, see Harry Rudin, *Germans in the Cameroons 1884-1914. Case Study in Modern Imperialism* (New Haven: Yale University Press, 1938); Helmut Stoecker, ed., *German Imperialism in Africa: From the Beginning until the Second World War* (London: C. Hurst, 1987).
4. German anti-slavery actions were halfhearted and often involved laws which were rarely enforced, particularly in the interior of Cameroon, but in 1905, the Germans carried out a punitive expedition against the Bamundu, who were accused of kidnapping people to be sold as slaves. On slavery in Cameroon, see Bongfin Chem-Langhëë, ed., *Slavery and Slave-Dealing in Cameroon in the Nineteenth and the Early Twentieth Centuries*, Special issue of *Paideuma* 41(1995); E.S.D. Fomin and V. J. Ngoh, *Slave Settlements in the Banyang Country 1800-1950* (Limbe, Cameroon: University of Buea Publications, 1998). On German policy toward slavery, see Andreas Eckert, "Slavery in Colonial Cameroon, 1880s to 1930s," in *Slavery and Colonial Rule in Africa,* eds. Suzanne Miers and Martin Klein (London: Frank Cass, 1999), 133-48.
5. Victoria is today the scenic coastal town of Limbe, which is popular with tourists. It was a slaving port of some local importance.
6. Today known as Bioko, Fernando Po was from the fifteenth to the eighteenth centuries claimed by the Portuguese. In 1778, it was ceded to the Spanish, who developed cocoa plantations there during the late

nineteenth century. On Fernando Po, see Sundiata, *From Slavery to Neo-Slavery.*

7. These relics are today in the Fondation Tabula, which was created in September 2000, and is located in Ekié, one of the neighborhoods of Yaoundé, the capital of Cameroon. The foundation has established a small museum in Lensap, which displays the history of Tabula and associated material objects.

8. Before colonization, there were several ways people of the Cameroon Grassfields became slaves. At the beginning, only criminals or people who had committed serious offenses could be enslaved. In such cases, enslavement was both a punishment and an opportunity for these individuals to be resocialized into their new roles as slaves. Similarly, war captives could be enslaved, and with time they would become subjects, warriors, or dependents of the victorious chief. They could also be ennobled. When the demand for slaves increased, kidnapping increased in the Grassfields. Those who were kidnapped were moved both to the coast where slaves were purchased for the Atlantic slave trade and to the emirate of Yola, where slaves were channeled through the *lamidats* of northern Cameroon to Hausaland and the Sahara. In the 1920s, there was still an underground traffic in slaves, although the Germans first, and then the British and the French, who took possession of Cameroon after World War I, had abolished the slave trade.

9. In 2003, a group of students and instructors at the University of Dschang founded the Association Esclavage Mémoire et Abolition to "protect the memory of and to fight against all forms of slavery or that resembling slavery." The association has its headquarters in Dschang, but it has sought to become a national organization. It has stimulated research on slavery, and has played a role in the creation of two museums—that of Bamendjinda and that of Dschang—while also contributing, through the sponsorship of public lectures, to debates on the heritage of slavery.

10. Interviews with Jean Tawembé, also known as Ndé Tabula, adopted son and heir of Tabula, 2003-9; Interview with Joseph Keugne, proprietor of the Tahiti Bar in Malabo, Equatorial Guinea, 2003; Fondation Tabula, Brochure, "Histoire réelle," 3. As Tabula's heir, Jean Tawembé has the few relics of Tabula's poverty-stricken life, and also has taken on responsibility for Bamileke rituals performed in memory of the deceased.

11. In reality, they were destined for plantation labor on the islands of Equatorial Guinea.

12. For young men trapped in slavery or forced labor, becoming a soldier seemed very attractive.
13. Here, Tabula's memory goes back to the time he spent on the plantation near Victoria.
14. Mama Abena was also from the southern Cameroons.
15. Probably the great-grandfather of the chief who ennobled Tabula.
16. According to the Fo Jean-Marie Tanefo, the last solar eclipse seen in Bamileke country and remembered by the people was in 1947.
17. The interviewer is referring to the life-cycle ceremonies and the ancestral rites, which are a crucial part of Bamileke sociality.
18. When a very young slave arrived, he was left in the care of a wet-nurse. This was confirmed by the Fo. This relationship was often maintained as the young slave grew up.

7. Songs of Sorrow, Songs of Triumph: Memories of the Slave Trade among the Bulsa of Ghana

EMMANUEL SABORO

Ghanaian folklore, especially among the Bulsa of northern Ghana, contains a rich repertoire of songs which evoke their collective experience of slave raiding and resistance to enslavement. The case for Bulsa is particularly interesting because, it is a culture that has grown out of violent struggle against predators.[1] Their songs articulate both the historical and social experience of a people who carved for themselves a unique cultural identity of resistance to slave raiding and enslavement. This chapter examines the motif of the *kanbong* or "slave raider" and how his image has come to be associated with oppression, tyranny, and devastation. Victory over him is celebrated as communal triumph over an alien force. In the songs, the term *kanbong* refers to the foreign slave raider specifically, but also, in a more general sense, to the destructive foreigner. My analysis is structured in two parts: The first provides a historiographical context for the songs. I discuss slave raiding activities in northern Ghana, and what the symbol of the *kanbong* has come to represent in the collective consciousness of the Bulsa as found in songs of lamentation and sorrow. The second part looks at songs of triumph and victory over the slave raiders. The chapter concludes by reviewing ways in which memories of the past have persisted in Bulsa folklore.

The Sources of the Data and the Analytic Approach

The art of singing within Bulsa culture is not learned formally. There are no organized structures for the transmission of this oral art. Children learn the songs informally from their mothers or from others within the community and they are passed on from generation to generation. There are no trained singers who recount the history as may be found in other African societies. The songs discussed here were recorded in different locations among Bulsa towns and villages. After each recording session, singers were asked to clarify certain terms. The focus of the analysis is on how various images associated with the *kanbong* are described in the song texts. The songs are analyzed as oral poetry with specific emphasis on how literary tools such as metaphors, allusions, symbols, and imagery are used to convey specific images of the *kanbong*.

Northern Ghana and the Slave Trade

The Bulsa today are a small population group of about eighty thousand people in the Upper East region of Ghana, not far from the border with Burkina Faso. Like many other inhabitants of northern Ghana and the neighboring Mossi, they speak a Voltaic language. It is called Buli and the tribal territory is Bulugu, also pronounced Buluk. According to Benedict Der, the intrusion of the long-distance slave trade economy into northern Ghana began in 1732, when Asanti conquered Gonja and imposed a tribute to be paid in slaves.[2] Similar obligations were then imposed on Dagomba, Mamprussi, and other states in northern Ghana. These states then met their obligations to Asante by raiding the more decentralized societies such as the Bulsa in what is now northern Ghana and Burkina Faso. Der argues that before this, slavery existed in northern Ghana, but was not widespread, especially in the more decentralized societies.

During the second half of the nineteenth century, a series of Muslim warlords equipped with modern rifles and horses invaded the area. There were also local strong men who emerged either as resisters or as allies of the invaders. Though the trans-Atlantic trade had ended, slave raiding and slave trading increased. The most important of these traders were the Zabarima, who came from an area near the present-day city of Niamey in Niger. They first entered northern Ghana in the early 1860s, as merchants, particularly of horses. They were hired by the Dagomba as mercenaries to help provide the tribute in slaves Dagomba owed to the Asante. Around 1870, the Zaberima started raiding on their own account.[3] Babatu became their leader in the late 1870s and expanded the scale of their activities to include a large area between the White and Black Volta rivers. Their methods were simple. They demanded cattle, cowries, or slaves from villages. Those who did not pay were raided, sometimes many times. Slaves were sold at Salaga and at other markets in the region. In the oral traditions, it is Babatu that is remembered as the *kambong*, though some of the raids may have been conducted by others. Songs speak of him going around capturing people. In the late 1890s, his ability to raid was limited by the arrival of French, British, and German troops in the area. In 1897, he was defeated by a French force, and retired to Yendi, the capital of Dagomba, where he died in 1907.

People employed many different strategies to deal with the invaders. Some retreated to caves or rocky outcroppings, where they could take refuge when Zabarima raiders approached. There is a song that says, "the slave raider is pursuing us and we are running away." The raiders then had to content themselves with sheep and goats. Others built walls, within which there were stores of food and grazing areas. Houses were often built close together so that horsemen who entered would have difficulty operating within the narrow spaces.[4] They also resisted through the use of arms. The Bulsa were particularly fierce resisters. The songs I have collected celebrate a victory near Sandema in a difficult battle at Akumcham, which means "death's sheanut tree" or "weeping sheanut tree." It is believed that Babatu's wife was captured and executed there. Today, the tree is no more, but a stone marks the spot. Some of the songs celebrate this defeat.

During the month of December every year, some of these songs are performed during the *feok* festival along with dances reenacting the resistance to, and defeat of, Babatu. The *feok* is a festival of thanksgiving at the end of each harvest season. Its original purpose was to thank the Gods and ancestors for ensuring a good harvest. It was an occasion for feasting, for merrymaking and for reconciliation. The songs are often also performed at funerals and other social gatherings.

The war dance commemorating Babatu's defeat is an important part of the celebrations. Similar to war dances performed elsewhere in Africa, it attempts to reconstruct the memory of collective resistance against slave raiding and the threat of enslavement. The performers in their war regalia dance and sing war and victory songs celebrating the heroic exploits of their fathers and the defeat of Babatu and his forces. They are supported by singing groups from the different villages. The *feok* festival has become one of the most significant events of the Bulsa calendar. It gives the Bulsa a sense of pride and communal identity. Memories of the devastation of the slave trade and of enslavement still linger on in the sorrowful tunes sung at the festival.

The *Kanbong* in Bulsa Collective Consciousness

The figure of the *kanbong* has become an important historical symbol associated with sad memories in the collective consciousness of the Bulsa. In the song texts, the *kanbong* is often associated with the Asante, who played a key role in the history of slavery.[5] Field interviews conducted in and around the Bulsa area suggest that the term has become synonymous with slave raiding, oppression, tyranny, the Asante, Babatu, and the foreign enslaver. The metaphor of the *kanbong* in the songs connotes cruelty, ruthlessness, a sense of loss, alienation, and misery. The term can also be used to refer to a crook, a cunning and manipulative person, or a wicked person, who never gives up.[6]

The songs articulate the experience of people under constant threat of enslavement. Some of them are songs of sorrow and lamentation against an alien system that violated the wills of the

Bulsa as human beings. The tone and mood of these songs represents what W.E.B. Du Bois refers to as "the rhythmic cry of the slave … the most beautiful expression of the human experience born this side of the seas."[7] Many, particularly the songs of women, are laments, which re-narrate the history of the Bulsa. The songs are a compelling story of a culture that emerged from constant fear to embrace a unique identity of resistance.

As Dan Allender has noted, "Music in a culture of sorrow is less likely to reinforce the status quo or beguile people with the 'good life.'"[8] According to Allender, songs of sorrow expose the need for cultural and personal redemption that will not come without intervention and rescue. Allender argues that many individuals know deep suffering, but few have been part of a culture that is defined by sorrow, that if one reads or listens to the art of these cultures, one is led not to despair, but to passionate hope. The greatest power in art, life, and faith comes from the soil of lament. Lament, according to Allender, embodies the passions of need, the fight against injustice, and implicitly the proclamation of hope. These songs are a verbal cry against injustice.

The Songs in Perspective

This section takes a closer look at the songs. Their texts have become a living testament that reminds Bulsa of a tragic and painful experience. The performers and singers of these songs, who are the descendants of those who were constantly pursued, share in this collective triumph. The first part of this discussion looks at the various images associated with the slave raider. One particular song runs thus:

> *The* kanbong *has come to attack me*
> *And I have no place to stay*
> *He attacked me and I am running*
> *And people are laughing at me.*
> *I do not have a place to stay any longer.*

The verb "to attack" evokes images of violence and aggression by an individual or a group on a people. It also suggests an invasion of personal and communal space. The expressions *"He attacked me and I am running/and I have no place to stay"* suggest displacement and a state of confusion. The *kanbong*'s predation within Bulsa land inhibited the peoples' creative abilities. People cannot develop when they are always running from slave raiders. This individual and communal flight has serious implications for development.

The *kanbong* is also seen within the context of his oppressive and predatory behavior. The song conveys a sensual imagery of pain and lamentation of the human soul. The song runs thus:

> *When the* kanbong *came to our community,*
> *Things are no longer the same*
> *The* kanbong *is going round*
> *our community capturing people*
> *Things are no longer the same.*
> *We are running away from the slave raider*

The word *yigi* in the vernacular text of the song as in "catch" or "capture" is suggestive of the use of force to deny a person of his/her freedom. It also suggests that people did not willingly surrender themselves to be enslaved but were forcefully and violently captured. The song repeats:

> *The* kanbong *is in the community capturing people. Things are no longer the same.*

The *kanbong*'s presence in the community altered normal life. Social and economic life was no longer the same. The threat of enslavement and slave raids affected local agriculture. That, these areas are still very poor is partly due to the history of predation. The line *"We are running away from the slave raider"* describes the plight of people more concerned with daily survival than with their future. Slave raiding led to a fragmented society. This is further captured in the lines:

138

When the kanbong *entered our land*
We could no longer socialize
When he entered into our land
We could no longer socialize
No more socialization
No more socialization
They came and drove us away
They came and drove us away

We could no longer socialize
When the slave raider entered our land
Where can you sit and socialize?
There is no more socialization in our community.
No more socialization
No more socialization

Fear and insecurity made socialization impossible. The image is of "psychological disorientation" where cultural clues, values, and the signs and symbols which guide social relations, are stripped away, as a result of the *kanbong*'s predation. The sense of cruelty and oppression experienced because of enslavement is noted in metaphors of death and devastation. The song says:

Look, I am feeling cold and hungry Kanbong!
I am feeling cold and hungry
The kanbong *who entered our land brought cold*
But we are no nearer home so that we can at least
*   drink water*
The household of Basiik *are suffering before getting home*

The feelings of cold and hunger suggest a sense of deprivation and misery. Being deprived of the *basic* conditions of human life is accentuated in the song in which the *kanbong* is presented as an embodiment of death and lifelessness itself. A specific line of the song says:

139

But we are no nearer home
so that we can at least drink water,

Some songs make specific reference to how slave raiding disrupted and interfered with the biological and reproductive capabilities of the people. Relevant portions of the song say:

No one runs away and leaves his/her children.
You do not run and abandon your own kind
With the presence of the kanbong
How can we have children again?

We are running away while abandoning our children.
I am running for my dear life.
I do not have time for children anymore.
I do not have time for children anymore

The song suggests that with the coming of the *kanbong*, mothers no longer had time for childbearing. Instead, the desire for survival and safety became their most prominent preoccupation. In one of the songs, the rhetorical question *"what do we still live for"* expresses a deep sense of despair. One image that stands out in this regard is the death metaphor. The death being alluded to in the song text is both physical and spiritual. An example of a song dealing with the condition of slave raiding and enslavement as death is seen in the following song:

When the kanbong *entered into* (Basiik) *our land,*
no one was left
He has killed all the people
And no one was left in the land
They say, when the kanbong *entered into our land,*
no one was left
All our people are finished

The kanbong *who entered into* Doning,
look, no one was left
All the people are dead
All our elders are dead
no one was left
The kanbong *who entered our land*
no one was left
All the people are dead and gone
How many have survived?
All are gone

This song is a dirge sung by the women and repeated several times during performance. The song captures images of death, devastation, and loss. The repetition of *"no one was left"* in the two stanzas emphasizes the destructive nature of slave raiding and enslavement precipitated by the *kanbong* and his cohorts. There is specific mention of Bulsa towns, Basik and Doning. One important point in the previous song and the following one is the stress on the word "All":

*He has killed **all** the people*
***All** our people are finished*
***All** the people are dead*
***All** our elders are dead*
***All** the people are dead and gone*
***All** are gone*

The specific reference to *"All our elders are dead"* is also of symbolic significance. The elders are repositories of communal wisdom and societal values. They are symbols of both the past and the future. Slave raiding and the process of enslavement thus disrupted this arrangement of passing on communal wisdom to the younger generation by violently uprooting the elders of the land.

Resistance and Victory over the *Kanbong*

Through the songs of victory, a bitter and tragic epoch in the history of the Bulsa is transformed into celebration. When the songs are performed annually, during their festival, there is a deep sense of communal pride. The songs of victory are songs of resistance. They are songs of deliverance and redemption from the *kanbong*'s domination and tyranny. In these songs of triumph, the image of war and violent confrontation is prominent. A song says:

> *We have eaten the medicine for death*
> *We have eaten the medicine for death*
> *We will strike and advance towards the enemy*
> *Without fear of death*
> *We have eaten the medicine for death*

This song celebrates bravery and resilience in the midst of predation from slave raiders. This song literarily talks of eating the medicine for death. The "eating" of medicine for death is suggestive of the use of charms and amulets as a part of the culture of warfare. Their use is indicative of a people's belief in the ability of the supernatural to influence the lives of the living. Charms and amulets appended to war regalia serve to protect the wearer from the enemies' weapons and encourage bravery and a determination to resist their oppressors.

> *We will strike and advance towards*
> *The enemy without fear of death*
> *We have eaten the medicine for death*

"Striking and advancing" is certainly not a feature of a passive people who acquiesced in their enslavement. Striking and advancing is suggestive of a violent confrontation. In one particular song celebrating communal victory, the people of Bulsa are emphatic:

Victory, victory
Victory, victory
Victory is not won twice
Victory, victory
Victory, is not won twice

This song has one stanza and is repeated several times and sung by men. The message of the song is clear: "*Victory is not won twice.*" The confidence in this declaration portrays bold and confident people whose determination, resilience, and fortitude brought them victory. A similar song of celebration is:

Where are the houses of the chiefs of the slave raiders?
The chiefs of the slave raiders have fled.
Where are the houses of the chiefs of the slave raiders?

Where are the houses of the chiefs of the slave raiders?

The chiefs of the slave raider have fled.

These songs are marked by the use of repetition, which takes varied forms: the repeating of metrical patterns, rhythm, internal echoes, refrains, and sometimes syntactic structure. In this particular song, the question "*Where are the houses of the chiefs of the slave raiders*" is repeated several times to achieve emphasis. This repetition also contributes immensely to the musical quality of the song. The drum accompaniment together with facial expressions and dignified steps by the war dancers all enhance the performance and elicit audience response. The second line of the song is more forceful: "*The chiefs of the slave raiders have fled.*" Active resistance led to the fleeing of the *kanbong*. On the metaphoric level, the song challenges the very institution of slavery. The rhetorical question "*Where are the houses of the slave raiders?*" is significant. In other words, "Where are the foundations of the slave enterprise?"

143

You should climb your roof-tops and see the slave raider
And his troops who are raiding the houses.
You should all climb up to your roof-tops
and see the slave raider who is raiding the houses

"You should climb your roof-tops and see the slave raider" is in a song of celebration announcing the victorious return of the warriors after defeating the slave raiders. The song is repeated several times and a call is made to the community to climb up to their rooftops to catch a glimpse at the notorious *kanbong* who is raiding the community. This song is performed with drum accompaniment and shouts of victory and ululations from women. After the victorious return of the warriors, Bulsa were called upon to share this collective victory. The "houses" metaphor goes beyond the physical structures in which people live to embody individuals, families, and the community.

The line *"Victory over the slave raider has brought us a sigh of relief"* is in another song that celebrates the defeat and overthrow of the *kanbong*. The song reinforces the sense of relief the people of Bulsa experienced as a result of the defeat of the *kanbong*. Some significant portions of the song run as follows:

Victory over the slave raider has brought us a
sigh of relief
Victory over the slave raider has brought us a
sigh of relief

The battle is ended and we are free at last
The battle is ended and we are free at last

Victory over the slave raider has brought us a
sigh of relief
Victory over the slave raider has brought us a
sigh of relief

The battle is ended and we are free at last
The battle is ended and we are free at last

In this song, the word *kanbong* is used alternatively with *tigurika* (Battle) in the second stanza. This suggests that the *kanbong* is a symbol of violence and oppression, whose defeat brought freedom at last. The repetition of the line *"The battle is ended and we are free at last"* is important. In another song, *"Our fathers have driven away the slave raider and he ran away"* also celebrates victory and communal triumph. Some significant parts of the song say:

> Our fathers have driven away
> the slave raider and he ran away
> The slave raider who entered our land
> was driven away by our fathers
> Our fathers have driven away
> the slave raider and he ran away
>
> Can't you see how our fathers could shoot arrows?
> Our fathers drove away the slave raider
> Can't you see how they are coming out with arrows?

Conclusion

Memories of slave raiding, enslavement, and resistance have played an important part in the collective consciousness of most African communities. The chief object of this chapter was to look at how the Bulsa of Ghana have preserved the memory of their enslavement and resistance through the expressive arts especially in their songs. Specific songs that deal with the activities of the *kanbong* and the images associated with him were sampled for discussion. The *kanbong* has become a major historical symbol of oppression and tyranny in the collective consciousness of descendants of the people who were under constant slave raids and threats of enslavement. His defeat and overthrow thus constitute personal and collective victory over an alien force that sought to legitimize the violation of the wills of the people. Even though the *kanbong* was finally defeated in northern Ghana, his presence led to such individual and communal devastation that it cannot be quantified.

145

Most scholars of the slave enterprise think that the slave trade and slave-raiding activities in Africa generally led to a depletion of the population.[9] In northern Ghana, the effects of slave raiding and of enslavement are still visible today. There is physical evidence of whole communities being completely wiped out. The song that says "*When the slave raider entered our land no one was left*" attests to this fact. The slave enterprise stifled individual and communal creative efforts, but the songs attest to resistance and resilience.

This chapter has discussed both songs of sorrow and lamentation and those of resistance. By articulating their plight, the Bulsa acknowledge the painful past but also encourage listeners to remember the resistance they offered to the constant predation on their people and culture. The songs present compelling evidence of the will to survive in the midst of adversity. They do not suggest collective passivity but communal strength and resilience. Through these songs, we see how the people have transformed an otherwise tragic event into a testament of cultural redemption. They have attempted to rewrite the history of the African experience of the slave trade by suggesting that the story about Africans should not always be about victimhood and subjugation, but also about individual and communal strength. The songs thus affirm a people's resolve and commitment to continue to resist systems and institutions that violate human dignity. In modern times, the Bulsa are no long resisting slave raids, but as they continue to sing the songs during funerals, festivals, and other social gatherings, they draw strength and inspiration from their forefathers.

Notes

1. N. J. Opoku-Agyeman, "The Living Experience of the Slave Trade in Sankana and Gwollu: Implications for Tourism," in *The Transatlantic Slave Trade: Landmarks, Legacies, Expectations*, ed. James Anquandah (Accra, Ghana: Sub-Saharan Publishers, 2007); A. Howell, "Showers of Arrows: The Reactions and Resistance of the Kasena to Slave Raids in the 18th and 19th Centuries," in *The Transatlantic Slave Trade: Landmarks, Legacies, Expectations*, ed. James Anquan-

dah (Accra, Ghana: Sub-Saharan Publishers, 2007).

2. Benedict Der, *The Slave Trade in Northern Ghana* (Accra, Ghana: Woeli, 1998), chap. 3.

3. Carola Lentz, *Ethnnicity and the Making of History in Northern Ghana* (Edinburgh, Scotland: Edinburgh University Press, 2006), chap. 1; J. J. Holden, "The Zabarima Conquest of North-West Ghana. Part One," *Transactions of the Historical Society of Ghana* 8 (1965): 60-83; Stanislaw Pilasewicz, *The Zaberma Conquest of Northwest Ghana and Upper Volta* (Warsaw: Polish Scientific Publishers, 1992); Franz Kröger, "Raids and Refuge: The Bulsa in Babatu's Slave Wars," *Research Review* 24 (2008): 25-38.

4. Benjamin Kankpeyeng, "The Slave Trade in Northern Ghana: Landmarks, Legacies and Connections," *Slavery and Abolition* 30 (2009): 209-21; Natalie Swanepoel, "Socio-Political Change on a Slave-Raiding Frontier: War, Trade and 'Big Men' in Nineteenth Century Sisalaland, Northern Ghana," *Journal of Conflict Archeology* 1 (2005): 265-93; Nathalie Swanepoel, "Every Periphery Is Its Own Center. Sociopolitical and Economic Interactions in Nineteenth-Century Northwestern Ghana," *International Journal of African Historical Studies* 42 (2009): 411-32.

5. On the role of slavery in Asante, see Akosua Perb, *A History of Indigenos Slavery in Ghana from the 15th to the 19th Century* (Accra, Ghana: Sub-Saharan Publishers, 2004).

6. Field Interviews, September 2005.

7. W.E.B. Du Bois, *Souls of Black Folks* (New York: Penguin, 1989), 265.

8. Dan Allender, "The Hidden Hope in Lament," *Mars Hill Review* 1 (1994). http://www.leaderu.com/marshill/mhr01/lament1.html

9. Patrick Manning, *Slavery and African Life. Occidental, Oriental and African Slave Trades* (Cambridge: Cambridge University Press, 1990); David Eltis and David Richardson, *Extending the Frontiers: Essays on the New Transatlantic Slave Trade Data Base* (New Haven and London: Yale University Press, 2008); Paul Lovejoy and Jan Hogendorn, *Slow Death for Slavery: The Course of Abolition in Northern Nigeria, 1897-1936* (Cambridge: Cambridge University Press, 1993).

8. Evoking the Past through Material Culture: The Mami Tchamba Shrine

ALESSANDRA BRIVIO

Tchamba is a *vodun*[1] consecrated to slaves, called in Ewe *ameflefle,* the "bought people." *Ameflefle* were the men and the women purchased in past times by the ancestors of present *vodun* Tchamba adepts. Tchamba or Mami Tchamba[2] is worshiped along what was called the Slave Coast, by only those families once involved in the slave trade. The *vodun* is consecrated to slaves who worked as domestic slaves, to slaves who married into their masters' families and thus became the ancestors to present-day worshipers, and to all those slaves sold away from Africa. In other words, Mami Tchamba gathers the spirits of all slaves who died far from their

Tchamba shrine, Lomé, January 2007

149

motherland. As noted by Pascal Lawson, a *vodun* leader in Cotonou, Benin: "Mami Tchamba is a *vodun* to remember our ancestors, who were slaves, who were [taken] from their motherland and who never went back to their villages."[3] During Tchamba ceremonies, the spirits of the deceased slaves possess the descendants of their ancient masters, who offer their bodies to the errant spirits.

The families involved in Tchamba all claim their ancestors owned many slaves; only infrequently do they admit that a "grandmother" was actually a slave who had married into her master's family. The reluctance to discuss one's slave ancestry (in contrast to the willingness to boast about an ancestor owning many slaves) was commented on in 2007 by Kokou Atchinou,[4] a Togolese leader of Tchamba and the descendant of a slave trader. According to Kokou Atchinou, "we all know who the slaves' descendants are in our families but it is not something we talk about,"[5] because it could compromise or even destroy our families' integrity. The stigma associated with slave status is still present even when they were fully integrated into their masters' families through marriage or childbirth. Talk about slavery is thought best discussed in secrecy, through "whispers and silences"[6] or, as in the case of Tchamba, through collective ceremonies and ritual practices.

Mami Tchamba represents a particular way for individuals and families to face personal and familial memories from the past. It is a ritualized memory, embedded in material objects and bodily practices that evoke different and disturbing traces of the past. It allows a variety of lineage perspectives to emerge in ways that speak silently (rather than discursively) about a common but contentious past.

In this chapter I will focus on the shrine's ritual objects as part of the rich material culture surrounding *vodun* rituals. I will argue that these objects on the one hand speak about the presumed ethnic origins of the slaves, and on the other they reveal the history of a land upset by death and violence. The architecture and the use of the spaces, the shapes, the colors, the smells, and the materials of the ritual objects are important sites where memories were planted and new meanings can grow. For example, in a Tchamba shrine, one observes that there is a careful disposition of ritual pots, each of which is thought to contain the spirits belonging to a particular ethnic group.

All of the pots, stools, and other materials that constitute the Tchamba shrine might be organized to evoke the image of a corpse waiting for the funeral. In this way, the Tchamba practitioners construct a symbolic body into which all the slave spirits might find a place to stay and finally to be celebrated. To interpret the symbolic corpse recomposed on the shrine, one needs to develop a comprehensive vision of local religious and mystical concepts. Indeed, Tchamba celebrates the tragedy of men and women, who died far away from their lands, their ancestors, and their divinities. Furthermore, as informers explained to me, a lot of slaves died on their way to the coast because they couldn't survive the trip or because they were killed by slavers. Today those dead ask for a proper burial. As they did not undergo funeral rites, they are considered to be "bad dead." The "bad dead" are unable to rejoin their ancestors, and in turn they are unable to become ancestors. They were forced into the position of breaking the continuity that held their lineage together, and as a consequence they haven't been able to find a place in the hereafter. For this reason these spirits are restless, not pacified, aggressive, and hot. They come back into their ancient adopted homes to annoy the descendants of their masters and to force the family into a dialogue with their spirits. By insisting on this dialogue, they emerge from oblivion and find a place for themselves.

The main feature of a Mami Tchamba shrine is the presence of a number of pots, different in number, shape, and color, aligned close to one another. Tchamba, in fact, brings together a number of different spiritual entities or divinities, in which each pot is said to "contain" a particular *vodun*. The more well-known and widespread, among those I encountered in Togo and Bénin, are Mama Tchamba herself, Bublume, Yendi, Mama Gae, Allah,[7] Donko,[8] and Losso.[9] At the same time, as noted by Kokou Gbosso, a priest of Mami Tchamba, in Cotonou, "it is really difficult to find all of [the deities] in the same shrine; for example I just have Bublume,

Yendi, Adoko, and Fulali, it depends on the number of slaves your family bought."[10]

The names of the deities associated with the Tchamba order are largely linked to the cultures and religions of northern Togo, Benin, and Ghana. Worshipers claim this is the case because it was from these areas that the slaves whose spirits they worship trace their origins.[11] In reality, the origins and identities of the enslaved are almost impossible to unearth. For Mama Tchamba worshipers, however, the past is open to invention and personal elaboration in support of their need to establish common and shared memories. In the absence of detailed knowledge about the actual villages from which the slaves came, the descendants of the slave masters have been forced to use general ethnic categories to welcome to their shrines the spirits of the slaves they once owned. For instance, Yendi is the name of a northern Ghanaian city, on the border with Togo. In the past it was an important center for the exchange of slaves, kola nuts, and salt. Tchamba is a present-day city in Togo, on the banks of the Mono River; it too had a large market, to which slaves from areas further to the north were conveyed and sold. Bolgatanga is a city in the Upper East region of Ghana; it served as one of the southern terminuses of the ancient trans-Saharan trade route that also hosted a slave trade.[12] And finally Bublume, according to Judy Rosenthal, seems to come from the term *Blu*, a name given to foreigners whose descendants were later integrated into the coastal villages of the Anlo-Ewe.[13] It is during ritual performances, when the spirits possess the bodies of the adepts, that the northern presence is more vividly expressed. The *trosi* (adepts) completely change identity and offer themselves to the foreign spirits: they speak northern languages, such as Kabre, Hausa, Losso, or Fulani; they dance Kabre music and drink *tchukoutou*, a Kabre alcoholic drink containing millet.

In the *vodun* practice, ritual objects are the actual sources of energy, power, and agency. Accordingly, the pots that are so central to Tchamba worship should not be understood as merely symbolic or representative. Rather, they concentrate all the energies surrounding the *vodun*. Equally important is the belief that the potency

"Bublume" during a Tchamba ceremony, Lomé, January 2007

of these energies or powers fluctuate, depending on the depth of knowledge of its *houno* (religious leader). A *vodun* is especially powerful if its leader has expert knowledge in how to mix different "ingredients" using particular plants (*ama*) and uttering specific formulas when installing the shrine, and when subsequently interacting with it. Because the *vodun* are dynamic entities, this focus on the ritual acts of collecting, preparing, inserting, and enclosing encourages worshipers to understand the relationship between human beings and divinities as one based on reciprocity, grounded in specific knowledge about how to manage cosmic power. The ritual acts performed by the *huono,* his containing and hiding the objects that he places in the containers, evokes the secretive, esoteric, and constantly evolving nature of the knowledge associated with the *vodun*.

153

Each *vodun* within Mama Tchamba must be understood according to its own peculiar features and actually each pot—made of aluminium or brass, or constructed from large pumpkins (calabashes) or clay—is a *vodun* associated with quite specific ritual objects, colors, dresses, bracelets, and necklaces. It is the material culture that allows worshipers to recognize and reconstruct the origins of the different slaves. It is almost a work in ethnography[14] that the Tchamba people perform in their efforts to establish a suitable location where errant and "hot" slave' spirits can rest and be pacified. While only the leaders know what the pots contain, worshipers recognize the individual spirits by the pot's color, by the type and color of the bracelets (*tchambaga*) that the adepts wear,[15] by the dress used during possession and, of course, by the language spoken by the spirits when they possess humans.

Each pot contains all the spirits associated with those slaves of a particular ethnic origin. All Bublume, for example, will be welcomed inside the black pots, while the brass pots are used to welcome those spirits associated with the town of Yendi. In other words, this classification of the spirits by color, influences all the material culture associated with the Tchamba orders: the bracelets' materials, the color and material of the shrine pots (brass, aluminum, or black clay), and the dress worn by the *trosi* during ceremonies as well as the color of the animals to be sacrificed. Their coats must be white, black, or yellow according to the *vodun* to which they are being offered.

The problem is how to discover the particular identities of the slaves who were attached to the present Tchamba adepts' families. This is necessary so that the adepts can recognize which of the spirits associated with Mama Tchamba they should welcome. One such adept, Pascal Lawson of Togo, explains how he has used knowledge of his family history to identity the origins of those slaves associated with his lineage:

> Once, in my family, we used to have slaves. All of them are now dead, but it is still possible to find their bracelets somewhere in the house or outside in the field

154

where they used to work.... You can [also] find them along the road, in the bush, or in the sea. You might see it and pick it up, but you don't really know its meaning; only after a while would you understand why you found it and finally that it is a sign of the vodun.... Anyway it is important to find out the origin of the slave, whose spirit is calling you [by having you find its bracelet]. They could have come from Monrovia, from Nigeria, or Gabon. You recognize them by their colors. The spirits of Bublume and Losso, for example, wear black bracelets. The Yendi's color is yellow and so its bracelets are made of brass; Danko's color is blue and its bracelets have three colors: white, red, and yellow.... In Tchamba there is also Mama Gae, whose colors are yellow and white, while Moriga is just a different name given to Yendi. Yendi is a woman, a divinity able to forgive.... Bublume is black; it is a strong spirit, one who does not forgive ... it is a woman, too. Mama Gae, who is a woman, is cool and it wears white. Even if the Tchamba *vodun* is worshiped all over Africa, these spirits come from the north of Togo and Benin; you can understand them just listening to their voices; they in fact speak Fulani, Mossi, and Kabre.[16]

To understand Mama Tchamba, it is important to realize that the histories associated with each divinity are not invented out of whole cloth, but rather are re-created in response to contemporary concerns and private histories.[17] We see this in Lawson's account that was just quoted. Lawson cited Monrovia as the origin of some slaves. He did so because there was a woman—a slave descendant- from Monrovia—in his own family. She was one of the wives of his grandfather, and was probably one of the freed slaves who returned to West Africa from America. So even if there are general rules for the identification and worship of slaves' spirits (like finding a particular colored bracelet in the sea), each person involved in this religious order modifies it according to his or her own personal history. Thus, according to Ablavi Laba, Mami Tchamba priestess in Baguida, Togo:

> I have Nana Kante [as a spirit that I worship] because my grandmother, who was a slave, was a Tamberman. Her family name was Benfo and she was from Kante. The master's family name was Aviti; he was from Ag-bogbo, close to Tchevié. The grandmother was the younger girl of a royal family; that's why I wear her ivory bracelet. In my family there are three more persons who wear the same type of bracelet. Others wear the iron ones, because they are linked to Bolgatanka, who were slaves of Mossi origins.[18]

Another feature of Mama Tchamba is the way in which it reveals the history of a land deeply scarred by death and violence. One sees this especially in the characteristics associated with a *vodun* named Ade. According to the local beliefs, Ade is a *vodun* to fear; it is hot and aggressive. Kokou Atchinou and Pascal Lawson, both of Togo, explained:

> In Tchamba there are spirits both quiet and angry. Indeed, some slaves refused to be caught or to be sold; they struggled against their destiny and for this reason they were killed ... anyway the corpses were useful for fishing cowrie [from the sea] ... the [slaves'] corpses were used in this way.[19] For these types of spirits there is a specific ceremony. We call the spirits Ade. Ade is the *vodun* linked to the slaves who suffered a brutal and violent death.[20]
>
> Ade is a warrior and a hunter ancestor, who fought in war and died during the battle though his corpse never came back. If you die in a road accident, drown, or are shot by a rifle, you will also become Ade. Anyway the real Ade are the past great hunters. They have now come back to ask for ceremonies because they are

lost in this world, existing in places where no one knows their origins. Actually, they have been abandoned.[21]

Evidence of the violence associated with Ade spirits is especially evident in the material objects associated with their worship, where the hunters and the prey are put together.

Tchamba shrine, Lomé, January 2007

During a *kpeta* (a big ceremony) in Lomé,[22] one or more white stools, set besides the pots, are dedicated to the ancestor who was involved in the slave trade as a trader (see Figure 3). The stools are not the common *togbesigbi*—the stools of an ancestor—but a *hosigbi*—a money stool. Only slave traders possessed them. Around the stools there are an ensemble of objects, symbols of both the richness and the violence embedded in the slave trade: cowries, chains, cords, sticks, bonds, and beads. During *kpeta*[23]all the ritual objects are visible to everyone. Usually they are hidden under a cloth except on Friday, when women charged with the

Tchamba shrine, Ouidah, July 2005

shrine's maintenance have to nourish and take care of all the *vodun*. As already underlined, the shrine is organized to resemble a corpse wrapped in a shroud.

To care for troubled and wandering slaves' spirits, the Tchamba adepts construct a symbolic body where the spirits can be celebrated. Even if not abandoned in the bush or in the ocean, their corpses did not receive the proper funeral. Instead they were buried in the *dzogbe*, a space reserved for people who died a violent death. According to the Ewe-Mina people of Togo and Bénin, the real tragedy for the enslaved was to die far away from their motherland and to have not received appropriate funeral rites. No one performed the ceremonies that would have allowed them to rejoin their ancestors and to become ancestors themselves. They were forcibly removed from their kin and, as a consequence, they cannot rest in peace. This is the reason why the spirits of the slaves come back to annoy the descendants of their masters. They want to emerge from

Tchamba shrine, Lomé, January 2007

oblivion and the silence to which their masters have condemned them. These spirits are "hot" and "bad," restless and aggressive, because sometimes they suffered a terrible and violent death and because they are still looking for a place to rest.

However, Ade is associated not only with the angry spirits of the enslaved but also with the hunters. Tchamba leaders claim that hunters caught slaves in the bush and brought them to the coast. In fact, according to local understanding, hunting was the main means that people used to catch slaves.[24] Ade, then, is a *vodun* devoted to both the hunters and to their victims. In Ade shrines, skulls of animals are placed beside *asen,* a "portable ancestor's shrine"; in Tchamba the slaves' spirits pots are positioned close to the masters' stools; the victims are placed beside the hunters; symbols of richness are mixed with symbols of violence. Tchamba adepts who pray at the shrine honor both slaves and masters. They reveal a

"Bublume" during a Tchamba ceremony, Lomé, January 2007

mythical and heroic past (as seen in the reverence for the spirits of the hunters) as part of their efforts to achieve a better future for all their families. Yet they also reconstruct the corpses of their deceased slaves in ways that evoke the violence of slavery. Nothing is denied; nothing is hidden. Rather, Tchamba adepts seek to build an "ethnography of the north" in a way to reconcile the different and conflicting strands of their familial past. By reconstructing the geography of slavery, by recognizing the slaves' cultural heritage, by imagining their habits and satisfying their desires, and by cooling their anger while also bringing them together with their masters, they seek a better, more prosperous, and pacific future.

Notes

1. *Vodun* is the name of the religion widespread in southern Togo, Benin, and eastern Ghana, and it is also the name attributed to the single entities (spirits or divinities) animating this religion. See, for example, Nadia Lovell, *Cord of Blood* (London: Pluto Press), 2002; Suzanne Preston Blier, *African Vodun: Art, Psychology and Power* (Chicago: University of Chicago Press), 1995.

2. I use Tchamba or Mami Tchamba, even if Mami Tchamba is often employed to mean the religious order to honor female slave ancestors, while Tchamba is used when there is no specific link to a female ancestor. On Tchamba, see Dana Rush, "In Remembrance of Slavery. 'Tchamba Vodun Arts,'" *African Arts* (Spring 2011): 40-51; Alessandra Brivio, "Nos grands-pères achetaient des esclaves: Le culte de Mami Tachmba au Togo et au Bénin," *Gradhiva* 8 (2008); 65-79; Judy Rosenthal, *Possession, Ecstasy & Law in Ewe Voodoo* (Charlottesville: University Press of Virginia, 1998).

3. November 27, 2006, Cotonou, Bénin.

4. Kokou Atchinou is the leader of GAMAT, the Groupment des Adorateurs de Maman Tchamba, in Lomé.

5. January 2, 2007, Bé, Lomé, Togo.

6. Sandra Greene "Whispers and Silences: Explorations in African Oral History," *Africa Today* 50 (2003): 40-53. See also Rosalind Shaw, *Memories of the Slave Trade* (Chicago: University of Chicago Press, 2002), and, on Bénin, Nassirou Bako-Arifari, "La mémoire de la traite négrière dans le débat politique au Bénin dans les années 1990," *Journal des Africanistes* 70, nos. 1-2 (2000): 221-31.

7. Allah is present in Tchamba because of the slaves' northern origin and their supposed Muslim faith. Many are the references to Islam. For example, Friday is chosen as holy day and *trosi* use a rosary as a necklace.

8. *Donko* or *adoko* is actually a general definition; in fact it is an Ewe word employed to mean "slave."

9. Losso people are a subgroup of the Kabre.

10. December 14, 2006, Fidjirossé, Cotonou, Bénin.

11. This is also the reason why to this day Mama Tchamba shrines welcome all "stranger" divinities from northern communities. On the relationship between the coastal people and the savanna ones, see John Parker, "Northern Gothic: Witches, Ghosts and Werewolves in the Savanna Hinterland of the Gold Coast, 1990s-1950s," *Africa* 76 (2006): 352-80; Parker and Jean Allman, *Tongnaab: The History of a West African God* (Bloomington: Indiana University Press, 2005); Charles Piot, *Remotely Global: Village Modernity in West Africa* (Chicago: University of Chicago Press, 1999).

12. Paul Lovejoy, *Caravans of Kola: The Hausa Kola Trade, 1700-1900* (Zaria, Nigeria: Ahmadu Bello University Press, 1980).

13. Rosenthal, *Possession, Ecstasy & Law in Ewe Voodoo*, 110.

14. Wendl Thomas, "The *Tchamba* Cult among the Mina in Togo," in *Spirit Possession: Modernity and Power in Africa,* eds. H. Behrend and U. Luig (Madison: University of Wisconsin Press, 1999), 111-23.

15. The bracelets are said to be left, in the past, by slaves. They are regarded as little "fetishes" charged with the presence, power, and identity of the linked *vodun*.

16. December 19, 2006, Cotonou, Bénin.

17. Rosalind Shaw, *Memories of the Slave Trade*, 12-15.

18. January 1, 2007, Baguida, Togo.

19. Alessandra Brivio, "Tales of Cowries, Money and Slaves (Togo)," in *African Voices on Slavery and the Slave Trade*, vol. 1, *Sources*, eds. Alice Bellagamba, Sandra Greene, and Martin Klein (Cambridge: Cambridge University Press, 2013).

20. January 2, 2007, Bé, Lomé, Togo.

21. December 19, 2006, Cotonou, Bénin.

22. January 13, 2007, Bé, Lomé, Togo.

23. *Kpeta* is a ceremony celebrated only once every five or even more years, because of the amount of money and energy it demands.

24. Actually, kidnapping played a major role in the supply of slaves in the early stage of the slave trade in the fifteenth century and then again in the last phase.

9. Slave Ancestry and Religious Discrimination in The Gambia

ALICE BELLAGAMBA AND MARTIN A. KLEIN

Memories of the Atlantic slave trade are actively preserved in The Gambia, where the government has pursued a heritage policy designed to attract the African diaspora. Every two years, visitors from Europe and northern America come to attend the Roots Homecoming Festival, which was first launched in 1996. While there, they often stop at the Albreda Slavery Museum, also inaugurated in 1996, and then go to James Island, where there are ruins of a European fort. In 2003, James Island was inscribed on the UNESCO World Heritage List, and in 2011, the government of The Gambia renamed it Kunta Kinteh Island to honor the memory of Kunta Kinteh, the ancestor whom the novelist and journalist Alex Haley celebrated in his novel *Roots*. The village of Juffureh, which was purportedly home to Kunta Kinteh, is another important site in the immediate proximity of Albreda. In Juffureh, visitors meet members of the Kinteh family and get acquainted with the traditions of rural Gambia. But in spite of all the efforts made to connect The Gambia to the history of the Atlantic slave trade, official initiatives keep downplaying the fact that in precolonial times slave dealing and slave holding were also an important part of Senegambian social life.[1]

As a matter-of-fact, the history of internal slavery and the slave trade predates the arrival of Portuguese sailors in the second half of the fifteenth century, and continued after Great Britain's first abolition of the slave trade in 1807. The end of slavery in The Gambia started only with the establishment of colonial rule in the later part of the nineteenth century. In 1894, parallel to the proclamation of the Protectorate of The Gambia, the British issued an ordinance against the slave trade, which gave enslaved men and women the possibility of buying their freedom and that of their relatives for the onerous fee of 10 £ for adults and 5£ for children; in 1906, this provision was extended to the eastern part of the country. In 1930, slavery was abolished definitively. Its social significance has survived though many groups today, both in Senegal and The Gambia, would like to be done with it.

The two sources presented in this chapter address the delicate issue of internal enslavement as much as the discrimination which throughout the twentieth century, and even today, have restrained the lives of Gambian slave descendants. Both speak of an area of the country, Badibu, which is particularly conservative on issues of slave ancestry. The first is an article published in a national newspaper in 2002, which comments on the Badibu custom of segregating slave descendants in a separate section of the cemetery. The second is an interview with Baba Suso, a Gambian griot—that is, a bard and oral historian; the interview was collected in 2008 by Alice Bellagamba and Bakary Sidibeh as part of a larger effort to track the legacy of slavery in contemporary Gambian culture. Baba Suso's narrative provides the background knowledge necessary to understand the conflicts between master and slave descendants which persisted in Badibu even after the legal abolition of slavery. It also points to the strategies that both social groups used to preserve mutuality and daily coexistence.

"People Are Not the Same!"

Sooner or later, any traveler to the Senegambia region will hear the phrase "People are not the same." This saying refers to the inclinations, thoughts, and desires of each human being but also to the diversity of social origins, as well as to different ways of interacting in social spaces.

Some of these differences are part of the colonial and postcolonial social stratification systems. There are those who are literate

164

and those who are not, people with white-collars jobs and others who toil in the fields. Some have enriched themselves by migrating and working in foreign countries. Others have never left their home villages. Each of these distinctions implies some sort of ranking. Civil servants and professionals, for instance, are socially on top of illiterate and rural Gambians. Then, and equally important, there are the social inequalities that come from the past. Some, although poor today, are the proud descendants of important precolonial leaders; some others are rich but their forefathers were slaves. There are also those who have a "caste" identity, like Baba Suso himself. This means that they descend from that part of the precolonial population consisting of professional endogamous groups, notably griots (or bards), blacksmiths, and leatherworkers.[2] In precolonial times, the distinction between freemen and bondmen intersected with the differences that separated noble and commoners, on the one hand, and members of artisan castes, on the other one. Artisans were free and could own slaves but ranked lower than the nobles and commoners who hired their services, and for whom they played the role of retainers. While some slaves were important as soldiers and as members of chiefly entourages and while others—especially those who were owned by the artisan castes—could learn the skills of their masters, the majority of slaves were employed in performing the much more arduous work of domestic chores and agricultural labor.[3]

When The Gambia, and some parts of Senegal, became peanut exporters in the middle of the nineteenth century, the demand for slave labor increased, and this, in turn, led to an expansion in internal slave dealing and slave holding. This process was linked to a series of religious conflicts that took place all over this part of West Africa from the middle of the century until the completion of colonial conquest which British sources called the Soninke-Marabout wars. The term *Soninke* refers to elite, sometimes pagan, but often lax Muslims who ruled most of Senegambia, and the term *Marabout* is used to describe the Muslim reformers and their followers.

In the early stages, Muslim leaders were concerned about protecting industrious Muslim peasants from pillaging by the slave soldiers, who served the various rulers. As they grew stronger, however, these slave soldiers took more and more of their own prisoners, whom they either incorporated as slaves into their entourages, or sold in exchange for muskets, gunpowder, horses, and provisions. As a result, on the eve of colonial conquest most areas of Senegambia had large slave populations, generally between 20 percent and 50 percent of the whole population. Although both the French and the British, as they took over, moved quickly to end slave raiding and slave trading, they were a little hesitant about attacking slavery itself, as they feared undercutting chiefs and local notables, who were indispensable allies in the administration. They did, however, refuse to return runaway slaves or to enforce slavery, giving the slaves an option. Slaves themselves, as a matter of fact, "were the most important agents in [their own] emancipation."[4]

Badibu and Slavery

Starting from the 1860s, Badibu, the region on the north bank of the Gambia River to which both of the sources featured in this chapter refer, was ravaged by the warring activities of Ma Ba Diakhou, a Muslim cleric and war leader, whose army, at a certain point, counted up to eleven thousand men.[5] The sociopolitical conflicts he ignited did not end with his death in 1867, as his successors and followers continued to fight and hence to produce captives, whom the Badibu Mandinka communities (villages like Kerewan, Sallikenye, and Saba) bought to meet their labor needs.

When the British took over in 1893, slavery was entrenched in the social life of the river. Chiefs and notables, who were the major slave owners, openly expressed their worries about abolition. Slaves, on their side, were looking forward to better living conditions. As soon as the slave trade was outlawed, and even before the 1894 ordinance, many of them left their masters. These were recently enslaved young men, mostly from the area south of the Gambia River, who had been acquired by Badibu traders in exchange for cattle and horses. While some of these young men returned home, others ran away from their masters and sought the protection of local chiefs, who were trying to increase the number of their dependants. Other slaves, especially those better integrated into their masters' communities, remained where they were. Colonial correspondence describes the latter category as "hereditary slaves," not first-generation slaves but men and women born into slavery.

Unable to acquire new slaves, as the slave trade had been halted, or to use force to retain their entourages (since colonial officials would free slaves who had been mistreated), masters were forced to gradually reduce their labor demands and exactions on slaves and slave descendants. They could not do otherwise, as the economy was heavily dependent on the competitive demand for manual labor for both the commercial groundnut cultivation sector and local use. This demand was intensified by the fact that only large households had the wherewithal to withstand famine, which in Badibu was a common occurrence. Renegotiations of bonds and rights between slaves and masters was a complex process that played out over several decades and involved a dramatic reduction of slaves' payments in kind or in labor.[6]

Despite these renegotiations, free men tried hard to maintain their higher status, often clinging to social distinctions even after the legal abolition of slavery and the disappearance of any economic differences between themselves and their former slaves. It is interesting to see, for instance, the kinds of strategy they used to increase the number of their slave retainers after the outlawing of the slave trade. Badibu was one of the first regions involved in the spread of commercial groundnut cultivation.[7] This meant that in addition to slaves, local communities used migrant laborers coming from as far as contemporary Mali, Guinea Conakry, and Guinea Bissau. In the first part of the twentieth century, migrants, who wanted to settle permanently, but could not demonstrate their free origins satisfactorily, were integrated into the ranks of the formerly enslaved. In addition, many of these immigrants, whether of free or slave ancestry, had no choice but to marry women of slave origins. Slave identity was matrilineally inherited, which means that

167

the children of these marriages are still today seen as descendants of slaves.

Marriage and religion remained the two most important battle grounds between slave and master descendants even when, by the late 1950s, slavery had lost all its economic significance and former slaves had only token obligations to their masters: a small payment to the masters and a few other services, like cooking during weddings and naming ceremonies, which they performed for compensation. With the spread of Islam in the course of the twentieth century, and with Islamic knowledge as a marker of social distinction, descendants of slaves sought religious education and became pious Muslims. In places like Kerewan, however, the stigma of their origins has remained. Our first document mentions that Kerewan slave descendants were buried until recently in a separate section of the cemetery. In other parts of the country, it has long been customary for the former master to pray on the graves of his/her "slaves" and to ask for forgiveness, so that their souls could rest in peace. In localities like Salikenye, the home village of Baba Suso, our second source, slave descendants were for a long time not allowed to sit in the front rows of the mosque. Even today it is difficult for them to become imams, except occasionally in an all-slave mosque. Some slave descendants, moreover, feel that for their pilgrimage to Mecca to be truly successful, they have to purchase their freedom within the traditional legal system, which, as Baba Suso explains in his narrative, has established a customary price for freedom of 66 dalasi.[8]

Our first document clearly emphasizes the role Islam can play as a force for liberation. In the aftermath of the colonial conquest, some Muslim religious fraternities helped slaves to find land and create new communities. In 2002, some Muslim leaders, critical of what they saw as the continuation of un-Islamic discriminatory local practices, encouraged their followers to consider all believers as equal in the eyes of God.[9]

An Article from a Gambian Newspaper

Religious Leaders Condemn Slave-Master System
The Independent (Banjul)[10]
January 25, 2002
By Momadou Bah
Banjul, The Gambia

Religious leaders across the country have unreservedly condemned the so-called slave and master system thought to be existing in Kerewan, where there was tension over who should be buried in the town's cemetery, which was being reserved for the so-called freeborn.

Describing such practice as unislamic and anti-civilization … with a deep rooted culture not only in the Gambia [but] also around Africa, the religious leaders asserted that so-called slave and master discrimination has been a socio-cultural belief that has its roots in history. They explained that because of this some people take it to be acceptable in religion. They added that this deeply rooted cultural belief has over the years led to a series of socio-cultural crises among people living together.

In an interview with *The Independent* the imam of state house mosque, Abdoulie Fatty, said that slavery had existed well before Islam and also alongside Islam but he noted that the type of slavery recommended and approved by Islam is when one refuses the call to Islam.

He added that our cultural way of acquiring slaves is not in line with Islam and therefore not recommended. He emphasized that all Muslims are equal before God and that the best Muslims are those who fear God the most. Imam Fatty warned against instigating violence, quoting a verse in the Quran which says that Satan is sleeping and that whoever wakes it will receive the curse of God. He also condemned the segregation of graveyards for so-called masters and their so-called slaves as unislamic and anti-civilization.

On his part the outspoken imam of Kaninfing mosque, Imam Baba Leigh, emphasized that Islam condemns anyone who treats his fellow human being as a slave. "In fact Islam has eradicated slavery using such a method like a freeborn marries a slave and delivers a child who is free." Imam Leigh said that segregating people in the graveyard is unfounded. He said that what is important is to fear God. He advised people to live together in a peaceful atmosphere and treat each other with love and affection and warned against segregating people at death. He also said what is important is to face God with good deeds in worship and God-fearing behavior. He finally called on Muslims to be tolerant and build mutual understanding and fraternity between them.

Sheikh Jibril Kujabi of the Tallinding Islamic Institute gave a historical account of Islamic ways of acquiring slaves and noted that it is only the Islamic way of acquiring slaves that is recommended. He explained that acquiring slaves during fighting a Jihad is legal; so is inheriting a slave captured in a Jihad or buying a slave captured during a Jihad. He warned that the other ways of regarding people as slaves is not Islamic and therefore cannot be accepted. Imam Kujabu asserted that there is nothing like segregation in Islam, citing the holy city of Medina where many slaves had lived together with Prophet Muhammad and his companions in peace without suffering discrimination as far as where they were buried were concerned. He further went on to say any aspect of culture that doesn't conform to Shari'a should be abandoned. He asserted that a Muslim is equal to all other Muslims. He warned people to desist from keeping slaves and segregating in graveyards. He added that burying the dead is an act of worship and that whoever takes part in it will be well regarded in the hereafter. Many other religious leaders expressed similar sentiments and appealed for tolerance, peace and understanding among Muslims and humanity in particular.

The Point of View of a Badibu Griot

The following narrative is the result of an interview that Alice Bellagamba and Bakary Sidibeh, former director of the National Council for Arts and Culture (the Gambian institution devoted to the preservation and promotion of the national cultural heritage), conducted in 2008 with Baba Suso, a griot and oral historian living in the capital city of The Gambia but hailing from Badibu. Like many other griots, Baba Suso migrated to the outskirts of the Gambian capital city, Banjul, in the course of the 1960s in order to attach himself to the new national elites of politicians, high civil servants, and professionals. For a good part of his life he earned a living by playing the kora—*the twenty-one-string lute typical of a Mandinka musician—and by offering his service as a mediator to the Banjul Badibu community. He was also involved in politics, first as a supporter of the People Progressive Party's (PPP)— which led the country to independence in 1965—and then of the National Convention Party, established by Sheriff Dibba, a politician from Baddibu, in 1975.*

By explaining the forms of discrimination against slave descendants, which he has witnessed in the course of his life, Baba Suso casts light on the resilience of the masters' supremacy. He also explains that slave descendants have used their social subordination as a strategy to carve out a niche in society. Baba Suso clearly illustrates the new hierarchies, based on education, wealth, access to the state, and to the international diaspora, which have emerged in colonial times and which today shape Gambian social life by ranking the literate over the illiterate, the civil servant or the professional over the rural farmer, the one who traveled over those who never went abroad. In this perspective, there is a linkage

171

*between the acceptance of slave ancestry—and of associated kinds
of discrimination—and poverty, lack of education, and a dearth of
opportunities. Slave descendants who have achieved a position in
the urban middle class, or who have enriched themselves by business or international migrations do not like to hear about the subordinate condition of their forefathers; neither is slavery a topic
to be openly discussed in public.*

I was born in Badibu Salikenye[11] originally. My mother was born
there but my father came from Wuli.[12] Anyway I know Badibu better than Wuli. Slave-master relationships used to be so formal in
Badibu that slaves and freemen did not live closely together. Even
at the village center, at the platform where men used to meet and
discuss, slave and freeman did not sit on the same platform.[13] The
former had to sit on a lower bench, which the freeman used to step
on to sit on the higher platform. They were not buried at the same
side of the cemetery. When you hear them say "take the body to
the left," it is a slave they are talking about. The cemetery was usually divided in the middle, the free on the right and the slave on
the left. Even when they prayed for the dead they placed them on
two different spots. When you hear somebody from Badibu saying
"This is our *korewo*," that means "dependant"; it is a slave descendant he/she is talking about.[14] Such forms of discrimination have
been common in Badibu until recently. Badibu Mandinka communities, apart from when they had to defend themselves from the attacks of the Wolofs, had no warriors who went to fight against
others and did not bring slaves back home. Their slaves were
bought. Normally people fought and captured slaves but most
Badibu slaves were bought. Slaves were generally given the surnames of their masters. This was to prevent them from identifying
themselves with their original surnames. For instance, they would
call a slave man Bakary Marong although his real name should
have been Bakary Fatty. When his relatives came to inquire
whether he was living there, they would usually ask for Bakary
Fatty. Then the reply would be: "We have a Bakary Marong here
and not Bakary Fatty!"[15] As you know, a man can resemble four

different others. He would resemble one man here and another one elsewhere. You would notice resemblance in both cases.

This practice of renaming the slaves has brought problems to Badibu today.[16] Recently, for instance, a large mosque was built in Kerewan, where, among the "slaves," there was an important old man. He had many wealthy children, but Kerewan "slaves" cannot pray in the first three rows of the mosque. So, when the old man prayed in one of these rows, they held him by the arm and told him "this is not your place to pray."

A Badibunka[17] fears a number of things, but he does not fear swearing by the Qur'an. A Badibunka would tell a lie and swear by the Qur'an, that is was true. But when a real Badibunka, that is a true son of the country, says something and forbids anyone from violating the agreement, no one dares to contradict that agreement.[18] "*Wulu-suwo*"[19]: do you know what that is? If I were your slave, and I—as a slave—bought my own slave out of my own toil, that bought slave was called *jong-ding-jongo*, meaning the grandson of an original slave. He later becomes a nephew within your lineage; that is what they call *wulu-suwo* in Mandinka. When the *wulo-suwo* insults someone, no one responds to that insult because he is considered to be "in the lowest of the law" [and not worth the effort of a reply]. No one in Badibu would insult the mother of such a man either as long as his mother was alive. They would prefer to be sent to prison themselves rather than cause him any suffering ...[20]

Q: *In Salikenye were you ever involved in a conflict with your ex-slaves?*

A: It happened. For instance, a conflict always developed when at a lineage meeting, a slave made a statement. Then, that person would be told to stop because the lineage meeting was not the place where their words were supposed to be heard. When you tell a person, "know yourself,"[21] it hurts that person. But he/she should realize who he/she is. Some people live until old age but fail to realize who they are even when they are told not to speak. If they

173

are not supposed to speak at a certain meeting, it is because of their lower status. It happened once to me, when I reprimanded a slave descendant. The man replied: "Do you call me a person of lower status?" I said, "Yes!" Then he continued: "I found your mother for your father and yet do you call me a person of lower status?" I replied: "I do not dispute that. That was what your father did for my grandfather.[22] That is what you are; it is your function."

We speak about some aspects but of others we are silent. That is history. Secondly, there is the question of spiritual leadership, notably the role of imam. In the mosque of Salikenye, announcements about communal services or compulsory services are never made.[23] In Fatajo Kunda, there is a small compound called Fatajo Kundaring.[24] Their elder was a very prosperous, prominent, and honest man. During Saikuba Dibba's[25] reign, he was asked to announce the demolition of a house. The family of Ceesay Kunda in which he belonged warned him not to mention the issue inside the mosque but to go outside. He did not want [to agree] but another man also asked him not to cause embarrassment. The man asked why he should not speak inside the mosque. The other man replied, "Because you belong to me." This statement caused a quarrel, which I cannot explain in details as his sons and grandsons live here. Some of them are my close friends; some others are fairly well off. If I explain that episode fully, even if you don't have a problem, I shall have a problem!

[Note: At this point in the interview, Baba Suso shifts from the description of the conflict to Badibu history, and he explains that the members of the Dibba family—to which Sheriff Dibba belongs—are not original settlers of Salikenye but Malian immigrants. In spite of this, they got the chieftainship in colonial times. It is interesting to compare Baba Suso's statement with what is found in a colonial report of 1931. This report states that "Sefo Karimu Diba Chaku ... he is the hereditary Headman of Salikeni, and enjoys the distinction of having been captured in his youth and sold as a slave, and subsequently freed."][26]

Badibu belongs to two people, namely, Kambi Jassi and Duta Juba Jassy. Kambi Jassi is at Suwarehkunda. There is a creek there called Kambi Creek. It was Jassi Marong who lived in the area. The Dibba [family] in Badibu do not belong to a royal family; they did not come from Mali with rulership. They were in search of their destiny; they did not come as rulers.

Q: *Did the quarrel we have just talked about result in a family conflict?*

A: It created a fight between the people. Different lineages and compounds opposed each other. They fought and during the fight more and more compounds joined in the fight. When a compound joined the fight, everybody got involved. Only the intervention of God and of good elders, who stood between the opponents, stopped the fighting. The elders who mediated said: "If any one crosses this line we shall deal with you." It was at a valley. Do you know that place? As you walk toward Salikenye mosque, there is a slope which divides Baduma and Basanto.[27] It marks the boundary between these two areas. When you cross it you go into the mosque. That was the line which was used to stop the two sides from reaching each other. Nonetheless, some marriages broke because of the fighting. Elders like Fasambojang Fatty, Falang Fatty, Jally Burama, Karamo Kanteh, [and] Fa Secka, who was a blacksmith, had to mediate to preserve the unions. These elders mediated between the conflicting families to end the dispute. I can't in fact tell the year it happened. It happened during Pierre Njie's period.[28] Other than that incident, the only conflict that occurred in Salikenye was between the families of Karum Chaku and the people of ChaKunda. It was a family quarrel between the Dibba. It was a conflict of succession, which was resolved through the intervention of two griots: namely Jally Burama and Wandifeng, who stopped the quarrel. What was the real cause of it? When you and I are both from a chiefly lineage, both of us would like to become chiefs of the same area. Each of us would meet different marabouts to seek prayers. When I gather people to campaign for my chieftaincy, you would approach some individuals so as to counter my authority, thereby causing many of them to defect to your side. When people come to me for information that you were the one going to different people to withdraw their support for me, eventually the fight would become open. They threatened each other; they did not take up weapons but after the threats, conflicts ignited between the two branches of the family and until now that fire is on. We know the families involved in this quarrel and no progress has materialized in those compounds. Saikuba Dibba was seeking chieftaincy. At that time, also Tapha Dibba, a prosperous businessman, was looking for office. In order to conquer support, he had given sixty-six donkeys to the villagers so that they could trade their groundnuts. Tapha was a generous man but Saikuba challenged him and became chief. Tapha could hardly bear it. Wherever Saikuba saw donkey dung with flies on top he would ask who owned the animal. They would say Tapha, and Saikuba would send a messenger to call him so that he would clean the dung. That was how Saikuba Dibba tormented Tapha. Tapha was Sheriff Dibba's father. The day Tapha was sentenced to imprisonment, he said to Saikuba Dibba: "I am going to prison but the day I come out of prison I shall find you a poor man and out of office. You shall not occupy the position." The day before Tapha was released, Saikuba was removed from chieftaincy. Their compounds were next to each other, so when Tapha came he stopped at Saikuba's gate and said to him what I told you has happened.... Saikuba Dibba died in Basse where he had moved after Tapha became the chief of Salikenye. When he attended Basse Chiefs conference [1956], Tapha went up to Saikuba to greet him. He told him Saikuba: "You prevented me from becoming chief but today I am the chief of Salikenye." Saikuba replied: "These three followers you brought along so that they could witness what you have told me; two of them are my slaves. But apart from you none of these people will be able to repeat what you have said."

Tapha and his followers returned to Mansakonko and spent the night there. The transport that was supposed to take them to Salikenye did not arrive. They took a boat to Balengo, where they disembarked. Two followers felt ill while they were on the boat. They did not arrive with the chief in his compound of Salikenye as they were supposed to. Instead, they were all taken to their own homes. One died that same day at midnight. While they were at the funeral, news of the death of the second one arrived. As Saikuba said, they would not relate what Tapha Dibba had said to him at Basse. Two of them, Tapha and another were freemen; the other two were slaves. Saikuba had predicted that the two slaves would never discuss with anybody what Tapha had said and so it happened.[29]

Q: *Who were the mediators who intervened in the first quarrel? Were they the only official mediators of the village?*

A: Before the elders were involved in mediation, the family griots and the leather workers had tried. Griots and leatherworkers were traditional mediators but when colonialism took over, only the leatherworkers kept this tradition. Then, those people who spent money on marabouts asked to become mediators.[30] This is how Jally Burama took over the position of mediator. He was one of those men who spent hundreds of dalasi to strengthen themselves spiritually. He became very influential. He used to say to people in conflict with one another: "I have come to you. Do you know what I am and what I represent? I know who you are. You used to open your shop or open your box and give me money. Now I do not require that; I wish to conquer what is in your heart." He always went spiritually well prepared, like a thief or a burglar prepared before an act. That was what griots also used to do. They tell you what you should do, and then you give them whatever they ask.

Q: *Let us go to Saba; what is the relationship there with regards to slavery?*

A: Slavery in Saba is more prominent than anywhere else in Badibu. Nothing has changed there. Elders have tried to preserve the custom of sharing the bride wealth which is due to "slaves" at the time of marriage. Youths have abandoned this custom, but the elders—who are the fathers[31]—still respect this custom. In Saba when you seek a wife from certain compounds, you have to provide the share of the bride wealth to the slaves. They call this share *fufalto*. Even if the marriage is broken, this part of the bride wealth is not refundable as it is for the slaves to consume.

The *fufalto* is different from what is commonly given to the brothers of the bride. The *fulfalto* is given to the other members of the family and the cross-cousins (who are also called slaves) when the bride is carried to the bridegroom's compound and during the consummation of marriage....[32] When the bride is taken at the husband's home, early in the morning cross-cousins bring warm water and knock at her door.

Q: *Which families in Saba owned slaves?*

A: Signateh, Makalow, Kamaso: those are the families which created a division in their cemetery. The side on the left as you walk toward the rice fields belongs to the slaves. On the right side are the tombs of the freemen. The situation still exists in Saba but the cemetery no longer retains the division. They now bury all the dead in the same area without discrimination. They have taken this decision because now land is becoming very scarce and some of the slaves, moreover, were married to freemen. According to Islamic law, when you find it difficult to find a wife among your own peers you can marry your slave. Some of these women were freed with sixty-six dalasi; you provide sixty-six dalasi for the back of the woman and sixty-six for the front and then you wash her to be free.[33] The back represents the fathers and the front the mothers.

Q: *In the old days, did the food and shelter of slaves differ from that of the masters? Did they live in separate compounds?*

A: Slaves lived with their masters as today maids are kept in compounds. That is why when the daughters of the masters went to live with their husbands; each was given a slave girl to live with her and to attend to her when she was cooking. The male slaves were kept in the compounds to farm for the master. If I were your slave,

my sons would farm for you. I would wait for you under the ve-
randa, you would issue orders, and I would carry them out. I would
wait for food to be prepared, breakfast and lunch, and take it to the
farm. My wives would be the cooks and your wives would dish it
out for the different parts of the family when the food is ready.[34]

Q: *During the regime of President Jawara, between 1970 and
1994, was there any land conflict between slaves and masters?*[35]
Were you aware of this?

A: I have heard about these litigations but the details are not clear
to me. The little I know about it is that they quarreled over land,
but I am not sure of what was said or done about the land issue.
Some say the land was originally obtained as a compensation for
a slave marriage. Let me explain. If people approach you, and you
are asked for the hand of your slave maiden so that she would be
married to a very loyal male slave or another man, in that case you
may decide not to ask money for your slave's bride wealth but land.
Then, you might give the land to the slave woman and say: "Make
a living out of it!" Some said that the grandfather of those who
presently own the land had a slave woman who was with him when
he was old and slow in movement, and that this man gave the piece
of land to that woman by saying, "Take this land to live."

Q: *Who demanded the land back, the master or the slave descendants?*

A: The grandchildren of the former master asked for the land to be
returned to them. They had been told that the land between their
farmlands and those of ex-slaves formally belonged to them. They
wondered why it came under the control of the ex-slaves, but I am
not sure about the details.

Q: *Was not the Conteh family involved in this dispute?*

A: This happened recently during the Jawara regime. The trouble was between the villages of Contehkunda N'jii and Contehkunda Sokoto. Sarbege Conteh and others were all slaves. In those days, nobody was rich like Sarbege Conteh. He was the man who bought a brand-new Ford truck and two new Bedford lorries! He put the rest of the money he carried back into his purse. Sarbege was in Contekunda N'jii; the meaning of N'jii is "Let us breathe!" as the elders had decided to move out of Contehkunda Sokoto to have more space to live. The whole village was made of slaves. Alhagie Seedy Conteh and Alhagie Julanding also lived in Contehkunda N'jii. The cause of the dispute was farmland, as they and their farmlands belonged to their masters. I will give an example. If I were your slave, you have your children and I am a grown-up man. We, I and my younger brothers, clear a farmland for you. Then we name that area after you. We also decide to clear another piece of land which we call *dingkunda*.[36] It is a tradition to establish a compound house called *dingkunda*. This is a social arrangement to provide for the "children" of the society. This farm called *dingkunda* brought about the dispute. The farm cleared for *dingkunda* became the source of all trouble. The people who cleared that area, that is, the slaves, had no strong descendants. The children they had were too young to fend for themselves, while the youths on the side of the masters were old enough and prosperous. The master's descendants began to migrate to Sierra Leone to better their lives and trade. Then migration to Europe began, and they also joined that flow. In the meantime, the children of the slaves had grown up and demanded the use of their land saying, "These are our fields!" The land which the masters cultivated was no longer fertile but the field that belonged to the slave, the *dingkunda*, was still fresh. So the slave descendants cleared it with the intention of starting cultivation. A serious dispute erupted and during the course of it some very unpleasant remarks were made, like "You, dirty slaves! What do you think of yourselves?" The elder of the slaves was sure he was socially and spiritually stronger than the elder of the master. So, he reacted to the insult and said that he would tie up the other elder when he met him. It became a fight between these two elders, and some people also lost their lives in the course of the fight. They shouted at each other and because of the fight they did not farm that year. Government sent some members of the National Guard who camped between the two villages until the end of the rainy season.

Q: *What happened afterward?*

A: The case was taken to a joint district tribunal.[37] They invited the famous and knowledgeable then retired district chief Mama Tamba Jammeh.[38] He came and told them what he thought about the case: "they and the land are both property of their masters, but the marabouts have already worked on the mind of chief Abou Khan, who was part of the joint district tribunal."[39] Eventually Abou Khan died.[40] They told Abou Khan: "Have you heard what Tamba has said?" Abou replied, "This man is finished; I don't accept his verdict!" Tamba asked: "Do you mean that my life is going to an end? I thought it was yours that would end." Abou left the court case and went back to Kuntaya where he died two or three days later. There were strong men in the past....

The man I mentioned earlier, Sarbege Conteh, was very wealthy. Now, Sheikh Sarbege, his son, is the head of the Conteh family and lives here, on the outskirts of the capital city. His real name is Jatta Conteh. Another son of Sarbege Conteh, Maa Conteh, is here too. God was very good with Sarbege Conteh. He had so much money that during the day he spread it out to dry; otherwise, the banknotes would be stuck together.

Let me tell you about the first incident at Contehkunda. As I have learned, an old man sat in the front row of the mosque, an elder who lived just nearby and used to be very wealthy, learned, and eloquent. He was highly respected; he had many children and daughters who were married to prosperous men. Though he was of slave ancestry, when he was going out he wore clothes that many freeborn could not afford. One day he stood in the front row of the mosque. They pulled him by his clothes and told to him: "This is not your position to stand; that is your place." But some people objected to this harsh treatment and did not agree on the fact that

181

slaves should not be allowed to pray in the front rows. The words spread and again a serious conflict erupted; they even fought. The matter could have become a police case if not for the intervention of Alhagie Jawara.[41] He actually put his hands into the affairs by sending men there to mediate.

He generously persuaded elders to intervene secretly and the police to withdraw from the case so that it could be solved. Socially, Alhagie never let it be known that he financed the settlement of the case; he hated publicity. Have you ever heard any griot praising him? When I got sick, I used to send people to inform him that I could not come to visit him because I was not well and he used to send me one thousand dalasis. When Alhagie Lalor Fatty died, whose daughter was married to him, the amount of money he spent for the funeral was enormous. So, the conflict began but thanks to his intervention it did not gain momentum.

A man called Alhaji Madi Ceesay was living in Foni Brefet. I was his first Quranic student. He lived there for more than ten years. He had several sons. In the village where he lived, there was a man acting as temporary imam, after the death of the imam himself. This was called Almamy Ceesay and was a slave descendant; his father was a freeman and his mother a slave. But youths did not know and although the man himself might have known, he did not speak about it. Without being aware of it, the father had married a woman of slave ancestry. As you know, the child of a slave woman inherits his mother's status, and the children of my slave's wife belong to me. The man was leading prayers in the mosque and the people asked another learned scholar, Alhagie Malick, to express his opinion on what was going on. When this happened, Almamy Ceesay asked: "Are you not satisfied with my leadership? Alhaji Malick knows me, and when the messenger was leaving to call him I gave him a letter." In that letter, Almamy Ceesay had raised a number of questions and Alhaji Malick replied back by letter. Alhaji Malick wrote back that he was very happy to hear about the imamship of his friend but that unfortunately he had to reveal him that he was not pure. It is only the freeborn who are appointed to lead as imam of a mosque. Alhaji Malik then explained to his friend and companion Almamy Ceesay his true origins: "It was from this compound that your mother hailed!" The matter created some noise but it didn't last long. What happened was provoked by the request of information the people made. Then they asked another man to come and lead prayers but this caused even more confusion, as Almamy Ceesay, the man of slave ancestry, continued to serve as deputy imam, and he was not only older but more learned than the new imam they had appointed.

Q: *What are the relationships between slave and master descendants today?*

A: They interact with mutual respect and consideration, through the difference is kept hidden. When they quarrel, it is difficult to control the situation because of the barrier which divides them. That barrier is that people expect each other to know their position and to act within its boundaries. Once, it happened to me in our compound. In the old days, when a child was born, his father's younger brother assigned a slave to him. I also had one. The son of this man [my former slave] is in Congo.[42] The son sent him money to go on pilgrimage to Mecca. I did not know much about this custom. This man [my former slave] told Alhagie Saiko that his son had sent money to go on pilgrimage but that he wanted to be washed.[43] The people said they could not free him; he had to come to me, in Banjul, as I was his master and I was supposed to wash him. Thus, he came and he asked me to perform the freeing ceremony. I did not know what to do. In those days, the father of Solo Darboe had a bus which ran between Banjul and Wuli. The man asked me to write a letter to my brothers at the village to inform them I could make the rite. It was difficult as at the time there was no one who could read English or Arabic. The letter was written in Arabic and somehow they managed to read it. In the end, I washed him for sixty-six dalasi. His relatives wanted to know why I did not ask for six thousand dalasis, and I replied that the customary practice is sixty-six dalasi.

One of his relatives just passed to visit me yesterday. I gave him a hundred-dalasi note but he complained that I had not taken into account the fare he paid to come and see me. He had traveled all the way from Lamin to this area, and according to him I was responsible also for his fare. I asked him how much it was and, as he replied three hundred dalasi, I added another two hundred dalasi to the hundred I had already given him. That is why slaves refuse to put an end to the institution of slavery. Masters would like to end it. At times, we see that slaves have beautiful daughters but if we ask them in marriage they tell us: "You are not supposed to marry this one!"[44]

Q: *When did politics enter this kind of conflict between slaves and masters? How did it work out at the time when the People's Progressive Party was talking about "one man, one vote?"*

A: When politics entered into our social life, those slaves who already resisted the idea of following their master all joined the People's Progressive Party, which at the time was called the Protectorate People's Party. If the master became a member of the People's Progressive Party and the slave chose to join the United Party this ended up in a fight. They could even take your farmland from you. They would say you could cultivate their land as you did not follow their political advice. There were many of these examples.

Q: *Those who were chosen for political leadership, like party chairman, secretary, mobilizer— were they slaves or the freemen?*

A: This is an interesting point. If you are observant, you would see that the leadership of a political branch as much as youth's leadership went either to the nephew of lineage head or to a foreigner or sometimes even a slave. Badibunka were reluctant to accept such kind of leadership. Now this is changing because of monetary benefits. People have realized that political leaders enjoy and participate in government. But in those days, they gave the leadership to slaves or other juniors of the lineage for the love they had either for the party or for the political candidate. They would say like this: "Because of our love for you, let us confer leadership to those who have the time and inclination for politics." Then the person, who answered their call at that moment, while you are present, he/she would get the leadership. They would give you a slave or another dependent but they think: "No, my own Lamin, no, no, no!" They would see politics as their direct concern.

Q: *Badibunka were among the first Gambian people to travel abroad. How did migration relate to slave ancestry?*

A: The Badibunka observed that the Serrahule were traveling to Sierra Leone to trade and followed them.[45] Serrahule were also going to Kiang and Senegal. They mostly traded in tobacco, incense, sweets, and cloth. In Sierra Leone, they also started to dig diamonds. Badibunka also joined this venture. When the masters went they often took a slave with them who was close in terms of age and friendship. If I want, I could invite a slave who was a friend of mine. I would tell him: "I want to go to Sierra Leone; would you come with me?" While going, he would carry both his bag and mine. In Sierra Leone, slaves were often successful where the freeman failed. That was why many freemen stayed in Sierra Leone. To travel with your slave and fail to succeed was the reason why many freemen never returned. Some masters who had money invited their slaves to come back with them. The slave would agree to return even if he did not succeed but the master could not tolerate the idea of going back along with a successful slave.

Q: *Who is richer in Badibu today, the slave or the master?*

A: In Badibu today, there are more rich slave descendants than freemen. By principle, hardworking people are always rewarded. The hardship that the grandparents and parents of slaves endured was rewarded by God. The grandparents of these people worked on the masters' farms and in their households. This is why God rewarded them. The balance between slave and master has changed today. Everyone will agree that the richest man of Badibu is Alhaji Jarawa and he is from slave origins.

Q: *Of those who have migrated to the capital city and surroundings, who do you think is more prosperous, the slave or the master?*

A: The slave is more prosperous than the freeman. Those free lineages that used to have twelve households now have three to four households, but the number of slave descendants increases all the time. Now we say to them: "You breed like frogs!" Things have changed; only God controls these changes. Within my own lineage today the only ones alive are myself, Karunka, Kaw, Soriba, Kebba, and Modou, but our slaves are countless and their children are more prosperous and progressive than ours.

Among our children today, one returned from abroad, fairly successful but they killed him. You must have heard about a young man who was stoned to death in his Benz car.... When he came, he gave us tickets to go to Mecca. He then asked us to wait for him. When he was about to come he was hit and his skull was broken. It happened three years ago. He was our elder brother's son. The murderer escaped and left the country. Today our family's hope is Jerreh. He built our compound in Lamin; also his elder brother who is in Freetown had started building a compound but the owner of the compound sold it before it was finished. I may be able to show you that compound one day. Jerreh managed to get empty land. A European woman helped him to join a football association in Europe and it was through this that he has been able to build the compound.

Today, parents should pray to God to grant a better future for their children and that is the only thing left for us to do.

Q: *Considering things that have taken place, why have the people not abolished slavery completely with all its stigma?*

A: Some people are ready to abolish it completely but some of the slave descendants are not willing to do so. If they agree to slavery being ended, then it should be ended but they do not want it to end. Some would like it to be wiped out completely but others do not wish to end it. Some people do not even want to hear the word slavery, even some freemen, if you refer to a person as a slave he would reply, "Please stop that sort of thing!" It is a thing of the past but at the same place, there slave descendants would call themselves as slaves and other people as their master; that is the problem.

Notes

1. Alice Bellagamba, "Reasons for Silence: Following the Inner Legacy of Slavery and the Slave Trade in the Contemporary Gambia," in *Politics of Memory: Making Slavery Visible in the Public Space*, ed. Ana Lucia Araujo (London: Routledge, 2012), 35-53; Bellagamba, "Back to the Land of Roots: African American Tourism and the Cultural Heritage of the River Gambia," *Cahiers d'études Africaines* 193-94, n.s. 1-2 (2009): 453-76.

2. There is a debate in Senegal on the persistence of old status-distinctions (and of "caste" in particular) and their interlacement with twentieth- and twenty-first-century social hierarchies and inequality. Penda Mbow, "Démocratie, droits humains et castes au Sénégal," *Journal des Africanistes* 70, nos. 1-2 (2000): 71-91; Abderrahmane N'Gaïde, "Stéréotypes et imaginaires sociaux en milieu haalpulaar: Classer, stigmatiser et toiser," *Cahiers d'études Africaines* 172, no. 4 (2003): 707-38; Roy Dilley, *Islamic and Caste Knowledge Practices among Haalpulaar'en in Senegal: Between Mosque and Termite Mound* (Edinburgh, Scotland: International African Institute, 2004); Beth A. Buggenhagen, *Muslim Families in Global Senegal: Money Takes Care of Shame* (Bloomington: Indiana University Press, 2012).

3. James Searing, *God Alone Is King: Islam and Emancipation in Senegal* (London: James Currey, 2002) and Sean Hanretta, *Islam and Social Change in French West Africa* (Cambridge: Cambridge University Press, 2009) look at the interplay of caste and slavery after abolition, and comment on the fact that freed slaves and slave descendants were turned into a sort of "pseudo-caste." Evidence from Baddibu and the north bank of the Gambia River point to the same conclusion. See National Archives of the Gambia, Bathurst, NGR1/19, Dr. Gamble's file on Slavery (previously CSO 76/19), 106-9.

4. Trevor Getz, *Slavery and Reform in West Africa: Toward Emancipation in Nineteenth-Century Senegal and Gold Coast* (Oxford: James Currey, 2004), XIV; Martin A. Klein, *Slavery and Colonial Rule in French West Africa* (Cambridge: Cambridge University Press, 1998).

5. John M. Gray, *History of The Gambia* (London: Frank Cass, 1966);

Charlotte Quinn, *Mandinko Kingdoms of the Senegambia: Tradition-alism, Islam and European Expansion* (Evanston, IL: Northwestern University Press, 1972); Klein, *Islam and Imperialism in Senegal: Sine-Saloum 1847-1914* (Stanford, CA: Stanford University Press, 1968), chap. 3; Klein, "Ma Ba ou la résistance forcé à la conquête Française en Sénégambie," in *Les Africains*, eds. Charles-André Ju-lien, et al., vol. 5 (Paris: Editions Jeune Afrique, 1977), 171-203.

6. P. Weil, "Slavery, Groundnuts, and European Capitalism in the Senegambia Kingdom of Wuli, 1820-1930," *Research in Economic Anthropology* (1984): 77-119.

7. K. Swindell and A. Jeng, *Migrants, Credit and Climate: The Gam-bian Groundnut Trade, 1834-1934* (Leiden, Netherlands: Brill, 2006).

8. The dalasi is the currency which The Gambia created in 1971, after having become a Presidential Republic in 1970. When Bellagamba started research in The Gambia, in 1992, $1.00 was worth 9 dalasi; today, $1.00 is exchanged at about 30 dalasi.

9. Searing, *God Alone Is King*; Sean Hanretta, *Islam and Social Change*. On Islam and the end of slavery in Sahelian Africa, see also Benjamin F. Soares, *Islam and the Prayer Economy: History and Authority in a Malian Town* (Edinburgh, Scotland: Edimburgh Uni-versity Press, 2005); Roger Botte, *Esclavage et abolition en terre d'Islam* (Paris: André Versaille, 2010); Brian Peterson, *Islamization from Below: The Making of Muslim Communities in Rural French Sudan, 1880-1960* (New Haven, CT: Yale University Press, 2011).

10. Established in 1999, *The Independent*—which was one of the most important non-government newspapers of the second Republic of The Gambia—was closed in 2006, after its journalists had suffered repeated attacks from government supporters and security forces.

11. One of Badibu's historical villages. In colonial times, Salikenye was a prosperous and populous community.

12. Wuli was an important precolonial polity of the Upper Gambia, which was crossed by trade routes linking the mouth of the river to the interior of contemporary eastern Senegal and Mali. Winnifred Galloway, "A History of Wuli from theThirteenth to the Nineteenth Century" (Ph.D. diss., University of Indiana, 1975).

13. This is the Mandinka *bantaba*, a large bench usually roofed or lo-cated under the shade of a big tree, where men used to meet and talk.

14. There are many ways to talk about slavery without mentioning it di-rectly. *Korewo* is one of the polite expressions, like *komakaa*, those who are in the back. Slaves had to play the role of supporters, while leadership was in the past considered to be a prerogative of freemen.

Other expressions are harsher, like "black ear" or "nine, never ten." The latter refers to the fact that the slave or descendants of slaves will never be complete social beings, and is documented in other parts of Sahelian Africa. See Claude Meillassoux, "État et conditions des esclaves à Gumbu (Mali) au XIX siècle," in *L'Esclavage en Afrique precoloniale*, ed. Claude Meillassoux (Paris: Maspero, 1975), 230-31.

15. Communities of the river Gambia used to change slaves' names in order to efface old identities. Badibu, moreover, was crossed by the main trade route linking the mouth of the Gambia River to the interior of Senegal and Mali. Badibu masters, as Bamba Suso tries to explain, did not want travelers to know the original surnames of their slaves as news easily spread along trade routes. It could always happen, and indeed it happened according to other oral narratives, that travelers looked for enslaved relatives in the communities they crossed. Surnames and genealogical information were, and are, one of the ways to identify people and their places of origin.

16. As slaves had the same surnames as their masters, after the end of slavery, it became difficult to distinguish those who were of free ancestry from those who were not within the same lineage.

17. Badibunka, or men or women from Badibu.

18. This means that Badibunka are very strict about the rules of their coexistence.

19. Literally, "born in the house." This term refers to second-generation or "hereditary" slaves, and, after the end of the slave trade, to all slaves in general, as first-generation ones disappeared.

20. When people are annoyed, they commonly insult each other by referring to their mothers' negative qualities. Baba Suso is saying that this is not done in the case of the *wulo-suwo*, as it would mean referring to the enslaved condition of his or her mother, and therefore also to her lack of honor. This would provoke psychological suffering which is considered too extreme. It also means that after the end of slavery, relationships between slave and master descendants have been ruled by quite strict norms about what should or should not be said about slave descendants.

21. This is a very common Gambian way to put people in their place, when they transgress the conventional boundaries of social interaction.

22. The father of the man, following the request of Baba Suso's grandfather, found a wife for his father. Parents arrange the marriages of their children, and they use intermediaries to identify proper candidates and present their request to the bride's family. People of slave

ancestry and artisans often do this kind of errand.

23. Making public announcements on behalf of the chief, the elders or state authorities is the responsibility of "slave" griots, namely griots whose forefathers were owned by griots' families.

24. Literally, "small Fatajo."

25. One of the colonial chiefs of Salikenye, the home village of Baba Suso.

26. National Archives of the Gambia, Bathurst, NGR1/19, Dr. Gamble's file on slavery (previously CSO 76/19, 79).

27. These are separate wards in the village of Salikenye.

28. Lawyer and leader of the United Party (one of the parties which were established in late colonial times), Pierre Sarr N'Jie was head of the United Party and chief minister of The Gambia from March 1961 to June 12, 1962. The period Baba Suso refers to was an epoch of rapid changes, when different groups questioned the customary social setup of rural society and the hierarchies consolidated in colonial times.

29. There is an understatement in this sentence. Masters could curse their slaves. The major obligation of slaves after the legal abolition of slavery remained that of respecting masters and not to withdraw their support. By following Tapha, the two men had betrayed Saikuba, who in turn revenged himself.

30. Baba Suso refers to men who invest in spiritual means and prayers provided by religious specialists (the marabouts) so as to strengthen their social influence. People respect them as they fear spiritual retaliation. In the narrative, Baba Suso explains that there are spiritual ways to prepare yourself when you need to convince people so that they would not refuse what you ask.

31. "Fathers" and "children" are a generational partition, which also sustains village organization. While the "fathers" are alive, the "children" are not supposed to interfere or to change things even if they are in their sixties.

32. Cross-cousins, that is, cousins from a parent's opposite-sexed sibling, have a joking relationship which allows them to tease each other "as slaves." Cross-cousins also perform some of the roles that in the marriage ritual would typically be performed by slaves. They cook, they fetch the firewood, and they also accompany the bride to the bridegroom and wait for the "first night" of marriage to be over. This kind of "slavery"—always called *jonyaa* in Mandinka—is considered to be different from the real one. But it also true that during the marriage ceremony cross-cousins, and slave descendants, join together to do the same things. What the cross-cousins are doing is a sort of living

memory of the important roles which in the past slaves, and particularly slaves born in their masters' household, performed in the ritual life of their masters. On Mandinka marriage ceremonies, see Ed Van Hoven, *L'oncle maternel est roi: La formation d'alliances hiérarchiques chez les Mandingues du Wuli (Sénégal)* (Leiden, Netherlands: CNWS Publications 36, 1995).

33. When the dalasi was introduced in 1971, it was worth about 5 Gambian pounds. This means that 66 dalasi roughly corresponded to the 10 British pounds established by the British for the freeing of slaves in 1894. Today, $1.00 is exchanged at about 30 dalasi; the price for freedom is therefore a little bit more than $2.00 (in U.S. currrency), even if some give a different interpretation of this requirement, notably that you have to multiply everything you bring to your master to ask for your freedom by 66, notably 66 kola-nuts, 66 sheep, and so forth. See the earlier reference to the value of dalasi.

34. It is interesting to note that while slave women cooked, free ones would apportion the food, and carefully supervise its distribution, so that each part of the family would get its share. The first and most important bowl was that of the family head, who often ate with friends or some of his retainers, trustworthy slaves included. Women and children would eat together. Elderly people, who could not move from their houses, would be provided with a separate bowl as would visitors. Family strangers would have their share as well as those busy working on the fields.

35. Jawara was the first president of The Gambia and the conflict we asked Baba Suso about took place in the early 1980s. Two villages, Contehkunda Sukoto and Contehkunda N'jii, the first belonging to former masters and the second to slave descendants, fought over a piece of land. The events are described in Bellagamba, "'Silence Is Medicine!' Ending Slavery and Promoting Social Coexistence in Post-Abolition Gambia," in *The Problem of Violence. Local Conflict Settlement in Contemporary Africa*, eds. Georg Klute and Birgit Embaló (Cologne, Germany: Köppe Verlag, 2012), 445-76.

36. Literally, "the small compound home." This was usually either a compound or a farmland for the juniors members of the family, like youths and of course slaves and slave descendants.

37. This is a court held by several district chiefs.

38. A very famous colonial chief, who stayed in office for long time. When the events took place he had retired but still he was consulted because of his knowledge of local history and customs.

39. Going to marabouts to influence the judgment of the court is a very common practice even today.

40. The Seyfo is the district chief.
41. The surname Jawara, who was one of the first presidents of The Gambia, Dawda Jawara, is quite common not only among the Mandinka but also the Serrahule. Here, Baba Suso refers to an influential elder from Badibu.
42. Over the years, many Senegambians have gone to the Congo to earn money.
43. The customary freeing of slave descendants consists of a ceremony of purification, which Baba Suso partially described before when talking about slave women and the freedom price of 66 dalasi. During the ceremony the slave descendant is washed, so as to wipe away the impurity of slavery. David Gamble witnessed such event in Niani during the late 1940s. David Gamble and A. K. Rahman, *Mandinka Ceremonies*, Gambian Studies n. 34 (Brisbane: University of California, 1998), 77-79.
44. One of the factors which, in colonial times, broke down slave-master relationships was masters' unwillingness to be economically responsible for their slaves, as customarily had been the case. Baba Suso asserts this point and explains that there is some economic advantage in claiming slave ancestry, as one is allowed to beg. Given the extremely difficult living conditions of colonial and postcolonial Gambia, the possibility of demanding help or money from master descendants is an advantage that has persuaded some to embrace the stigma of their slave status in order to secure social support. The comment about marriage is interesting as well. Actually, freemen can marry women of slave ancestry, but as a sort of revenge for the fact that slaves cannot marry freemen; people of slave ancestry often prefer to give their daughters either to foreigners settling in the country or to men of the same social condition. They might also fear that their daughters would suffer humiliation in the compound of a freeman.
45. The Serrahule, known elsewhere as Soninke, have a long tradition of trade and were among the first Senegambians to engage in labor migration in other African countries and in Europe. François Manchuelle, *Willing Migrants. Soninke Labour Diaspora* (Athens, Ohio, and London: Ohio University Press, James Currey, 1997).

10. Memories of Slavery and the Slave Trade from Futa Toro, Northern Senegal

MAKHROUFI OUSMANE TRAORÉ

Introduction

Futa Toro is situated on the south bank of the Senegal River.[1] It is an area in which millet and rice are grown and lies between the desertic Ferlo of Central Senegal, where a short rainy season makes agriculture difficult, and the sand dunes and dry plateaus of Mauritania. Futa Toro residents claim descent from Tekrur, a province of the medieval Ghana empire, whose ruler converted to Islam in the eleventh century. The name of the principal inhabitants of Futa Toro, the Tokolor, comes from the term *Tekrur*. Between 1776 and 1781, a group led by Muslim clerics called *torodbe*[2] drove out their previous rulers and formed a strongly Muslim regime.[3] After the successful jihad, the religious leader of the movement, Sulayman Baal, was invited to become chief. He refused the offer and suggested that Abdel Kader, the military leader of the jihad, be offered the position.[4]

In April 2007, I did interviews in this former kingdom of Futa Toro, in Golléré, a village of around twenty-seven hundred people in the department of Podor. My informants were two descendants of slaves, Kalidu Diallo (b. 1934)[5] and Amadu Tidiane Sow (b.1950).[6] I also interviewed two nobles, Bocara Dème (b. 1913),[7] and Samba Bubu who was eighty-five at the time of our conversations. Interviewed separately and together, these four men were chosen with the main objective of describing and analyzing Futa Toro social stratification and its inequalities. My goal was to give

193

voice to slave descendants and to describe how they stand within the system of social stratification, how they view past forms of enslavement, and how they feel about discrimination associated with slave ancestry today. By comparing the testimony of nobles with men of slave descent, I sought to analyze how dominant social groups manipulate the overall representation of the Futa Toro social order, by obscuring certain historical facts like the connection between Futa Toro Islamic leadership and the Atlantic slave trade. In the set of interviews presented here, Kalidu Diallo, Amadu Tidiane Sow, Bocara Dème, and Samba Bubu focused on the late nineteenth century, when the slave trade was between African slavers and African slave users. They all also told tales of the eighteenth-century slave trade and relations between Futa Toro slavers and the French, which remain vivid in the social memory.[8] By following these recollections, researchers can cast light on how slavery and the slave trade are remembered in present-day village collective memory.[9]

Society, Slavery, and Enslavement in Futa Toro

As in many other West African societies, the three unequal social strata of precolonial Futa Toro, nobles, artisans, and slaves, are significant today in spite of the political, social, and economic changes which have taken place since French conquest in 1891. Social inequality reinforced the social and political hegemony of the dominant social groups, and for the purpose of this chapter, it helps us to better understand the history of domestic slavery and the slave trade in the contemporary collective memory of Futa Toro's people. In this part of the Senegambia, Islam became religiously and politically dominant in the course of the eleventh century. When in the late eighteenth century the Futa Toro's rulers were supplanted by new theocratic elites, Islam turned into a tool of state construction, one which the new rulers used to legitimize and reinforce inequality. Some one hundred years before the emergence of this new theocratic elite, between 1673 and 1677, a Mauritanian marabout named Nasr el-Din mobilized populations across northern Senegal and southern Mauritania, who had been victimized by slave raiders and attacked traditional aristocracies who had failed to protect them. The profound dichotomy between the powerful and the powerless created by the slave trade in the Wolof, Pular-speaking, and Sereer states stimulated this movement, which briefly controlled most of northern Senegal. Resistance to slave raiders was also a factor in the eithteenth century *torodbe* revolution of 1776, but once in power, the *torodbe* opposed neither slavery—a part of the social structure—nor the enslavement of others.[10] Instead, they used Islam to justify slave holding and slave dealing by claiming the right to subjugate those who had not yet converted. Islam as a religious ideology thus served political power. Though the *torodbe* revolution triumphed in the name of militant Islam, it never ended the segregationist dichotomy characterizing inegalitarian social structures. The ideology of Islam has confirmed the low status and contempt in which lower social groups are held by Futa Toro maraboutic and aristocratic elites and has reinforced their political and economic power. Today, memories of slavery linger in Futa Toro society and shape its internal social and political relations, as much as the behavior of both master and slave descendants. Slave ancestry is stigmatized, and slave descendants' access to land (the most important resource in Futa Toro) is mediated by the clientelist relationships they have developed with their former masters since the legal abolition of slavery.[11]

Histories Remembered by Enslaved Descendants

As a general rule, it is unusual for members of low-status groups in Senegal to make remarks that betray a consciousness of the social inequalities on which society and its social stratification are built. This kind of restraint is even stronger in rural and conservative areas like Futa Toro where many descendants of slaves censor what they say about slavery in front of nobles. When someone is able to talk openly, like Kalidu Diallo did during our 2007 conversations, it is indeed a rare and precious occasion:

The slave trade is a very delicate subject.... No torodbe will admit that an Almamy [*a common Muslim title used by rulers of the* torodbe *regime*] exchanged slaves with Europeans for arms or with Moors for horses.... The Almamies submitted to the Europeans. They were not there for the people, but rather for the whites, with whom they cooperated and whose directives they enforced. They did not openly sell slaves because it was contrary to their temporal and spiritual mission. They were supposed to provide the people with security and protection.... However, they used subterfuges to sell slaves to the whites and the Moors.... By contrast, Almamy Eliman Boubacar Ciré was a wise man, a sage, a man of great learning....According to my father, he was a man of great stature... who treated us [*the slaves*] generously and in whose reign the slaves began to learn the Quran.

This important testimony draws our attention to two historical details that are worth highlighting. First of all, Kalidu Diallo states that Boubacar Ciré was a nineteenth-century Almamy in Futa Toro. This is not the case, however, as his name does not appear among those Futa Toro rulers who bore this royal title. Boubacar Ciré instead may be a reference to another individual who bore the title Saltigi and was thus known as Saltigi Boubacar Ciré.[12] Saltigi Boubacar Ciré reigned several times in a conflict-ridden period in the early eighteenth century. It was he who is remembered as the first ruler to recognize the right of slaves to have access to Koranic education.[13] Kalidu Diallo's tale about slave's rights under Futa Toro rulers could also be applied to another competitor for the throne and successor of Boubacar Ciré, Saltigi Bubu Musa. According to Mamadu Sek (interview conducted in Mantes-la-Jolie [France], April 2008), Saltigi Bubu Musa was also against the slave trade. He never agreed to commercial relations based on the slave trade with a French trading company.[14] According to our informant Mamadou Sek, the populations of Futa-Toro recalled and admired

Bubu Musa's anti-slavery sentiments. His political, social, and economic success reinforced his popularity among the populations of Futa-Toro and gained their support for his reign in spite of the French opposition to his power. [15]

Despite these memories of nobles who were against the slave trade, slave descendant Kalidu Diallo, notes that the eighteenth- and later nineteenth-century Almamies of Futa Toro were heavily implicated in the slave trade, a point of view which is confirmed by French sources from this period.[16] Once in power as a result of the *torodbe* revolution of 1776, Muslim leaders maintained segregation within the social structure in spite of having initially preached against the slave trade.

Slave and Noble Memories in Futa-Toro Compared

Kalidu Diallo and Amadu Tidiane Sow, slave descendants, and Bocara Dème, and Samba Bubu, nobles, present themselves as members of the community of Golléré and as Futanké, that is, as members of Futa Toro's society. Of this group only Kalidu Diallo is willing to speak of a foreign origin. His father was captured in a jihad in Macina and then taken to Futa Toro.[17] This is an important detail because it means that he was a *maccube galankobee*, or "a slave descended from a war captive." His father wasn't necessarily a slave in his society of origin. Bocara Dème and Samba Bubu belong to the nobility while Amadu Tidiane Sow is a slave whose family had long lived in Futanké society. It is also worth underlining that all see themselves as part of the same community though they have very divergent views on the slave trade. Kalidu Diallo makes clear that the voice of a slave, his history, and his heritage have three different roots, that of the family of his master, that of the community of slaves, and finally, that of the collective memory of the village:

> I want to state first that I am the son of a slave because my father was bought in Macina and taken to the Futa Toro just after the defeat of Amadu.[18] Thus, all of what

197

I know and will tell comes to me directly from my own family, that of my masters, or from discussions among slaves, often held under the leadership of our chief. We discuss the history of the village, of its founder, our history, and that of our adoptive families. However, there are things that I have personally lived through here in Golléré and in the Futa Toro thanks to my numerous commercial trips, notably to Ogo, Kanel, Madina, Ndiabe, Hayde Laaw, and Bodee [*other Futa villages*] to run errands for my master or to engage in commerce. I have also talked to griots, and the essence of our discussions are of great interest for our history as slaves.[19]

Although they were members of Futanke society, the slaves of Golléré were part of a subcommunity organized well enough for them to preserve their own history, as Amadu Tidiane Sow explains:

We slaves had our own chief, the *jaaraf*. The first slave jaaraf in Golléré was called Bubu Sy. It is a policy of nobles (who saw that we had a strong community [among ourselves] with a desire for emancipation) to authorize us to elect a spokesman to conciliate us....Our masters, who [sought to] put us at our ease, entrusted commercial missions to us and even put other slaves at our service.... The slave born in the Futa is very proud and has a certain margin of maneuver in contrast to the slave sold or to be sold who has no liberty.... [We were known as *maccube*; in contrast there is the *maccudo*.] A *maccudo* is a captive who has became a domestic slave. Eventually, people no longer know his origin, [but still] he is someone who has been sold, who has nothing, who is nothing, and who lives in someone else's home. In brief, he is someone who is lost and has difficulties and problems of adaptation.[20] There are nobles who have the right to sell slaves. Under the authority of the

Almamy, they sent slaves they had taken via Jolof to Gorée. Even if the Almamy did not sell them directly, they were implicated. By contrast, here at Golléré, there were *maccube* to whom slaves were given and who sold them.

The nobles present very different testimonies, which are more filtered and more censored even though they do not legitimate domestic slavery. Samba Bubu clarifies how the collective memory of the nobility has been preserved:

I am a member of the royal family and I descend from the last Eliman of Mbumba. My grandfather was Almamy Ali Ceerno and was the origin of a line of Almamies like Boubou Racine and Mamadou Baal of Golléré. My information comes essentially from two sources: those from my family transmitted by family and those transmitted by family griots…. Every *dimo* [noble; pl. is *rimbe*] family has griots who preserve its history and traditions. These griots can also play the role of mediator and help to reinforce and solidify relations between members of the family…. Different versions of these traditions come from different sources, which mean that traditions present an apology for one family and denigrate others. There are two types of griot, the good and the bad. They are masters of the word…. Experiences I have lived through involve the kidnapping of children by Moors, who take them to Mauritania as slaves…a member of my family was kidnapped and reduced to slavery and we had to ransom him…or the story of one of our slaves who fled the house and took refuge at Mbumba and was then taken back to Golléré by force by my father…. Any individual taken prisoner in a distant territory was sold by his master. But learned men did not sell slaves. Only unbelievers were sold as slaves…. The Almamy did not dare to sell slaves…. The

Almamy was a wise man, prudent, someone who obeyed the Quran and applied shari'a.

Nobles, like Samba Bubu, are extremely conscious of their history and their social milieu. He admits openly that slavery shaped the social stratification and is part of its functional mechanism. This testimony made by this noble converges with that made by Kalidu Diallo.

Slave descendant Kalidu Diallo associates memories of slavery with his identity as a member of Futa Toro society [a Futanke] and with his present status as a slave from war and from commerce. Remembering that his father was a *maccube galunkobee,* that is, a "slave taken in war," Kalidu Diallo is similar to Samba Bubu in describing a Futanke society where domestic slavery and the slave trade were an integral part of a sociopolitical system.

> In Futa Toro, there were differences between the *maccudo* who could be sold and the proper *maccudo.* The real *jaam*[21] or *maccube* was a domestic slave, who lived in the chief's house and had a plot of land and a family. He could even become a member of the family. He usually took the family name of his master. His children were part of the master's family and could at any time buy their freedom. The *maccudo* who was sold or could be sold came in most cases from those captured in jihad.[22] These were given the harshest tasks, especially in agriculture. Any time the master felt the need, he could sell them because there was no affective tie that united them. …Captives of jihads or slaves bought in distant territories were usually sold to Futankobé [or Futanke], that is to say, into the local trade, to Moors in exchange for horses and salt, or to Europeans in exchange for firearms. In Futa Toro, any free person had the right to buy or sell slaves to anyone he chose. Only the Almamy had no right to sell slaves.

Kalidu Diallo's account echoes the description of slavery made in 1721 by Nicolas Despres Saint-Robert, the director of the French commercial company: "The wars made by the Moors against the Fulbe and the pillage of the Laobes—elephant hunters—by the Great [Nobles] has forced them to retreat toward the Gambia River."[23] For Saint-Robert, the raids of the Moors and of the Futa nobility were having the same effect, notably that of pushing Fulbe communities to seek refuge further south, along the Gambia River, in order to escape from enslavement. The noble, Bocara Dème, concedes that the slaves of Golléré issued from such a process, but according to him:

> In Futa Toro, slaves were never sold to Europeans. There were slaves that we bought somewhere else on commercial voyages who were brought here as domestic slaves and others that we captured in the course of jihads against pagans like the *ceddo*. ...[24] Here in Golléré, we had many domestic slaves who ended up integrating into the family and adopting the master's name.... We have slaves bought by my father and grandfather who today carry my family name: Dème. But whatever their social status today, they remain what they are, that is to say slaves. ... Among them, we have those who came from jihad or from sale and who often come from distant regions. Those brought from distant regions were often sold to Futankobé, that is to say, to other people in the region. By contrast, what we know of the Almamies of Futa Toro is that they introduced people to Quranic knowledge and applied the shari'a. Almamy Ceerno Suleyman Baal suppressed the Horma, a tax that people paid to the Moors. Other Almamies like Almamy Ibra and Elimane Amadu Moctar brought well-being to Futa Toro while solidly implanting Islam. There were also many kidnappings of people of Golléré by the Moors.

This account by Bocara Dème was supported by noble Samba Bubu, interviewed separately, at eighty-five years of age and a descendant of the founder of Golléré. Following his reconstruction, his father used to go to Mali to buy slaves, who, once at Golléré, were put to work in agriculture and long-distance trade.

By contrast, slave descendant Kalidu Diallo tells of his experience as a slave trained to trade for his master. He brings out the tie between the slave trade, the process of enslavement, and the socioeconomic system of Futa Toro. Acording to Kalidu Diallo:

> The trade in human beings was an essential part of the life of the Futankobé. Everyone competes in trying to possess the greatest number...the more one possesses, the more he is respected by his peers ...and a Futankobé in difficulty can always sell his slaves to someone else in exchange for cattle, sheep, or goats. ... The Almamy did not openly sell slaves because it was contrary to his spiritual and temporal mission; he was obligated to provide security and protection to the people, but he often gave slaves to the governor of Ndar as a present [*Ndar was the African name for the French capital, St. Louis*]. Often Almamy Ibra returned to the Futa with firearms, which he had purchased from the Europeans of Ndar in order to make jihad.... To tell the truth, these slaves were never asked if they wanted to convert to Islam. I recognize nevertheless that it is a delicate question because never or almost never would a *torodbe* say that an Almamy sold slaves to the Europeans or exchanged slaves from the Futa Toro with the Moors for horses. Some persons were sold as punishment for a theft or murder. The sin of adultery was also punished by the application of shari'a, particularly if the author or authors were noble. By contrast, if it was a noble woman and a slave, the slave was automatically sold under the orders of the Almamy or his master.[25]

Golléré descendants of slaves, like Kalidu Diallo and Amadu Tidiane Sow, describe how slaves' integration in Futa Toro society always depended on the master, who could give them an easier life by entrusting them with commercial responsibilities. According to Amadu Tidiane Sow, the slave in this position could have a bit of freedom by contrast to the slave destined to be sold or who had difficulty adapting to Futanké society. According to noble Bocara Dème, slaves of his family always ended up integrating and adopting its family name while remaining locked into a slave's social status. Adaptation and integration in the Futanke community did not afford, however, any guarantee to slaves and their descendants:

> Prisoners of war became slaves, but they were never sold to Europeans because any Almamy or imam who did so put his reputation at risk and those who did so were ridiculed by the people. Sometimes, the Almamy sold slaves to the Europeans or to Moors that the Futanke bought in Macina, Kajoor, or Bawol, who were exchanged for salt or cattle or given to the governor of Ndar with the knowledge of the people. The Almamy had become a direct collaborator of the governor. Likewise, the troops of the Almamy needed horses to make jihad and exchanged slaves for horses and firearms. Slaves could also be exchanged for cattle, sheep or goats.... But we must emphasize that we only sold to the Moors captives who refused to convert to Islam. ... The Almamy did not sell slaves directly, but did so through intermediaries, in particular, members of his entourage. People who wanted to sell slaves went to St. Louis. As for the Moors, they crossed the river with salt and horses to buy captives taken in jihad. ... The slave trade was practiced in two ways: one could acquire slaves during a jihad and those who refused to convert would be sold as slaves to the Salsabé, i.e., Moors. By contrast, other persons were reduced to slavery for having committed adultery, murder or even theft.... Shari'a

applied then and the guilty person was whipped, but in extreme cases, he was sold as a slave in order to acquire horses and firearms for holy war and under the order of the Almamy even if that order was never public.

In the imagination of Futa Toro nobility, the slave trade remained an activity not associated with the Almamiyat [the *torodbe* regime], even though Bocara Dème admits that Almamies were involved. For them the Almamies were all marabouts and scholars who systematically refused to allow the establishment of Europeans on their lands. They brought the people science, Islam, and the shari'a. For example, the leader of the *torodbe* revolution, Suleyman Baal, is said to have suppressed the Modu Horma, the seed tax that the Moors imposed on the Futanke.[26] For noble Bocara Dème, only those captives who refused to convert to Islam were sold. When this argument was presented to slave descendant Kalidu Diallo, he disagreed strongly. For him:

> Never or almost never would a *torodbe* say that the Almamy sold or exchanged slaves for salt or horses. To tell the truth, war captives were never asked whether they wanted to convert to Islam; on the contrary, they were sent directly to Ndar and sold to the Europeans.

According to the Futanke nobility, the slave trade was practiced elsewhere among the Wolof *ceddo* or among the Sereer or the Moors, who raided Futanke. Bocara Dème tried to exonerate the Almamiyat on another form of enslavement practiced by the Moors, namely child kidnapping:

> The Moors came to steal children. In leaving Futa Toro, these children, who were often nobles, lost that status and became slaves. There were many of our people who were taken and led by force to the other side of the Senegal River. Sometimes, these people returned to Futa Toro after several years of slavery in Mauritania....

> I still remember the story of a *torodbe* child seized by the Moors and led into slavery. He was sent by the Quran teacher to look for wood to make a fire at the Quranic school. Several years later his children returned to Golléré to search for their father's roots and his activities as a noble.

Even if the Futanke of Golléré tell of the slave raiding and kidnapping done to them by others, it is difficult to find in the version presented by nobles a real image of the state and the Almamy implicated in the slave trade or in enslavement. Though the noble Bocara Dème reports that his father bought slaves in Mali, he does not state that Almamies were associated with such activity. Only the voices of descendants of Futanke slaves can inform us about the history of the slave trade in Futa Toro. According to slave descendant Kalidu Diallo, everyone presents a version that presents his family in a favorable light:

> Information varies strongly because every group wants to speak well about its ancestors. If we take the *torodbe*, they will always speak well of their family. They will present them as scholars, sage men prudent in judgment. In brief, they were men of God whose daily occupation was the study and teaching of Quran and hadith.

Like Kalidu Diallo, slave descendant Amadu Tidiane Sow discusses the nonegalitarian social structure and the imagined glories of a noble past in which the slave is in an inferior position: "The *torodbe* is a noble who keeps three things: land, mosque, and chiefship."

Depending on how slave descendants stand within the social structure and how they interpret its inequalities, both slave and noble narratives of slavery involve controversy over what parts of the past should be significant in the present. Past events are remembered differently. For example, there is no agreement on whether slaves were sold and if so, which ones, or on whether or not Futa

Toro Almamies sold slaves. These memories, in turn, are linked to the persistent discrimination that slave descendants keep facing in Futa Toro society. From their perspective, memories of slavery and the slave trade have been manipulated, as was Islam, in order to justify existing inequalities in access to land and education. Slave descendant Kalidu Diallo, for instance, explains:

> They are silent on evil done by the Almamy, who was a dictator. And as for our group [the slaves], they only speak very negatively. They will even say that we are damned. By contrast, there is a negative aspect of the authority of the Almamy on which they are silent. And the griot praises certain groups and acts like a parasite. . . . Thus, versions differ according to social groups and persons.

Kalidu Diallo's words contrast with the vision of the noble Samba Bubu, who, in spite of his paternalistic rhetoric, continues to see slaves as inferior—he uses the analogy of sheep—and still sees them as a heritable part of his family's patrimony:

> Relations between slave and master are those of a shepherd and his herd, but a certain loyalty unites them. The slaves are a family patrimony that I inherited when I got married. They are part of the family but they cannot marry members of my proper family.

Slaves were alien, and their descendants continue to be seen as outsiders even if their families have lived for several generations in the Futa. That is why slave descendant Kalidu Diallo tells an anecdote on the process of enslavement and of reproduction in Futanke society:

> We have the history of Samba Aljuma who was reduced to slavery as a boy of fourteen months although he was with his mother, Yacine. Possibly this was the result of

a battle. He was taken to the Almamy's capital at Mbumba, where he was offered to Tenduk. Today, there are many slaves at Golléré, who are descendents of Samba Aljuma.

Kalidu Diallo recognizes that his origins are from elsewhere and that his father was transported from Macina to Futa Toro after a military defeat. He recognizes that others, like his father, were sold to the Moors. Although all this happened after the end of the Atlantic slave trade, he articulates slave memories from that earlier period. He cannot accept the paternalistic vision of the nobles. That is why he adds that the Almamies were close to the Europeans:

> They used subterfuges to take slaves to the governor of St. Louis as presents in the name of good relations according to what the *torodbe* said. Even if they solidly implanted Islam, security, and the protection of Futanke territory, Ibra Almamy returned many times with firearms for jihad after going to St. Louis with slaves.

Conclusion

When dealing with collective memories of slavery and the slave trade, historians have to be particularly careful. First, this type of source is not chronologically precise, and many informants might collapse together events that occurred at different times in the history of the same society. Memory is flexible and can mix reminiscences of the late nineteenth century with those of the eighteenth century. It may also attribute to persons acts and relationships that could not have taken place. Still it helps identify events, names, and localities which are not mentioned in the archival record. Secondly, collective memories are far from being consensual. The sources presented in this chapter have shown the different ways in which descendants of slaves and nobles narrate their common past. The conclusion is that the understanding of slavery is shaped by the position of the person in the social structure. The abolition of slavery in French colonies in 1848 and then the effective end of slavery in rural Senegal in the early twentieth century have not changed this reality. For the descendants of the slave, the narrative is more than a simple quest for honor or a paradigm of victimization. It rests on the role played by the Futanke aristocracy. As for this aristocracy, reference to the slave trade is mitigated by a concern to justify and legitimize their social class and to assert their rights to control the descendants of their former slaves, whom they continue to see as personal property.

Futa Toro social stratification has resisted any modern influence. After the first round of interviews held in Futa Toro in 2007, I continued to make inquiries about the history of slavery and the slave trade in France, and more precisely in Mantes-la-Jolie, a Parisian working-class suburb with a large immigrant population. Senegalese are second only to the Moroccans among the immigrants. Most of them hail from Futa-Toro. My main informant in Paris, who I interviewed in 2008, one year after my research in Golléré, emphasized very proudly and very clearly the strength of social stratification even though this community of Futa Toro immigrants has been living in France since the 1970s, when they came attracted by the development of the automotive industry and by De Gaulle's immigration policy.

Notes

1. Several regions colonized by the Fulbe (people of the Futa), have been called Futa, for example, Futa Jalon in Guinea. The name Toro may have come from the province of that name, which was renowned for the war-like abilities of its chiefs.
2. The Haalpulaar (*pulaar*-speaking) society is divided into three major social groups: The nobles are subdivided into *torodbe, fulbe,* and *sebbe (*warriors) and *subalbe* (fishermen). The second group is constituted of artisans subdivided into *waylube* (smith), *maabube* (weavers), *lawbe* (woodworkers), and *sakeebe (*leatherworkers), and the third is the *maccube* (slaves). Omar Kane, *Le Fuuta Tooro des Satigi aux Almaami, 1512-1807* 2 vols. (Ph.D.diss., Université Cheikh Anta Diop, Dakar, Sénégal, 1986).
3. The previous regime, the *denianke*, was founded in 1490. Its leaders

were also Muslim, but the *torodbe* were critical of their involvement with the French and their inability to protect Futa Toro from Mauritanian slave raiders.

4. David Robinson, "The Islamic Revolution of Futa Toro," *International Journal of African Historical Studies* 8 (1975): 185-221; Oumar Kane, *La première Hégémonie Peile: Le Fuuta Tooro de Koli Tengella à Almaami Abdul* (Paris: Karthala, 2004), 403-604.

5. Interview held in Golléré (Saint-Louis region, Senegal), April 3, 2007.

6. Interview held in Golléré (Saint-Louis region, Senegal), April 2, 2007.

7. Ibid.

8. According to David Robinson, "One [social] division of the Tokolor is the *torodbe* the "beggars for alms" who formed the leadership and much of the membership of the Islamic reform movement in nineteenth-century West Africa and became the ruling class of the Almamate, a new dynasty of Muslim clerics. The *torodbe* and other Tokolor are part of the Futankobe ("those of Futa") ..." Robinson, "Islamic Revolution of Futa Toro," 188. Roy M. Dilley elaborates: "The ideological vision constructed by the *torodbe* clerics at one and the same time maintained 'caste' distinctions and forms of cultural separation, but yet attempted to embrace all social categories into a global conception of a social totality." Dilley, *Islamic and Caste Knowledge Practices among Haalpulaare'en in Senegal: Between Mosque and Termite Mound* (Edinburgh, Scotland: Edinburgh University Press, 2004), 99.

9. According to Boubacar Barry: "Up until the fifteenth century, the contact between Senegambia's Atlantic coast and European maritime powers gave to Futa Toro and other Senegalese kingdoms an unprecedented importance. That contact, especially with Moors and French, brought about deep economic, political, and social transformations in Futa Toro. From that point to its abolition in 1848, the slave-trade was one of the important staples of an international trade that linked Futa-Toro in an international market between Africa, America, and Europe." The period after the Atlantic slave trade saw the establishment of European economic control of Senegambia. In 1891, Futa Toro became a French territory after being conquered and annexed. Boubacar Barry, *Senegambia and the Atlantic Slave Trade* (Cambridge: Cambridge University Press, 1998), 35, 241.

10. Ibid., 50-54.

11. See also Jean Schmitz, "Islamic Patronage and Republican Emancipation: The Slaves of the Almaami in the Senegal River Valley," in

Reconfiguring Slavery: West African Trajectories, ed. Benedetta Rossi (Liverpool: Liverpool University Press, 2009), 85-11; Jean Schmitz, "Islam et 'esclavage' ou l'impossible 'négritude' des Africains musulmans," *Africultures*, numéro spécial: Esclavages. Enjeux d'hier à aujourd'hui 67 (2006): 110-15; Abderrahmane N'Gaïde, "Stéréotypes et imaginaires sociaux en milieu haalpulaar: Classer, stigmatiser et toiser," *Cahiers d'études Africaines* 172, no. 4 (2003): 707-38.

12. Boubacar Cire is also mentioned by the French National Archives. Archives Nationales de la France, Colonies C6-9, 18 June 1725. He probably reigned as Saltigi of Futa-Toro from 1716 to 1721 and then intermittently, until 1725. Boubacar Cire was also the ruler of Futa-Toro who called in the Moroccans in 1716, to assist his ascent to power and gave them the opportunity to interfere in the affairs of Futa-Toro. According to Barry, *Senegambia and the Atlantic Slave Trade*, 88-89, "From that date, the kingdom was put under an obligation to pay the Mudo Horma, a seed tax."

13. Islam tells masters to teach their slaves religion, but most nobles only taught a few simple prayers. A few admired figures did teach their slaves to read the Quran and with the end of formal slavery, many former slaves sought a religious education.

14. Archives Nationales de la France, Andre Brue, "Correspondances du Sr, Andre Brue Directeur General de la Compagnie du Commerce du Senegal," Colonies C6-6, 6 April 6 1720.

15. This was a period of conflict and outside intervention in the interest of the slave trade by both the French and the Moroccans. In 1725, Samba Gelaajo Jeegi became *saltigi* with French support and reigned until 1731. Bubu Musa was ruling in 1736, when he attacked some French boats, and reigned from 1738 to 1741. Samba Gelaajo is the subject of an epic that tells of his bravery and is sung to this day. His wars provided the French with slaves. See Barry, *Senegambia and the Atlantic Slave Trade*, 88-91.

16. Archives Nationales de la France, Paris, "Copie de la traduction de la lettre du roi Almamy à M. Blanchot en date du mois de mars 1789." Colonies F 3- 62, 1789. The Senegambian revolutionary movements of the seventeenth and eighteenth centuries, from Nasr-al-din to Suleiman Baal, were opposed to the slave trade on Islamic principles, but once in power, these theocracies ignored their earlier principles. From my perspective, a sincere and real Islamic movement against slavery should have started by eliminating the social disparities and inequalities, which allowed the flourishing of slavery within and from the social structure.

17. In spite of the fact that Macina was already Muslim, it was conquered by the Futanke jihad leader Umar Tal in 1862, but Umar Tal was killed there two years later. The area was subject to bitter warfare for another thirty years. Kalidu Diallo's father was probably enslaved in these wars.

18. Amadu Tidiane Sow was the son of Umar Tal. When Amadu Tidiane Sow was defeated by the French at Segou in 1890, his Futanke followers were expelled and forced to return to Futa Toro. Most took their slaves with them on a march still remembered for its suffering and loss of life. Kalidu Diallo's father was probably on that march. Martin Klein, *Slavery and Colonial Rule in French West Africa* (Cambridge: Cambridge University Press, 1998), 106.

19. Griots or bards were the traditional historians in African society. They were passed down within a hereditary caste.

20. He has moved here from talking about the *maacudo*, who have been integrated into the community to talking of the *maccube-galunkobee*, who had been captured and can be sold or disposed of in any way his captor wishes.

21. Slave in Wolof. Same as *maccudo*.

22. He is distinguishing between slaves born in the community, who could not be sold, and those who had been captured and were subject to sale.

23. Archives Nationales de la France, Saint-Robert, Colonies, C 6-6, 28 March 1721. The Lawbe are an artisan group within Futa Toro society, who specialize in wood carving. The punishment for adultery by enslavement was based on an interpretation of shari'a, the moral code and religious law of Islam.

24. The *ceddo* were slave soldiers in many Senegambia states. Because they were strongly opposed to Islam, the word was often used for people and states that resisted the Muslim jihads.

25. Shari'a was widely studied in the Futa Toro and across much of West Africa. According to Paul E. Lovejoy, "In the Seventeenth and Eighteenth Centuries, Islamic schools across western Africa taught the principles of slavery that derived from Ahmad Baba," a medieval West African writer, Islamic author, and jurist, 1556-1627, who lived in Timbuktu. His writings influenced justifications of jihad to protect Muslims from wrongful enslavement and to sanction the enslavement of the enemies of jihad, even those enemies who were Muslims. This reveals the contradictions in linking enslavement with religion." Lovejoy, "Slavery, the Bilad-al-Sudan and the Frontiers of the African Diaspora," in *Slavery on the Frontiers of Islam,* ed. Paul E. Lovejoy (Princeton, NJ: Markus Wiener Publishers, 2004), 12-13.

The example of the Futa Toro theocracy helps us to understand that using militant Islamic principles of Jihad and **shari'a** does not prevent inequalities between different social groups and can increase them.

26. The *Modu Horma* was a payment in kind imposed on the Futanke by powerful Mauritanian tribes. The *torodbe* revolution of 1776, led by Suleyman Baal and Abdul Bokar Kaan, was partly against this tax.

Glossary

Ade	In *vodun* terminology, the spirit of a hunter who died violently
Ajami	Arabic script used to write many African languages
Almamy	Rulers in many West African Muslim states; it comes from the Arabic *el-imam*
Amadi	Freeborn Igbo; among the Aro, the term usually refers to nobles
Ameflefe	"Slave" in Ewe
Aro	A slave trading group that dominated Igbo areas and much of the hinterland of the Bight of Biafra
Association Esclavage Mémoire et Abolition	An association formed in Cameroon to protect the memory of slavery and fight against modern forms of the practice
Bamileke	An ethnic group in south-central Cameroon
Bantaba	A wooden platform where men in Mandinka villages gather
Bariba	Ethnic group that dominated Borgou; also called Baatombu
Bellah	Songhay-Zarma term for a person of slave origin among the Tuareg; the Tamacheq term is *akli* (singular) and *iklan* (plural)
Boo	An ethnic group in Borgou in northern Benin; also called Boko
Borgou	A kingdom in northern Benin
Ceddo	Slave warriors among the Wolof of Senegambia
Dalasi	Currency of the Gambia; the U.S. dollar is equivalent to about 30 dalasi

Denianke	Ruling dynasty of Futa Toro from 1490 to 1776
Dimdinaado	Freed slave among the Fulbe
Dimo	A freeborn Fula; the plural is *Riimbe*
Donko	An Ewe and Akan word for "slave"
Ekpe	A secret society that regulated commercial relations in the Bight of Biafra
El Hor	An organization formed among the Haratine of Mauritania to fight for greater freedom
Endam Bilali	An organization of slave descendants in the Futa Toro of Senegal
Eye	Public recitations of genealogy among the Aro
Feok	A festival of Thanksgiving among the Bulsa of northern Ghana
Fiqh	Islamic books of law
Fulbe	An ethnic group, mostly pastoralists, found across the Western African savanna from Senegal to Chad
Fulfulde	Language of Fulbe; also called *poular*
Ganda Koy	A militia organized among the Songhay and among Bellah dependents of the Tuareg in a civil war in Mali in the 1990s
Gando	An umbrella term to designate people of slave descent in Borgou in northern Benin, although not all Gando are of servile origin
Grassfields	An area of south-central Cameroon that supplied many slaves
Griot	An occupational caste found in the western part of West Africa; its members were musicians, praise-singers, bards, and historians
Haalpulaar	Speakers of *poular* or *fulfulde*, the language of the Fulbe
Hadith	Sayings of Prophet Mohammed; a major source of Islamic law

Hajj	Pilgrimage to Mecca
Haratine	Among the Bidan of Mauritania, people probably of slave origin who are dependent on the Bidan; similar to Bellah
Horma	A tax paid to Moors by people of Futa Toro before 1776
Ibiniukpabi	An Aro oracle that played a major role in the slave trade
Ihu	A system of homage among the Aro, in which a person sacrificing an animal gave parts to a superior
Imam	Leader of prayer in a Muslim congregation
Izu	A four-day market cycle or market week among the Igbo
Jihad	In Islam, a war fought for the expansion of Islam; similar to the "just war" doctrine among Christians
Jong	Slave in Mandinka; the word is pronounced *jon* among the Bambara and *jom* among the Malian Mandinka
Juffureh	Supposedly the native village of Kunta Kinteh in the Gambia
Kabre	An ethnic group in northern Togo that was a source of many slaves
Kanbong	Image of the slave raider in the folklore of the Bulsa of northern Ghana
Korewo	Dependent in Mandinka; a polite term for "slave"
Kpeta	A major ceremony held intermittently among *vodun* worshippers
Kunta Kinteh	The central character of Alex Haley's novel *Roots*; came from the Gambia
Laawol Fulfulde	An organization formed among the Fulbe speakers of northern Benin to combat their

	political marginalization
Maccube	Slaves among the Fulbe; the singular is *maccudo*
Malekite	A school of Muslim law important in West Africa
Mandinka	Major ethnic group in the Gambia; found also in Senegal, Mali, and Guinea
Marabout	Muslim religious leader; the term was also used during the 19th century for leaders of a faction in Senegambia that waged jihad and took many slaves
Mawla	Clients who were former slaves; in most African Muslim societies, manumitted slaves did not sever their relationships with their masters but rather became clients
Mazi	Title of respect among the Aro
Middle Belt	A region that runs east to west across Nigeria and includes the confluence of the Niger and Benue Rivers
Muezzin	Man who calls believers to prayer in a Muslim congregation
Murgu	A system in northern Nigeria in which a slave gradually pays off a preestablished price for manumission
Ndar	Name of the city of St. Louis in several Senegambian languages
Ndimaaku	An honor code widespread among freeborn Fulbe; similar to *pulaaku*
Ohu	"Slave" in Igbo
Oru	Another spelling of *ohu*
Pulaaku	An honor code widespread among the Fulbe; similar to *ndimaaku*
Riimaybe	Slaves among the Fulbe born into the community
Sahel	Arid strip of grassy savanna south of the desert

Saltigi	Title borne by Denianke rulers of Futa Toro
Sebbe	Warriors among the Fulbe of Futa Toro
Seemee Allah	An organization formed among Gando of northern Benin to fight against their exploitation; originally broke away from Laawol Fulfulde
Shari'a	Muslim law
Soninke	Opponents of Marabout faction in wars of the 19th century in The Gambia; means "givers of libations." Soninke is also an ethnic term for the Serrahule or Sarrakolé of the Senegambia
SOS-Esclaves	An anti-slavery organization in Mauritania
Tchamba	A *vodun* cult in southern Togo in which descendants of masters worship the spirits of their slave mothers; also called Mami Tchamba
Tchambaga	Bracelets worn by Tchamba adepts
Tekrur	A medieval kingdom based on the Senegal River
Timidria	An organization of slave descendants among the Tuareg of Niger that struggles for greater rights in Niger
Tokolor	Fula-speaking people of Futa Toro
Torodbe	Muslim clerics who led an 18th-century revolution against the Denianke of Futo Toro and created a Muslim state; also spelled *tooroBe*
Vodun	An indigenous religion in coastal West Africa based on spirit possession; also called voodoo and important in the Caribbean and in Brazil
Wulu-suwo	Among the Mandinka, slaves born into slavery—means "born in the house"; also spelled *woloso*

About the Contributors

Alice Bellagamba is Associate Professor of Social and Cultural Anthropology and African Studies at the University of Milan-Bicocca in Italy. She has long fieldwork experience in The Gambia and neighboring Senegalese regions. Currently, she is completing a research project—combining archival, oral, and ethnographic sources—that addresses the end of slavery in colonial Gambia, as well as the tracks that a past of internal slave dealing and slave holding have left in contemporary Gambian society.

Alessandra Brivio is an anthropologist. She did postdoctoral work in Anthropology at the University of Milano-Bicocca. Her research interests are Africa religions and the memory of slavery in Africa. She has conducted field research in Benin, Togo, and Ghana.

Sandra E. Greene is Professor of African History at Cornell University. She is the author of *Gender, Ethnicity and Social Change on the Upper Slave Coast* (1996), *Sacred Sites and the Colonial Encounter* (2002), *West African Narratives of Slavery* (2011), and numerous articles. She has also been president of the African Studies Association (U.S.).

Eric Komlavi Hahonou is Associate Professor at the Department of Society and Globalisation, Roskilde University (Denmark) and member of LASDEL (Laboratory for the Study and Research of Social Dynamics and Local Development, Niger). His work addresses issues of citizenship, domestic slavery, and governance in the context of democratic decentralization reforms in West Africa. Among his publications are "Past and Present Citizenships of Slave Descent: Lessons from Benin" (2011) and "Slavery and Politics: Stigma, Decentralisation, and Political Representation in Niger and Benin" (2009). He is currently working on a monograph entitled

219

Slavery, Citizenship and Politics in Benin and is coauthor of the documentary film *Yesterday's Slaves: Democracy and Ethnicity in Benin* (2011).

Martin A. Klein is Professor Emeritus at the University of Toronto, where he taught African history for twenty-nine years. He is the author of *Slavery and Colonial Rule in French West Africa* (1998) and has edited a number of books, including *Breaking the Chains: Slavery, Bondage and Emancipation in Modern Africa and Asia* (1993) and, with Claire Robertson, *Women and Slavery in Africa* (1983). He has served as president of the African Studies Association (U.S.) and the Canadian Association of African Studies.

G. Ugo Nwokeji is Associate Professor in the African American Studies Department of the University of California, Berkeley. His publications have covered the slave trade as well as the colonial and postcolonial political economy. His book *The Slave Trade and Culture in the Bight of Biafra: An African Society in the Atlantic World* (2010) won the 2011 Melville J. Herskovits Book Award from the African Studies Association.

Damian U. Opata is Professor in the Department of English and Literary Studies, University of Nigeria, Nsukka, and currently heads the department. He has written widely on African literature and especially on Igbo history and philosophy. His most recent book is *Ontologies, Values and Thought in the Igbo World View* (2012).

Lotte Pelckmans is an anthropologist, currently conducting post-doctoral research at Leiden University in the Netherlands. It centers on biographies of the leaders of anti-slavery movements in West Africa. During 2010 and 2011, she was Assistant Professor in Anthropology and Development Studies at the University of Nijmegen, The Netherlands. Her Ph.D. research (2005-2009) at the African Studies Centre in Leiden resulted in a book entitled *Travelling Hierarchies,* which describes the maintenance of hierarchical relations inherited from the slave past among Fulbe migrants in Mali and reflects her interests in issues of mobility, slavery, hierarchy, and multiple identities in West Africa.

Emmanuel Saboro is a lecturer at the Department of English, University of Cape Coast, Ghana. He is currently pursuing a Ph.D. at the Wilberforce Institute for the Study of Slavery and Emancipation (WISE) at the University of Hull in England. His research interests include cultural trauma and memories of slavery in Ghanaian folkore, the interface between history and literature, slavery folksongs, and African-American literature.

Zacharie Saha is a Senior Lecturer, Head of the Department of History, and Coordinator of the Masters in History at the University of Dschang in West Cameroon. He is the president of Association Esclavage-Mémoire & Abolition. He is the author or coauthor of numerous articles and books on slavery, colonialism and colonial cartography, conflicts management, and culture of peace. He is an active member of the NGOs Action Stratégique pour un Développement Durable and Knowledge for All.

Makhroufi Ousmane Traoré is currently teaching at Wagner College on Staten Island in New York. He has published "State Control and Regulation of Commerce on the Waterways and Coast of Senegambia," in Carina E. Ray and Jeremy Rich, eds., *Navigating African Maritime History* (International Maritime Economic History Association, 2009). His Ph.D. dissertation will be published under the title *Slave Trade and Diplomacy in West Africa, 1500-1800*.

www.ingramcontent.com/pod-product-compliance
Lightning Source LLC
Chambersburg PA
CBHW020702270326

41928CB00005B/234